T0328367

"Grant provides an eminently practical guide to harnessing the hidden potential within our minds to become better leaders. Psychologists and neuroscientists have known for some time that the vast majority of leadership behaviors are programmed subconsciously. Beautifully annotated, this book provides a helpful explanation of the tools required to hack the subconscious and, in doing so, dramatically improve leadership effectiveness. An essential read for inspiring leaders and for those in the business of developing the next generation of leaders."

**Bradley Hastings**, Business School, University of
New South Wales, Australia

"Time working with Grant is effortless. He has the amazing ability to get you into flow quickly where ideas and insights present themselves in abundance. He has done a wonderful job taking what he brings in his one-to-one coaching and team leadership sessions into this book. Filled with a balance of theory, personal experience and quick exercises, *Tailored Approaches to Self-Leadership* is a must read to stay mindful and resilient in today's new normal of rapid change."

**Quentin O'Mahony**, General Manager, Singapore CAE Flight Training

"With over a decade of working with leaders to implement change, I read with excitement on what Grant has developed. He puts complicated ideas and research into bite-sized portions for leaders to comprehend and apply. He also suggests practical ways to apply these principles into your work so that you can get results."

**Kenneth Kwan**, Leadership Speaker and Author of
*Small Steps to Big Changes*

"A highly entertaining book that will keep you reading on! The book provides lots of great analogies which bring out the message Grant wants you to take away. Grant provokes your mind to think hard – something great leaders value."

**Christian Chua**, International Speaker, Business Motivator

"In *Tailored Approaches to Self-Leadership*, author Grant Bosnick has masterfully blended psychology, neuroscience, stories, and real-life examples to not only make behavioral change possible, but to make it simple, too. A must read for anyone looking to strengthen their self-leadership!"

**Brenda Bence**, Global Executive Leadership Coach, and Author of
*The Forgotten Choice: Shift Your Inner Mindset, Shape Your Outer World*

"Self leadership will be the difference between the people who lead and the people who only follow. Grant has written a highly accessible and timely book that allows you to hit the self-leadership highway in an accelerated manner. Filled with applied activities, it is not just a book to read but a book to use to up your game."

**Dr. Tanvi Gautam**, Multiaward Winning Executive Coach,
President of Asia Professional Speakers and Top 100
Leadership Thinkers to Watch (2022)

"*Tailored Approaches to Self-Leadership* unleashes your potential for higher productivity and performance. Grant Bosnick has crafted an elegant book with an engaging balance of applied neuroscience and practical tools. For a game-changing experience to develop your self-leadership skills and your leadership of others, this is a book to enjoy and apply."

**Ron Kaufman**, *New York Times* Bestselling Author, *Uplifting Service*

"For 41 years and in 63 countries I've been helping leaders grow, change and develop, and I have noticed that the number one thing that stands in their way is their ability to change a lifetime of habits. The will is there but they have been brainwashed into thinking that changing our habits is difficult. But what if we knew that change is easy if you have the right knowledge and the right tools? Grant's new book *Tailored Approaches to Self-Leadership* provides that knowledge and those tools. What is super cool about his approach to this topic is that he makes the process easy by providing a change assessment that shows you where you need to focus, and then with laser-like precision he provides the bite-sized knowledge and tools that enable you to make a breakthrough in areas that are most important for YOU. Grant's comprehensive model outlines what is needed to apply self-leadership for behavioral change and then provides just the right amount of information to get you moving. If you really want to understand the psychology and neuroscience that will catapult you to the next level in your life as a leader look no further, *Tailored Approaches to Self-Leadership* was written just for you."

**Philip Merry**, Ph.D., CEO, PMCG and Author of *The 9 Key Keys of Synchronicity*

"Wow, what a read! This book is full of great ideas and tools to keep you performing and living at your very best! If you're ready to change your beliefs and transform your life, this book is a must. Get ready to become more self-aware as you become engaged in your own journey of self-discovery and mastery. Enjoy the ride!"

**Scott Friedman**, Author of *Celebrate! Lessons Learned from the World's Most Admired Organizations*

"If you have time to read only one book to improve your self-leadership, make it this one. Bosnick has artfully created the "all you need to know reference manual" to self-leadership. He saved us countless hours by wrapping the world's most relevant and powerful, research backed leadership principles into one easily digestible and immediately applicable source."

**Grant "Axe" Rawlinson**, The Team Decision Making Coach & Human Powered Explorer

# Tailored Approaches to Self-Leadership

This book provides a uniquely adaptable approach to develop awareness (of self, others and one's environment) of self-leadership through real behavioral change. Through neuroscience, psychology and behavioral science approaches, each chapter will help readers make their learning and development personal and take it to a deeper level.

With a tip of the hat to the gamebook format where you choose your adventure, readers are encouraged to take an original online self-assessment quiz to determine the challenges and priorities they are presently facing. The quiz then provides a suggested reading order of chapters to address these growth areas. Each of the 18 chapters explores a different theme related to self-leadership and are written in such a way that one can read them in any order. Filled with practical activities, reflective questions and personal anecdotes, Bosnick encourages readers to understand behavior from the "inside-out" of neuroscience and how the brain works, while also keeping an eye on the "outside-in:" how we understand others and how others see us.

Combining research-backed principles with tried-and-tested exercises, this is a book tailored for leaders of all levels, professionals in a transitory phase of their career, as well as those just starting out in the working world.

**Grant Bosnick** is the Managing Director of YES (Your Empowering Solutions), author, consultant, keynote speaker and executive coach. He has worked with 100+ Fortune 500 and FTSE 100 companies to cocreate people strategies to help organizations build a trusting, collaborative culture and develop leaders to transform their behavior to lead themselves, others and perform at a higher level. Originally from Toronto and now based in Singapore, he has lived in Asia Pacific for over 20 years.

GRANT BOSNICK

WITH A FOREWORD BY
MARSHALL GOLDSMITH

# Tailored Approaches to Self-Leadership

A Bite-Size Approach Using Psychology and Neuroscience

LONDON AND NEW YORK

Cover image: © Richard Drury / Getty Images

First published 2023
by Routledge
4 Park Square, Milton Park, Abingdon, Oxon OX14 4RN

and by Routledge
605 Third Avenue, New York, NY 10158

*Routledge is an imprint of the Taylor & Francis Group, an informa business*

*British Library Cataloguing-in-Publication Data*
A catalogue record for this book is available from the British Library

*Library of Congress Cataloging-in-Publication Data*
A catalog record has been requested for this book

ISBN: 9780367649357 (hbk)
ISBN: 9780367649333 (pbk)
ISBN: 9781003127000 (ebk)

DOI: 10.4324/9781003127000

Typeset in Joanna MT
by Newgen Publishing UK

Access the companion website: http://selfleadershipassessment.com/

This book is dedicated to all those who have influenced me to navigate my self-leadership journey: Marshall Goldsmith, Dr. Stephen R. Covey, Ken Blanchard, people close to me, among others; and to all of you reading this, to chart and navigate your personal self-leadership journey. May you choose your own leadership venture and transform your self.

# Contents

**Figures**

**Tables**

# Foreword
*Marshall Goldsmith*

For over 40 years as an Executive Coach and Behavioral Psychologist, my mission has been to help people achieve positive, lasting change for themselves, their teams and companies. When Grant told me about this book and the work he's doing to help people achieve behavioral change, I was intrigued.

From my experience as a coach to many of the world's top business leaders, I have learned that the methods I teach are easy to understand, yet difficult to do. As Grant discusses, lasting change requires a focused mindset, becoming aware of environmental triggers, and using the support systems around yourself to keep yourself on track. *Tailored Approaches to Self-Leadership: A Bite-Size Approach Using Psychology and Neuroscience* shows how you can stay engaged in your personal growth in a very practical way. Filled with more than just stories, this book's research on neuroscience will help you unlock the keys to how and why your brain works the way it does ("inside-out") and understanding others and how they see you ("outside-in"). Combining this important knowledge with simple, yet powerful steps will transform your life, at home and at the office.

Whether you are just starting your career, or a long-time leader in a career transition, this book provides a bite-size approach to reach a higher level of self-leadership through real behavioral change. Begin this book with the self-assessment to determine your own focus and unique journey. From your results, review the suggested order for reading the chapters to personalize this journey for you and help target the most important elements quickly.

For over 20 years, Grant has partnered with Fortune 500 and FTSE 100 companies and leaders at all levels, using psychology and neuroscience to help people transform their behavior to lead themselves better and perform at a higher level. Grant's keynotes and training sessions have helped thousands of people around the world improve their lives and companies in radical ways.

I truly believe in the power of the mind and the limitless abilities of each person to become better than they were yesterday. My advice is to read this book, follow its advice and create a more fulfilled, rewarding and enjoyable life.

**Marshall Goldsmith** is the Thinkers50 #1 Executive Coach and New York Times bestselling author of Triggers, Mojo, and What Got You Here Won't Get You There.

Introduction

# One

In *Thus Spoke Zarathustra*, Friedrich Nietzsche wrote about the *Ubermensch* or, translated into English, the "Beyond-Human," "Overhuman," or "Superhuman;" the ability of humans to go beyond average and reach a heightened transformational state of being. This book adopts this thinking, with real practical tools and exercises to engage you, the reader and take your learning journey deeper and transform your self-leadership style.

This book provides a bite-size approach to develop awareness (of self, others and one's environment) to help you – whatever level of leader you are in an organization or if you are just getting started or if you are in a career transition – to reach a higher level of self-leadership through real behavioral change.

There are 18 content chapters in the book, each exploring a different theme related to self-leadership. As far as possible, I have tried to make the chapters MECE (mutually exclusive, collectively exhaustive). Think of it like going to the gym. When we go to the gym, we bench press to work our back muscles, do arm curls to work our biceps, leg press to work our quads and so on. It is the same with our brain and our behavior. Each of the chapters in this book works on a different part of our brain and behavior, and together will then help us lead ourselves better to transform our self-leadership style.

Through neuroscience, psychology and behavioral science approaches, each chapter will help you make your learning and development personal and take it to a deeper level. Filled with lots of examples and my own personal experience, the practical tools and exercises will help you to immediately apply it for yourself. Centering around the themes of personal development, transformational leadership, personal effectiveness, mindset and behavioral change, each chapter is concisely written to allow the learning to sink in and have a transformational impact. Moreover, the book adopts an "inside-out" and an "outside-in"

DOI: 10.4324/9781003127000-1

approach: "inside-out" from the neuroscience and how the brain works and "outside-in" from understanding others and how others see us.

In this book, we focus on the self and as the self relates to others. There is a lot more about leading others, interacting with others, fostering relationships, and group dynamics. To help us develop ourselves and self-leadership, we will look at who we are and who that person is in relation to others.

To get the most out of this book, I have designed a tool to assess the challenges and priorities you are facing right now, at this point in your life. This will then give you a suggested order to read the chapters. As mentioned earlier, the chapters are designed in a way that you can read the chapters in whatever order you wish. This will help determine your unique focus and personalize the journey for you.

When I was a child, I grew up with a series of novels called "choose your own adventure" books. In these books, the reader could make choices and, based on the choice, turn to a different page in the book to continue the story to make it personal for them. I have made this book like this too – a "choose your own adventure" self-leadership journey.

If another chapter is interesting to you, feel free to adjust the order to suit your adventure. Overall, this journey is about having more executive control of our brain and our conscious experience. This is the key to leading ourselves and leading a fulfilling life.

This book intends to be a voyage through the realms of our mind, charted with navigation tools of psychology and neuroscience. Like all adventures worth having, it will not be an easy one. It will require some mental effort, a commitment to reflect and think hard about your own experience. Without this, you will not gain much from what follows.

This challenge is both easier and more difficult than it sounds: easier because the ability to do so is entirely within your hands; difficult because it requires a discipline and tenacity that are relatively rare in this present era.

Control over our consciousness and behavior is not simply a cognitive skill. At least as much as rational thinking, it requires the commitment of emotions and will. It is not enough to know how to do it; you must do it. It is not only about "know how," it is, even more so, about "show how." And this is never easy. It is a challenging journey, but definitely one that is worthwhile and full of rewards.

Good luck on your adventure!

Enjoy the deep journey of transforming your self-leadership style!

To get started, visit www.selfleadershipassessment.com or scan the QR code for the simple assessment to plan and choose your own self-leadership journey.

Goals

# Two

Often when we think of goals, we think of the target and reaching the target: setting the goal and reaching the goal. However, goals are much more than just the desired endpoint. They also include the small steps we take, the path we choose to get there, victories along the way, obstacles that may challenge us and the strategies we pursue. We can think of this like a road trip. A road trip is much more than simply the destination. It also includes the pit stops along the way, the milestones, the roads or paths travelled en route, the bridges we cross, the speed we drive, and how we prepare for the journey. It is all of this, as the parts of the road trip, and also how all of this is synthesized together.

### Goal Setting

In the road trip metaphor, goal setting involves deciding the destination, planning the route, packing the gear and making sure the vehicle is ready to make the journey.

To get the most value out of this chapter, right now, think about one goal or aspiration that you have for yourself. This could be a professional one or a personal one. How would you define it? What route would be a good one to take to get there? What gear will you need for it? How are you going to make sure that you, the vehicle, are ready to make this journey? Think about this now to get the most value out of this chapter.

You don't need to have full answers right now. This is an iterative process. So, we can come back to this to fill in more later. For example, at the time of writing this book, as a professional speaker, I had spoken to hundreds of people at offsites or sales conventions. Now my target is to speak for higher hundreds or thousands of people, at larger events, possibly using hybrid technology to reach wider audiences. This is the goal I've set for myself, and I am now working on pursuing it.

What is one goal that you have? Think about that now.

DOI: 10.4324/9781003127000-2

### Goal Striving

This involves navigating the route to the destination, managing roadblocks and deciding when to stay on the road, when to take a pit stop and when we need to take a new road. It involves understanding our mindset, when to go fast, when to go slow and when we need to take a break and rest.

Let's explore now some ways to help us strive for our goal.

#### Force Field Driving Us

According to Kurt Lewin's *Field Theory*,[1] a goal is embedded not only in the individual but also exists within the "field" around the individual (i.e., there is a desired target within the "field" around us that drives us to pursue the target). Between us and the target, there is a "drive force" or "drive field;" and as we get closer to the target (or the perception of being closer), the strength of the force increases.

Like in our road trip, and we've all experienced this, as we approach the destination, we get excited and our energy picks up. The same happens in sports, in a race. As we approach the finish line, it nudges us to give that little extra. In dragon boating, which is a competitive canoe racing sport, we call it a charge. We put in that extra effort and we feel the "force" pull us toward it.

For example, I received an RFP (request for proposal) about a year ago to design an intervention to help the Senior Leaders of a global financial services company. My goal was to win this contract. We had four months to prepare the proposal and then the client would make a decision two months after that. I remember it was exciting preparing the proposal and then we were waiting for two months. Within the two months, the client came back to us three times with questions and to understand more; and we pursued it with such tenacity because we wanted to exceed their expectations. As we approached the two-month decision point, I could feel the excitement grow inside me and it grew to a peak right up until the decision day. And, we got it. We won the contract.

Right now, for yourself, think about one big goal you had from the past. When you first started it, how much pull did you feel toward it? Then, as you got closer to achieving it, how much more pull did you feel toward it? We can use this pull or "drive force" to propel us as we get (or perceive ourselves getting) closer to our goals. It's a powerful feeling, just like the excitement of approaching the destination on a road trip.

Charles Carver and Michael Scheier's *Cybernetic Model*[2] posits that goal theory is like a computer pursuing a goal: we continuously test if what we are doing is helping us get closer to the target or further away. It becomes a loop that we continuously go through, comparing what we are doing and whether it is helping us or not. This helps us choose what to do and what not to do. We will dive more into this later.

Moreover, our goals exist in a hierarchy: smaller loops are more concrete and specific; larger loops are more holistic and encompassing. By asking "why" questions, we move up in the hierarchy, from the concrete and specific to the bigger picture. When we ask "how" questions, we move down the hierarchy, from the big picture to the concrete and specific. If we get stuck at a low level in the hierarchy, we can lose sight of why we are doing this; likewise, we can get stuck in the higher levels of why and neglect to consider the actions (the "how") to achieve it. This hierarchy allows us to contextualize what we want in the bigger picture and simultaneously look at lower-order action steps we need to take. It gives us the *will* and a *way*. And at the very top of the hierarchy is an ideal version of ourself, so that all actions toward our goals (i.e., the lower-level "hows") will always be integrated with the ultimate "why" – ourself.

Neuroscience has also shown us that the "how" system in the brain operates entirely differently than the "why" system in the brain.[3] "Why" thinking engages networks for intention and mental state reasoning, whereas "how" thinking engages networks for action preparation and object identification. One critical skill for goal pursuit in the long run is the ability to switch adaptively between "why" and "how" modes of thinking to enable flexible movement throughout a goal hierarchy. With our road trip metaphor, we can think of moving up and down the hierarchy like joining the dots on a big picture map, which can help us then to take an alternative route when our original course is blocked, one that still gets us to where we ultimately want to be.

For example, in 2015, on a sunny day, I moved to Singapore (from Japan, where I had spent 17 years). Besides consulting companies on people strategy and designing interventions to foster their growth, I am also a music and arts producer and music composer. In Singapore, my new home, I was very excited to collaborate with others and put on an amazing and big performance. I put the team together and then was looking for events to play. However, in order to play the bigger events and get established, the organizers need to see exactly what the show looks like before they will book it. Therefore, I would have to produce my own events first in order to get established.

The challenge for me, at that time, was that my mind was not very good at long-term thinking and planning; rather, my mind thrived "in the moment" and being spontaneous. However, organizing an event requires long-term thinking and planning. So, I could either have found a partner and outsourced it or developed my own skills and mindset. I opted for the latter: to develop my mind to think long-term planning and pursue this goal.

Figure 2.1 shows a hierarchy of this goal, with my ideal self-image at the top, then cascading down into the specifics.

The "System Concept" represents the highest level – our ideal self-image – whatever that means to each of us. The "Principles" are the next level down – higher-level goals within our hierarchy. The "Programs" are the downstream concrete projects or strategies to reach these higher-level goals. Each program, moreover, can be broken down into the specific steps to deliver on that program. Notice also that there are multiple principles that make up our ideal self-image, and multiple programs that can help us reach each of the principles.

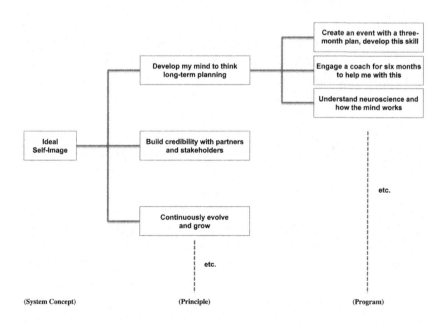

**Figure 2.1** Goal Hierarchy

**Exercise**

*Goal Hierarchy*

Use a piece of paper or an app on your computer to create your own goal hierarchy.

1.  What goal are you currently working on? It could be a professional one or a personal one. It could be a specific, concrete program you are working on, or a higher-level principle goal.

2.  If it is a specific program, ask yourself "why am I doing this?" to get to the principle level. Keep asking "why" questions until the answer is "to create my ideal self-image." If it is a principle goal, ask yourself "why am I doing this?" to connect it with your ideal self-image.

3.  Then, on the principle level, ask "how can I do this?" to get more specific, concrete programs. Multiple programs are okay, and in fact desirable, as we could do them all to pursue the principle goal, or these could be alternatives that we could choose from (like alternative routes on our road trip).

When you ask "why?," you connect to higher-order principles; when you ask "how?," you connect to lower-order concrete programs or strategies.

Execution Strategy

As mentioned earlier, with each level in our goal hierarchy, we continuously test if what we are doing is helping us get closer to the target or further away. It becomes a loop that we continuously go through, comparing what we are doing and whether it is helping us get closer or not. This helps us choose what to do and what not to do, and to measure the success of our efforts.

Figure 2.2 represents this loop system for my goal hierarchy example.

Notice with each level, there is a loop that we will go through to test and compare what we are doing to make decisions, refine what we are doing and execute our strategy.

Let's now break down each loop into the component parts. Figure 2.3 shows a close up of a loop and what each part means.

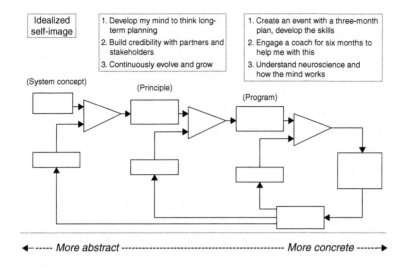

**Figure 2.2** Execution Strategy – High-Level Overview

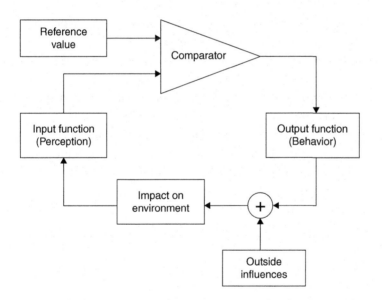

**Figure 2.3** Goal System Loop[4]

The "Reference Value" is the goal, stated as time-bound and measurable. For example, lose 5 kg in two months. The "Comparator" describes our current state or ability with respect to that goal to set up a "gap" and a "test" to measure our progress. This establishes where we are now and where we want to be.

The "Output Function" are the actions and behavior that we will do to help us reach the target. "Outside Influences" are people or things that will positively or negatively influence our progress; these then are motivators or obstacles for us. "Impact on Environment" is the outcome or results from our efforts plus outside influences.

Based on this, we then determine our "Input Function," which is our perception of where we are now as a result. We then use this to test with the Reference Value and Comparator. If we have achieved the goal, then we are finished. If we have not, then we go back through the cycle, executing new actions or behaviors, or delving deeper into the ones we're already doing, or trying to increase the positive outside influences, to help us close the gap even more and achieve our targets.

Figure 2.4 illustrates the loop for the example of my principle goal "Develop my mind to think long-term planning."

First, I looked at where I want to be (Reference Value) and where I am currently (Comparator). Then, I listed different actions and behavior I could take and the outside influences (both positive and negative). The result of this (Impact on Environment) is the outcome from my efforts plus outside influences. Based on this, I then determined the perception of where I am now (Input Function). Since I did not achieve the goal, I would then continue through this loop, refining my actions or behavior and/or increasing the positive outside influences.

On a more granular, lower level, Figure 2.5 (on page 12) illustrates the loop for the example of my program "Create an event with a three-month plan to develop my skills," which falls under the fourth action to "Test out a small project."

In this case, I successfully achieved the goal and learned a lot in the process. In this example, I mention two actions: "Use implementation intentions and social accountability." We will talk more about this later in the last section of this chapter.

Goal: Develop my mind to think long-term planning

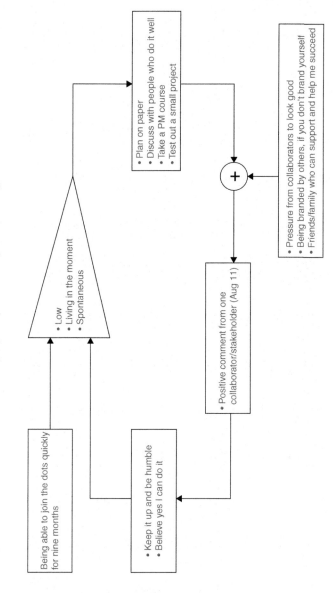

**Figure 2.4** Execution Strategy – Functional Level 1

11  **Goals**

Goal: Create an event with a three-month plan to develop this skill

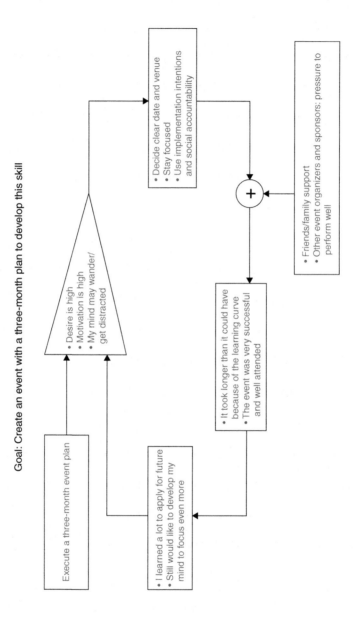

**Figure 2.5** Execution Strategy – Functional Level 2

**Exercise**

*Execution Strategy – Functional Level*

Using the guide below and template on the next page (Figure 2.6), create your own Execution Strategy Loop. You can choose either one of your programs or one of your principle goals.

Guide:

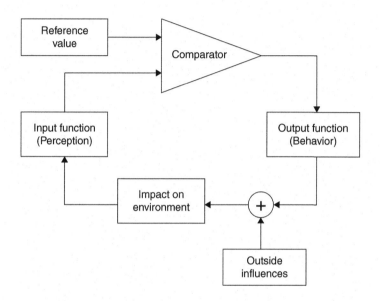

Goal System Loop

1. Write the program or principle goal as the "Reference Value," making it time-bound and measurable.
2. For the "Comparator," describe your current state or ability with respect to that goal to set up a "gap" and a "test" to measure your progress.
3. Fill out the "Output Function" (the actions and behavior you will do to help you reach the target) and "Outside Influences" (people or things that will positively or negatively influence your progress).
4. Spend a week executing the actions and behavior and record the "Impact on Environment" (the outcome or results from your efforts plus outside influences).
5. Based on this, what is your perception of where you are now as a result? Record this in the "Input Function." Test this with the

Reference Value and Comparator. If you've achieved the goal, then you're finished. If not, then go back through the loop again, executing new actions or behaviors, delving deeper into the ones you're already doing or trying to increase the positive outside influences, to help you close the gap even more and reach your destination.

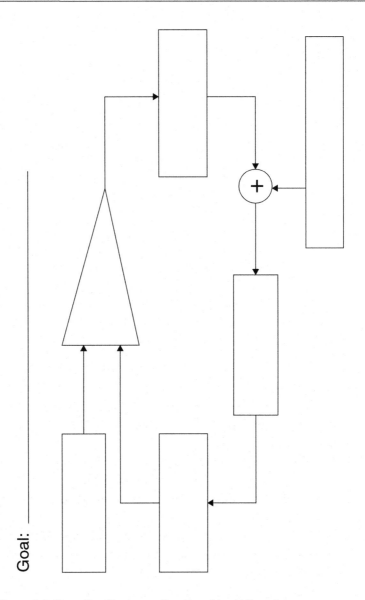

**Figure 2.6** Execution Strategy – Functional Level Template

### Derailers

As we pursue our goals, circumstances or situations may change and we may get derailed. This is like roadblocks on our road trip. When we hit a road-block, it stops us in our tracks and we need to think what do we do next.

Three of the main roadblocks or derailers we might face include:

1. **Unforeseen Circumstances** – something unexpectedly happens, whether in our professional or personal life, and this derails us in the moment.
2. **Depleted Energy** – it takes effort to live our lives and pursue our goals; sometimes we may deplete ourselves of our energy or will-power in pursuit of these.
3. **Competing Commitments** – there are many things that we may want to do in our lives: we want to do A and B and C; sometimes we may have to decide or prioritize what we do.

Thinking about yourself, which of these derailers are you most likely to fall into? Are you experiencing any of them right now?

In Chapter Three: *Inspiration and Motivation*, we dive into different forms of motivation and how this can help us to stay focused. If this resonates with you, perhaps read this chapter next.

Now, let's look at how to change our goals into habits, which will help us maintain our momentum and help us recover from derailments.

### From Goals to Habits

Goal striving needs a lot of cognitive effort, such as attention, working memory and self-regulation. Over the long haul, these can make us tired or we lose focus. A more sustainable and effortless way is to use more "automatic" processes such as habit. In our road trip metaphor, this is like cruise control, so that we can conserve our precious resources and maximize our drive to the target. This also helps us recover from derailers and maintain our momentum.

To create a new habit, we need to train the X-system, the automatic thinking system within our brain. And the key to training the X-system is repetition; repeating the new behaviors so that they become habitual. In research done by Phillippa Lally et al. (2009), it takes on average 66 days to form a habit, and this can vary widely depending on the behavior, the person and the circumstances. In Lally's study, it took anywhere from 18 days to 254 days for people to form a new habit. The researchers also found that missing one opportunity to perform the behavior did not materially affect the habit formation process. In other words, it doesn't matter if you mess up every now and then. Building better habits is not an all-or-nothing process. Sometimes, we may get discouraged if we mess up or feel a small setback. Brush it off and keep going. This is how habits are formed.

Two ways to help us stay on track and turn new behavior into habits are through social accountability and implementation intentions.

### Social Accountability

"Social Accountability" means telling others our intention or prediction about our behavior; this will then increase the chance we will act on it. The social world provides a very important force that helps us maintain or derail goals because other people are a very powerful contextual influence on us (Lieberman, 2013). Other research by Fitzsimons and Shah (2008) has begun to explore how "instrumental others" can help us achieve our personal goals when we draw closer to them. So, if we seek out and engage with people who will help us, this will allow us to set better targets, learn more from our mistakes and those of others and sustain our efforts on the long road toward success. These accountability partners will help us stay focused and accountable to our goals, and help us get back on track if we get derailed.

---

**Reflection**

**Social Accountability**
What three people will be your network of Social Accountability? What specifically will they do to help you be accountable to your goal?

| Name | What Do |
|------|---------|
| 1 | |
| 2 | |
| 3 | |

---

### Implementation Intentions

An "Implementation Intention" is a statement of intention to do something when faced with a potentially difficult situation. This links the new habit and the environment triggers and helps us to imagine what potential hazards might be on the road ahead and to plan for them to the extent possible. We make an implementation intention by creating a preconceived if-then statement that pairs a particular eventuality with a specific action to deal with it (Gollwitzer, 1999).

For example:

1. If I get stuck and feel frustrated, I will talk to others (from my social accountability network) to help me work through it.
2. If I lose my focus, I will remind myself of the project plan and how all the parts fit in.
3. If I have trouble creating the plan or get confused or lost, I will consult and discuss with those I am socially accountable to.
4. If other collaborators feel that they are not getting the most out of this, I will discuss with them to see how we can create more value.

---

**Reflection**

**Implementation Intentions**
Imagine the worst potential hazards (for yourself or others) that might derail you from your goal (e.g., you get stuck, frustrated, lose focus, trouble doing something, others' feelings, unexpected circumstances, competing commitments, etc.); write three implementation intentions.

| | | |
|---|---|---|
| If | then | |
| If | then | |
| If | then | |

---

Connect to Your Personal Vision or Mission

Another way to help us contextualize our goals in the bigger picture of our life and connect it with our ideal self-image is by writing a personal vision or mission statement and aligning what we want with that. In our road trip metaphor, this is like a globe or world map. It is all-encompassing, and all road trips can fit into it.

There are several ways that we could write a personal vision or mission statement. Here are three simple ones to get started on it. We may then want to revisit it and revise it; or reword it into something that is stickier for us and resonates deeper in us.

1. Make a list of ten "ing" verbs that describe what you do. Then make a list of ten nouns that describe what you do. Then pick one from each list and combine them together. Perhaps, as you do this, you may think of other words that resonate more. Feel free to choose these, even if they are not part of the original ten. When I did this, after about 30 minutes of reflection, I chose "orchestrating connections." Have some fun with it and choose something that resonates with you.

2. Write ten statements about yourself that start with "I want to ..." Then prioritize the statements in terms of what truly resonates with you, what excites and energizes you for your personal vision or mission of your life.

3. As a visualization exercise, imagine it is your 80th birthday party and all your family, friends, colleagues and every significant person in your life that you have ever known are there. Whether they would be alive or not at that point, include them all (including parents and grandparents). This is your day and they are all there to celebrate your life. And then think, what would you want each of them to say about you? Reflect on each of these people and write a tribute statement about yourself – what you would want them to say about you.

---

**Reflection**

*Personal Vision or Mission Statement*

1. Choose one (or all) of the techniques above and write a personal vision or mission statement about yourself. Think of this as your ideal self-image at the very top of your goal hierarchy. For now, think of this independent of any downstream goals; rather focus on your life and ideal self-image in the biggest possible way. (*Make a note here.*)

   _____
   _____
   _____
   _____
   _____
   _____
   _____

---
---
---

2. Wait a few days or a week, then revisit it. Revise it, reword it, make it stickier to resonate even more with you. And then reflect how your principle and downstream program goals align with this.

3. Revisit your personal vision or mission statement from time to time (every three months or six months). Reflect on it, making it even more stickier and resonant, and aligning even more with your principle and program targets.

## NOTES

1 Lewin, K. "Field theory and experiment in social psychology." *American Journal of Sociology*, 44(6), 868–96. May 1939.

2 Carver, C. S. and Scheier, M. *Attention and Self-Regulation: A Control-Theory Approach to Human Behavior* (Springer Series in Social Psychology). Springer. New York. 2012.

3 Spunt, R. P., Falk, E. B. and Lieberman, M. D. "Dissociable neural systems support retrieval of how and why action knowledge." *Psychological Science*, 21(11), 1593–8. 2010.

4 Carver, C. S. and Scheier, M. *Attention and Self-Regulation: A Control-Theory Approach to Human Behavior* (Springer Series in Social Psychology). Springer. 2012.

# Three

We cannot motivate others; we can only inspire them. Motivation comes from within and is within all of us. Inspiration can come from any-where – within us, around us, through us. Others can inspire us. And we can inspire others. In this chapter, we explore different kinds of inspir-ation and motivation, and how to have more of it.

## Inspiration

Inspiration is moving people, or being moved ourselves, to be excited about achieving something. It's about seeing or doing things differently, or changing our thinking, feeling or who we are, now and for the future.

We can be inspired by things and we can be inspired by people.

We can also inspire others.

### Inspiration from Things

What inspires you?

I recently pulse checked this with some people I know from different parts of the world. Just informally, I sent out a message to ask them what inspires them. Here is what they said:

- Books, Music, Film
- Music, Art, Film
- Books, Dance, Play
- Music, Nature, My kids

I then asked them, which book, music, art, dance, film or other inspired you and why did it inspire you?

For me, I chose the following:

- Books: Nietzsche inspired me very much because he had the words for what my mind was already thinking.

DOI: 10.4324/9781003127000-3

- Music: Canadian band Rush inspired me because they blend classical and rock music together, with very deep thought-provoking lyrics.
- Film: Quentin Tarantino's *Pulp Fiction* inspired me because it was the first nonlinear film I saw, and it really expanded my mind for how to see narratives.

Here is what others had to say:

- Mozart for his infinite creativity. Picasso for seeing the world differently. The boy who harnessed wind for overcoming limiting circumstances to invent and solve problems.
- Book: *Power* by Jeffrey Pfeffer because this book challenged the way I perceive power. It was quite inspiring to understand that power does not always corrupt.
- Dance: I find all forms of dance inspiring since it is the most beautiful form of expression across cultures.
- Play: In the busyness that surrounds us, I find inspiration in play – to just be. To put everything else aside and just be in the moment, to enjoy and get reminded of my childhood every time I play a game.
- A walk in nature, especially the sky and sea, inspire me. Songs with deep meanings such as Leonard Cohen. Kids remind me how simple life is and being happy.

Inspiration from People

We are also inspired by people.

For me, Steve Jobs, Richard Branson and Oprah Winfrey have inspired me. Steve Jobs and Richard Branson combined being a rock star and a CEO and had a "following." Steve Jobs's 2005 commencement address for the Stanford University graduating class was also extremely inspiring. Oprah Winfrey inspired me because she is the richest self-made woman in the world and is an amazing inspiration for so many people.

Who inspires you and why?

Again, I pulse checked this with the same people from different parts of the world. Here is who inspired them and why:

- Elon Musk for diversity of interests and committing his own money to back projects.

- Michelle Obama – to maintain her own and not be overshadowed by the status of her husband – now, that's something!
- Eckhart Tolle (German spiritual teacher) for the wisdom he has about life's purpose.
- Nelson Mandela for standing up against the oppressors in South Africa in a peaceful way, enduring incredible hardships and then becoming South Africa's first black President.

Now, what is it about these things and people that inspire us so much? They inspire us because they give us hope for the future – personally for our own life to be better; for all of humanity to be better people; and for the Earth to be a better place. They show us a new way of thinking, of being, and help us to see a better way for the future. And they make us feel good, emotionally and mentally.

### The Neuroscience of Inspiration

Research has shown us that inspiring stories and images produce oxytocin in our brain.[1,2] Oxytocin is the neurochemical that facilitates feelings of trust. Inspiration also produces dopamine in our brains (Ashby et al., 1999; Depue and Collins, 1999), which is a neurochemical associated with motivation and reward.

Moreover, the concept of neuroplasticity underpins inspiration. Neuroplasticity is the brain's ability to form new connections and reorganize itself as a result. Through inspiration, our brain is literally restructuring itself as we connect ideas together to form new ideas. The process of inspiration carves out new pathways inside our brain.[3]

In Chapter Seven: Insight, we talk more about this neuroplasticity and how new connections are formed in our brain. If this resonates with you, perhaps read this chapter later.

Also, by recalling what inspires us, it will prime our brains for more inspiration. In positive psychology, this is called *appreciative inquiry*. So, when we reflect on what inspires us, it primes our brains to be even more inspired.

### Inspiring Other People

Likewise, we can also inspire other people. Some people may enjoy it more than others. Some may be better at it than others.

There is a lot involved in how to inspire other people. In different chapters in this book, we look at it through different lenses. Specifically, in the following five chapters we look at inspiration through the lenses of the chapter titles:

Chapter Ten: *Persuade and Influence*
Chapter Fifteen: *Relationships and Authenticity*
Chapter Seventeen: *Trust*
Chapter Eighteen: *Empathy*
Chapter Nineteen: *Presence*

When you get to each of these chapters, reflect also how this is helping you to inspire others.

For now, we can just think of our qualities and how they might inspire others. For example, being creative, being a good listener, our sense of humor, our leadership abilities, the energy we bring, etc. Think of the different qualities that you have and how this can inspire others.

---

**Reflection**

**Inspiration**

1.  What inspires you? Books, music, art, dance film, other? What specifically about that thing inspires you? (*Make a note here.*)

    _____
    _____
    _____
    _____
    _____

2.  Who inspires you? What specifically about that person inspires you? (*Make a note here.*)

    _____
    _____
    _____
    _____
    _____

3. What is one quality about yourself that could or does inspire others? How can it inspire them? (*Make a note here.*)

_____

_____

_____

_____

_____

### Motivation

Motivation is what drives us to do what we do.

#### External vs Internal Motivation

External motivation is outside of ourselves and includes things like money, reward, punishment, recognition, awards, credentials, and so on. Internal motivation is what drives us from the inside and includes our psychological needs and core values.

Both of these are important – I do like recognition and awards – but research has shown that internal motivation has even more sustainable impact than external motivation alone.[4] In this book, we focus on internal motivation and how this can help us to have a greater and longer-term impact – for ourselves and for others around us.

#### ACRES Needs

For the past 100 years, researchers and psychologists have studied our human needs. In Chapter Twelve: *Change*, we review some of the history of this and how it relates to our feelings of reward and threat. If you want to know more about this, feel free to read Chapter Twelve later.

In terms of our internal motivation, we are talking specifically about our psychological needs. Different people have called these different names. I call them our "*ACRES*" needs, which include our five psychological needs:

**Autonomy** – a feeling of control and choice.
**Competence** – feeling valued and respected for our contribution.
**Relatedness** – a fundamental need to belong and be accepted, to have social connections.
**Equity** – perceiving decisions and actions as fair.
**Sureness** – predicting what's going to happen moment to moment.

When what we do satisfies all of our ACRES needs, then we feel truly motivated internally.

For example, one peak experience that I had, which I mentioned in Chapter Two, is when I received an RFP (request for proposal) about a year ago to design an intervention to help the Senior Leaders of a global financial services company. With all our preparation, I could feel the excitement grow inside me and it grew to a peak right up until the decision day. And, we got it. We won the contract.

And so, when I reflect on this peak experience, I can see how it satisfied all of my psychological needs:

- **Autonomy**: I created the solution/proposal and made the decisions.
- **Competence**: I could use my skills, knowledge and competencies; and I felt valued for this.
- **Relatedness**: it brought me closer together with the other collaborators and partners; and one theme of the project is inclusion and making human connections.
- **Equity**: yes, I think things were fair for all of this.
- **Sureness**: well, nothing is really that sure now is it? However, I feel that we do have a very good chance to secure future projects as well too, and we're talking about that now.

As a result, this experience satisfied all of my psychological needs to a great degree and I felt extremely motivated.

Also, as mentioned before, by recalling positive experiences, it primes our brain for even more positive experiences (*appreciative inquiry*). So, by recalling these peak experiences where our psychological needs were satisfied, it primes our brain for even more peak experiences.

As another example, one of my clients told me that they spearheaded a major project for one of their customers. He recalls how he satisfied all of his psychological needs:

- **Autonomy**: he could lead the project and make decisions.
- **Competence**: he had specialized knowledge and skills to add value to the project.
- **Relatedness**: it inspired his team; built rapport with customers and exceeded their expectations.
- **Equity**: his team felt included; and he and his team all felt things were fair.

- **Sureness**: the project was so successful that the customer wanted annual ongoing support globally.

---

**Exercise**

*Motivation:"ACRES" Needs*

1. What are some examples of external motivation for you? (*Make a note here.*)

   _____

   _____

   _____

   _____

   _____

2. Recall a peak experience, one that satisfied you by accomplishing something important. As you reflect on it, how did you satisfy your five psychological needs of autonomy, competence, relatedness, equity and sureness? (*Make a note here.*)

   _____

   _____

   _____

   _____

   _____

3. How can reflecting on this experience motivate you even more? (*Make a note here.*)

   _____

   _____

   _____

   _____

---

Core Values

Understanding what our core values are, and getting alignment with what we do and our goals, is very satisfying. When we have alignment with our core values and what we do and aim to do, then we feel truly motivated internally.

Figure 3.1 has a list of 40 common core values. Reflecting and understanding more about our top core values will help us make decisions and take actions along our journey in life.

For example, for me, having gone through this list, my top five core values are as follows:

First list:

- Creativity, Excitement/Enthusiasm, Integrity, Respect, Compassion, Courage, Fairness

Shortlist to five:

- **Creativity, Integrity, Compassion, Courage, Fairness**

Prioritized (with an example how it plays out in my life):

- **Integrity** – making decisions from principles and sound judgment.
- **Compassion** – putting myself in other people's shoes to see and feel the situation from their perspective.
- **Courage** – looking at myself in the mirror and seeing the things that are good and the things to improve.
- **Creativity** – expressing myself and generating new ideas to help other people.
- **Fairness** – thinking of all people involved, and making decisions and taking actions with everyone in consideration.

### Approach Motivation vs Avoidance Motivation

Approach motivated people are more motivated by gain than loss; avoidance motivated people are more motivated by loss than gain. For example, salespeople tend to be more approach motivated; people in compliance or legal tend to be more avoidance motivated. Approach-driven people will look for the benefits that they can gain; avoidance-driven people will look for the risks to avoid.

For example, in business, I tend to be more approach motivated as it is the benefits that can be gained (for myself and our clients) that propel or motivate me forward. When I brush my teeth, however, I tend to be more avoidance motivated, as I would like to avoid getting cavities.

One of my friends, however, is the complete opposite. Rachel, who works as a Director in Regulatory Affairs for a large cosmetics company, tends to be more motivated by avoiding risk and other loss (both professionally and emotionally) with the decisions and actions that she takes.

Likewise, in the movie *Moneyball*, Brad Pitt says, "I like to win. You get on base, we win. You don't, we lose. And I hate losing. I hate it. I hate losing more that I even wanna win." The approach motivation is strong – to win. However, the avoidance motivation – not to lose – is even stronger.

| | |
|---|---|
| **Achievement** | **Humanity** |
| **Adventure** | **Humor** |
| **Authenticity** | **Integrity** |
| **Balance** | **Justice** |
| **Beauty** | **Kindness** |
| **Compassion** | **Leadership** |
| **Contribution** | **Learning** |
| **Courage** | **Love** |
| **Creativity** | **Loyalty** |
| **Excitement/Enthusiasm** | **Openness** |
| **Fairness** | **Optimism** |
| **Faith** | **Peace** |
| **Fame** | **Religion** |
| **Fitness** | **Respect** |
| **Freedom** | **Security** |
| **Friendship** | **Self-Respect** |
| **Fun** | **Spirituality** |
| **Happiness** | **Success** |
| **Harmony** | **Wealth** |
| **Honesty** | **Wisdom** |

**Figure 3.1** Core Values

**Exercise**

*Motivation: Core Values and Motivation Strategy*

1.  What core values are your key drivers for internal motivation? Select five from the list and prioritize them. Then give an example for each where it has played out for you in your life. (*Make a note here.*)

    _____

    _____

    _____

    _____

    _____

2.  If you adopt an approach motivation strategy, what are the rewards you can gain? If you adopt an avoidance motivation strategy, what is it you'd want to avoid? Which is more motivating for you: gaining the reward or avoiding the risk? And if both, what ratio: 70–30, 50–50, 40–60, etc.? (*Make a note here.*)

    _____

    _____

    _____

    _____

    _____

## NOTES

1 Gerrig, R. J. Experiencing Narrative Worlds: On the Psychological Activities of Reading. New Haven, CT: Yale University Press. 1993.

2 Gimbel, S., Kaplan, J., Immordino-Yang, M., Tipper, Gordon, C. A., Dehghani, M., Sagae, S., Damasio, H. and Damasio, A. "Neural response to narratives framed with sacred values." Annual Meeting of the Society for Neuroscience, San Diego. 2013.

3 Thrash, T. M. and Elliot, A. J. "Inspiration as a psychological construct." Journal of Personality and Social Psychology, 84, 871–89. 2003.

4 Deci, E. L. and Ryan, R. M. Handbook of Self-Determination Research. Rochester, NY: The University of Rochester Press. 2002.

Mindfulness

# Four

In this modern world, we are constantly distracted (smartphones, music, Facebook, Twitter, Instagram, advertising, horns, cars, trucks, dogs, others talking, beautiful people). We are overwhelmed with potential distractors.

This morning, when I woke up, my alarm was going. Then I checked the notifications on my phone and emails; then Facebook and Instagram. Then I got up and made some coffee and sat down at my desk to work. And then delivery trucks came by, school buses for children, workers cutting the grass, dogs barking, and there is construction going on in the neighborhood. There are so many potential physical distractors around me. And this is just a normal day.

For others, going to the office or working in a café, there are also people walking around, more cars, advertising and people who may talk to us. Plus multiple other sounds and sights all around us – so many things that could possibly distract us.

Moreover, modern work culture has a myth that we are more productive when we power through. Therefore, we email colleagues at all hours, and they respond, usually within minutes. Or we ask employees to show up early or stay late and they do. This requires us to be always-on, and it impacts our well-being and mental abilities. In the days before cell phones, internet or email, work actually ended at 5 pm. At today's pace, we are always on and overwhelmed by potential distractors.

And then, there are also all the internal distractors. We may think about the pressure of looming deadlines, relationships with people that may not be as strong as they could be, preoccupation with memories, judging ourselves and our own abilities, ruminating about events, thinking about the future and/or feeling emotional triggers from changes in our life. All of these can distract our thinking and our attention as well.

When we open up our computer in the morning and notice the growing list of tasks and projects, the number of calls we have to make,

DOI: 10.4324/9781003127000-4

the volume of work we need to do, and everything else that is going on in our life, it is easy to become so consumed that we neglect our basic health, become stressed and feel anxious. In this heightened state of stress, our nervous system is overactive, leading to increased cortisol, which, if experienced in prolonged periods, can result in illness and disease. In Chapter Six: *Physical Health*, we dive into how physical health impacts our brain and our performance. If this resonates with you right now in your life, perhaps read this next. In this current chapter now, we will focus on *mindfulness* – what it is, how to develop it and the many benefits of it.

Before we get to this, let's take a moment to assess our usual day at this point in our lives, and all the potential external and internal distractors that we may have.

---

**Reflection**

*Distractors*

1.  Take a moment now to think about all the potential external distractors that you may have. Think about everything that is around you right now. All the sounds and sights, objects and people. List them up here.

    _____

    _____

    _____

    _____

    _____

2.  Now, take a moment to think about all the potential internal distractors that you may have. What is happening in your life now that might distract you from focusing on your goals or work? List them up here. Just list them up; don't think about them.

    _____

    _____

    _____

    _____

    _____

3. How would you feel if you had more "executive control" of your attention – to be able to block out distractors and focus on whatever you choose to focus on? (*Make a note here*).

_____

_____

_____

_____

_____

### What Is Mindfulness?

We hear this word often. A Google search produces "About 379,000,000 results (0.59 seconds)." There are many definitions of it. And each of us can think about what does it mean to us.

To help us all get on the same page, here are a few definitions from the biggest dictionaries and some of the founders of mindfulness:

*A mental state achieved by concentrating on the present moment, while calmly accepting the feelings and thoughts that come to you, used as a technique to help you relax.*

(Oxford English Dictionary)

*The practice of being aware of your body, mind, and feelings in the present moment, thought to create a feeling of calm.*

(Cambridge English Dictionary)

*The practice of maintaining a nonjudgmental state of heightened or complete awareness of one's thoughts, emotions, or experiences on a moment-to-moment basis. Also, such a state of awareness.*

(Merriam-Webster English Dictionary)

*The practice of giving complete and non-judgmental attention to one's present experience, used as a stress-reduction technique.*

(Collins English Dictionary)

*A moment-to-moment awareness of one's experience without judgment.*

(American Psychological Association)

*The awareness that arises from paying attention, on purpose, in the present moment and non-judgmentally.*

(Jon Kabat-Zinn)

It seems, then, to be both a mental state AND the practice of reaching that mental state.

We can think of *mindfulness* like a Jedi's mind in the movie series *Star Wars*. It's like *the Force*.

In the original *Star Wars*, Obi-Wan Kenobi told Luke Skywalker, *"Well, the Force is what gives a Jedi his power. It is an energy field created by all living things. It surrounds us and penetrates us; it binds the galaxy together."*

In *The Empire Strikes Back*, Yoda says to Luke,

Size matters not. Look at me. Judge me by my size, do you? Hmm? Hmm. And well, you should not. For my ally is the Force, and a powerful ally it is. Life creates it, makes it grow. Its energy surrounds us and binds us. Luminous beings are we, not this crude matter. You must feel the Force around you; here, between you, me, the tree, the rock, everywhere, yes. Even between the land and the ship.

And in *Return of the Jedi*, when Luke returns to Dagobah to see Yoda, the wise old Jedi who trained him in the ways of the Force, he finds him on his deathbed. At the age of around 900 years old, Yoda finally dies. Right before he goes, though, he imparts to Luke some very sage advice about how to use the Force. He says, *"Remember, a Jedi's strength flows from the Force. But beware: Anger, fear, aggression — the Dark Side, are they."* He wants to make sure that Luke keeps his emotions in check and doesn't slip into the Dark Side.

And so *mindfulness*, like *the Force*, is the practice AND the mental state of purposely bringing our attention in the present moment without evaluation.

### Attentional Deployment

In order for us to be *mindful*, to focus and keep focus, we need to have "executive control" of our attention.

On the most primitive level, our brain (through the *amygdala*), consciously and unconsciously, alerts us to all stimuli in our environment (a snake, a bear, a beautiful person). It is the same also with emotional and social stimuli (a feeling, relationships, communication). The *amygdala* then guides our attention to the most important stimuli. Reward and novelty also guide our attention on this primitive level (e.g., receiving email, Facebook likes and comments). This makes us hyper-attuned to all the information coming in.

For example, imagine walking approaching a road to cross it, and you hear a car coming from the right or left side at a high speed. The *amygdala* alerts us of this and we stop whatever we were doing and immediately turn our attention to the car approaching.

Or, imagine, the reward we get when a notification comes in of an email or Facebook likes, and we immediately turn our attention to that to feel the rush and joy of that.

With all these stimuli coming in, on a higher level of thinking, we therefore need to select where our attention will be. How we select is influenced by what we perceive to be most important, the task at hand and our emotions at the moment.

For example, as I sit here writing this book, there are many other things happening around me and in my life: client work; deadlines for proposals; a neuroscience course that I am taking to upskill myself; a video I need to record for a professional speakers association of which I am part of the executive committee; and so on and so on. Plus other emotional experiences happening in my life: a global pandemic; friends and family; and my own stress, triggered by memories or other events in my life. All of these compete for my attention. Through "executive control" of my attention, I purposely deploy my attention to writing in order to focus and keep my focus.

Moreover, in a famous experiment called "The Invisible Gorilla," by Christopher Chabris and Daniel Simmons, participants are asked to view a video of a group of six students passing a basketball between them. Half of the players are wearing a white shirt and half of them are wearing a black shirt. Viewers are then asked to count the number of times the players with the white shirts pass the ball. During this video, a person in a gorilla suit walks across the screen. The majority of viewers do not even notice this. When our attention is on one particular task, we can become like a racehorse with blinders on, seeing only the task at hand, and creating "perceptual blind spots" in our view of the situation and what is happening at the moment. As a result, our attention and focus can become too narrow, and we miss a lot of what is important.

In order for us to truly focus, on the big picture and the details, on everything that is important, we need to have "executive control" of our attention. This means evaluating the current state of ourselves and our environment, guiding our attention to what is most important to us, and tying the actions we are doing to our goals. Imagine it's like GPS. At any moment, you can pinpoint where you are, zoom out to see the big picture or zoom in to see the details. This GPS, or "executive control," helps us to truly focus on what is most important.

We can also think of it like being on the dance floor and then choosing to go up to the balcony. Down below, on the dance floor, this is where all the action happens, where we spend most of our time. Then, when we go up to the balcony, we can see a much wider bird's eye view. We can survey the whole landscape and see better how everything fits together. Then, we can choose another part of the dance floor and then zoom into that. Through the "executive control" of our mind, we can then zoom in and out.

To do this requires a high level of *arousal*, the mental state of being awake to what is around us, which leads to increased heart rate, sensory alertness and readiness to respond. Optimal *arousal*, moreover, is not the same for everyone; case by case it will be different. Some people can handle more; others less. And if we go over the edge, then we become strained and anxious, feel anxiety, and our performance will go down. Therefore, we need optimal arousal for focus and high performance. In Chapter Fourteen: *Resilience*, we dive into the Yerkes-Dodson Law, which shows the relationship between stress or *arousal* and performance.

Moreover, in order for us to focus and keep our focus, we need to be mindful. *Mindfulness*, as described in psychology, is a process (or practice of such) with two components: (1) orienting our attention purposefully to the present moment and (2) approaching our experience in the present moment with curiosity, openness, nonjudgment, nonreaction and acceptance.

There is also evidence from studies that being *mindful*, being aware of the present moment without grasping on to judgments, improves our immune function, enhances a sense of clarity and increases empathy and relational satisfaction.[1,2]

Being mindful and developing "executive control" of our attention creates new connections and neural pathways in our brain (neuroplasticity) – which aids us in focusing to reach out goals, performing at peak levels, solving complex problems, having insights and regulating our emotions.

### Developing Mindfulness and Executive Control of Our Attention

We can, however, train our attention to focus, through mindfulness exercises. One of the founders of mindfulness, Jon Kabat-Zinn, said, "You can't stop the waves, but you can learn how to surf." In other words, we can't stop the distractions or mental clutter, but we can learn to control our attention.

Mindfulness training is getting more and more popular in the business world as well, and many large corporations have been incorporating mindfulness into their culture. For example, companies such as Google, Apple and Procter & Gamble offer mindfulness coaching, meditation breaks and other resources to their employees to improve workplace functioning. As a result, mindfulness has been found to increase employee well-being, lower levels of frustration, lower absenteeism and burnout, as well as an improved overall work environment. Through mindfulness we can increase focus and perform at a higher level.

We can think of it like a mental muscle; we can build it to become strong, just like going to the gym to work out, and it can become weak if we don't train it. One effective way to develop mindfulness is through meditation, sitting quietly, turning our minds inward. We will talk more about this later. Another way, and we will talk about it first, is through PQ Reps.

#### PQ Reps

I often find myself rubbing my fingertips together with such pressure that I feel the ridges on each finger. Or rubbing my thumb and index finger across my lips. Or focusing my ears on the ambient sounds in the room. I have done this for years, and when asked what I was doing, I said that I was thinking.

Then recently, I came across the concept of PQ Reps. Coined by Shirzad Chamine, PQ Reps stand for "positive intelligence quotient repetitions" and are small, laser-focused exercises that consciously and purposely deploy are attention to one specific sensation. One rep is ten seconds of laser-focused attention doing one of these exercises; or, if we do it for two minutes, uninterrupted and with complete focus, then that would be 12 reps.

In the same way that we would go to the gym to lift weights to build our physical muscle, doing repetitions of weight-lifting, PQ Reps build our mental muscle. Doing these throughout the day develops our "executive control" of our attention and recharges our brain; and we can do them anywhere, anytime. We should be aiming to do at least 100 reps per day, especially first thing in the morning, after lunch, anytime we feel our energy go down, and before important meetings, presentations or other activities that require our complete focus. I'm doing them right now in between typing words.

There are several different ways and exercises that we can do this by focusing and deploying our attention to one specific sensation. We will introduce several of them here. Try them all and choose the ones that work best for you.

### PQ Reps with Touch

Close your eyes and rub your fingertips together with such pressure that you feel the ridges on both fingers. Feel what this does to your brain as you do this. Make little circles clockwise; then counter-clockwise. Then, make circles going inwards; then circles going outwards. Feel what it does to your brain as you do this. Do this for about 30 seconds or a minute.

Another exercise you can try:

Close your eyes and relax your body. Then, starting from the top of your head, direct your attention to your forehead and your eyebrows, tensing those muscles up as tight as you can. Then tense up the muscles in your nose and your cheeks and your ears. Then tense the muscles in your jaw and your whole head, holding it like this all tensed up for about ten seconds. Then release all that tension and feel the muscles relaxed again. Then, repeat this same process with your shoulders and arms and hands; then to your chest and stomach; then to your hips and legs. Each time, tensing the muscles one area at a time for about ten seconds, then releasing it and relaxing. This should take only about two minutes.

### PQ Reps with Breath

Paying attention to your breath is another way.

Close your eyes and deploy your attention completely to your breath. Feel the rise and fall of your chest or stomach. Feel the difference in your brain as you inhale and as you exhale. Feel the difference in the temperature as you inhale and as you exhale. Do this for 30 seconds or a minute several times throughout your day.

### PQ Reps with Sound

Close your eyes and focus on all the different sounds you can hear – the ambient sounds in the air and the sudden sounds that may happen. Then focus your attention on the farthest sound you can hear. Really stretch yourself to hear the farthest possible sound you can. Then draw your attention to the closest sound you can. This is probably the sound of your own breathing. Listen to the sound of your breathing as you inhale and exhale.

We can also do this with many of the natural daily habits that we have. When you are having a shower, listen to the sound of the water spraying out of the shower and the sound of the water as it hits your body or the floor of the shower. When you brush your teeth, listen to the sound of your toothbrush inside your mouth, and then of the sound of the mouthwash as you swish it around.

### PQ Reps with Visual

Choose something in your room that you see right now and focus your eyes on it. Look at it with such intensity that you see the rich textures, the shades of colors, the way the light reflects off of it. Look at it for a minute or two with such intensity that you see all the beautiful visual aspects of it.

Another exercise you can try:

When you go for a walk, choose one color that you may not see so often, like orange or pink. Then, as you are walking, look out for things or people with that color: signs, objects, vehicles, clothing, packaging and so on. Deploy your attention and focus on all the things you see that are that color.

### PQ Reps with Smell

When you make coffee in the morning or are cooking food, close your eyes and focus your attention on the smell of the coffee or the smell of the food. Breathe in deeply and pay attention to all the rich aroma and beautiful smells in the kitchen.

When you have a shower, close your eyes and focus your attention on the smell of the shampoo or the soap. Breathe in deeply and fill your nose with all the beautiful smells in the shower.

When you go for a walk, keeping your eyes open for safety, breathe in deeply and notice all the wonderful smells outside. This could be the flowers blooming, a person's fragrance in the air, fresh cut grass or the smell of restaurants as you walk past. Focus your attention on all the smells around you as you go for a walk.

PQ Reps with Taste

When you sit down for your next meal, as you put a forkful or spoonful of food in your mouth, really notice all the rich flavors of it. Close your eyes to focus even more. With each chew and bite, really focus on the beautiful tastes of everything you are eating, or of the wine or coffee you are drinking.

By doing these *PQ Reps* throughout the day, it will develop the mental muscle in our brain, just as going to the gym develops the physical muscle in our body. Incorporating these *reps* into our daily routines and activities, over time, will develop our "executive control" of our attention and the *mindfulness* of our brain.

---

**Exercise**

**PQ Reps**

Develop your *mindfulness* and "executive control" of your attention through *PQ Reps*. Go through the list of *PQ Rep* exercises introduced above and try them all out one at a time. Feel what each of them does for your brain.

Do them regularly throughout your day, every day, and find the ones that work best for you. You can do them when you take a break, while you think, while you're listening to others, showering, brushing your teeth, etc. Try to do at least 100 *reps* every day (remember 1 *rep* = 10 seconds, so 1 minute would be 6 *reps*) to have more control over how you deploy your attention and more control over your brain.

---

Meditation

Meditation is another very effective way to develop *mindfulness*, by sitting quietly and turning our minds inward. As mentioned before, *mindfulness* is a process (or practice of such) where we orient our attention purposefully to the present moment and approach our experience in the present moment with curiosity, openness, nonjudgment, nonreaction and acceptance. Meditation is a conscious and deliberate practice to help us do this.

The first step in meditation is to learn to become aware of the difference between bottom-up sensory experience and the top-down chatter of our narrative minds. In other words, we need to learn to quiet our mind and to allow ideas to just come and go, without holding on to any of them; and to focus our awareness on the present moment, without judgment, and on the sensory experience we are having.

There are many ways that we can do this, some of them more complex than others. To keep things simple, especially for people who are new to it, we will outline two simple ways below.

1. **Counting breaths slowly to 30.**
   Sit quietly on the floor with your legs crossed. Use a cushion or block to give yourself a little more elevation to make it easier. If the floor is uncomfortable for you, then sit on a chair with your back straight. Then close your eyes and breathe very deeply and slowly. Focus on your breath and start counting your breaths until you reach 30. If you lose count, go back to one and start again. Once you have finished, gently open your eyes.

2. **Set a timer.**
   Another way to do this is to set a timer. Sit quietly on the floor with your legs crossed on a cushion or block, or on a chair with your back straight if the floor is uncomfortable for you. Set a timer for five minutes, choosing a gentle sound, like chimes, for when the timer expires. Close your eyes and start breathing deeply and slowly. Allow ideas to come and go, without holding onto any of them. If you notice yourself focusing on an idea, just let it go gentling, drawing your awareness to your sensory experience: sounds, smells, feelings, sensations. When the timer expires and you hear the chimes, gently open your eyes. As you get better at this, you may choose to increase the time to 10 minutes or 15 minutes.

I remember several years ago, when I first started meditating, I was going through a lot during that period of my life. I was finding it hard to sleep, I had a lot of stress, and there was a lot of negative top-down chatter in my narrative mind. I felt like I was always on, and I just wanted it to stop.

I wanted to make my mind like a TV set that I could turn on and off at will. So, I decided to learn to meditate.

At first, I found myself focusing on ideas and thinking about them really deeply, after all I studied philosophy in university and I thought this is what I should be doing. Then, the people who were teaching me to meditate told me just to let the ideas come and go, come and go. It took me a year of practice to finally understand what this meant and to make my mind like a TV set that I could turn off and on as I liked. I learned for myself that thinking was like talking to myself, and that meditating was like listening to myself. So, rather than thinking deeply about ideas, I listened to myself, paying attention and increasing my awareness of the sensory experience around me. This really helped me to deal with what I was going through at that time and to have more "executive control" of my mind.

---

**Exercise**

**Meditation**
Develop your *mindfulness* through meditation.

If you already have your own meditation practice, do this now for the time that you usually do this. Think about how this practice helps you to focus more, be more awake to and aware of what is around you and inside you, and to have more "executive control" of your attention.

If you do not have your own meditation practice, try the two simple methods outlined above. Then see for yourself how this can help your focus, awareness, "executive control" and purposefully being in the present moment.

## NOTES

1 Davidson, R. J., Kabat-Zinn, J., Schumacher, J., Rosenkranz, M., Muller, D., Santorelli, S. F., Urbanowski, F., Harrington, A., Bonus, K. and Sheridan, J. F. "Alterations in brain and immune function produced by mindfulness meditation." *Psychosomatic Medicine*, 65, 564–70. 2003.

2 Siegel, D. J. *The Mindful Brain: Reflection and Attunement in the Cultivation of Well-Being*. New York, NY: Norton & Company. 2007.

# Five

Stare at a clock for 1 minute and wait for it to change – it will seem like it takes forever. Completely engage and immerse yourself in your work and time will seem to pass effortlessly or seem irrelevant. What makes this difference?

Coined by Mihály Csikszentmiháyi, in psychology and neuroscience, flow is the mental state of being fully immersed in a feeling of energized focus, full involvement, and enjoyment in the process of the activity we are doing. In essence, it is characterized by complete absorption in what we do, performing at the edge of our capabilities, peak performance. In this state, it feels effortless, as if things are flowing together.

Researchers credit flow with most athletic gold medals and world championships, major scientific breakthroughs and significant progress in the arts, but this might only be the very beginning of the revolution.

We are in micro flow all the time; it's always there. When we look for it, then we can ride it into jacked flow. We can train ourselves into flow. And heighten our performance.

This usually occurs when our body or mind is stretched to its limits in a voluntary effort to accomplish something challenging and worthwhile. Flow experience is, therefore, something that we make happen; it is not something that happens to us. For a child, this could be placing the last block on a tower she has built, higher than any she has built so far; for a runner, it could be trying to beat his own personal best record; for a pianist, mastering an intricate musical piece. For each of us there are thousands of opportunities and challenges to expand ourselves.

Flow depends on our ability to control what happens in our consciousness moment by moment. Each of us has to achieve it on the basis of our own individual efforts and creativity. We are in control of consciousness when we have the ability to focus attention at will, to be oblivious to distractions, and to concentrate for as long as it takes to achieve a goal, and not longer. In Chapter Four: Mindfulness, we dove deep into how we

DOI: 10.4324/9781003127000-5

can develop this ability to control our attentional deployment and focus at will on what we choose to. If you haven't yet read this chapter and would like to develop your ability to have more executive control of your brain and how you can deploy your attention at will, perhaps read this first, then come back to this chapter. When we can do this, we usually enjoy everyday life even more.

When we are in flow, with full concentration, laser-focus and complete absorption in what we are doing, we are functioning at top peak performance, and the experience is so engaging that it is almost painful to slow down. We are in a state of mind that creates an optimal experience for us and propels us to push forward with such tenacity that we feel like we are "flowing." This is why Mihály Csikszentmihályi called it flow.

As a result, one of the most universal and distinctive features of flow is that we become so involved in what we are doing that the activity becomes spontaneous, almost automatic. We stop being aware of ourselves as separate from the actions we are performing. In Mihály Csikszentmihályi's book Flow, he says:

> A dancer describes how it feels when a performance is going well: "*Your concentration is very complete. Your mind isn't wandering, you are not thinking of something else; you are totally involved in what you are doing …. Your energy is flowing very smoothly. You feel relaxed, comfortable, and energetic.*" A rock climber explains how it feels when he is scaling a mountain: "*You are so involved in what you are doing [that] you aren't thinking of yourself as separate from the immediate activity …. You don't see yourself as separate from what you are doing.*"[1]

For example, for me, besides being a consultant, I am also a music producer and drummer and have been drumming for about 40 years. When I am drumming, I am so absorbed in what I am doing that it is as if time stands still. I feel such laser-focused attention in the activity of drumming. It is so enjoyable. I feel the rhythm inside me and feel one with the rhythm. I feel my arms moving, lifting them up and letting gravity pull them down. My body and mind are one, working together, to play the different rhythmic patterns. And this allows me to perform at the highest level.

Also, when I design a presentation, I also get myself into flow. I will wake up in the morning, have a clear idea of what I want the presentation to be and then just start into it. First, I storyboard with pencil and paper. I fold a sheet of paper into 16 squares, then draw a box in each of the squares. I then start plotting the storyline, zooming in and out of the details and the big picture, sketching visuals for it or making a note of a particular image I would like to use. Then, I review the storyline and look for any gaps and fill those in. Then, I am ready to open PowerPoint and design the slides. Starting with the big picture, I make the same number of slides as squares in my storyboard and put the titles in. For many of the slides, I can use slides from previous presentations as templates, changing the text. Then, I look for the images that I want for the image slides and design any new ones that I need. Then, I do a final check, and I am done. This whole process will take me about half a day. And my brain is in such a state that it propels me to push forward, with such sheer enjoyment that I forget about time and even eating.

I remember also several years ago, I had a job designing and building flower gardens. I remember that once I had laid out all the flowers in the design we wanted, we would then just start planting. And we just planted and planted and planted. We were so absorbed in what we were doing that time stood still and it felt effortless. I called it "power planting," and it was so engaging, that we just enjoyed it and loved it. In this state, I could plant 2,000 flowers in a day.

---

**Reflection**

*Visualize Yourself in Flow*

We have all been in flow before and we have all ridden the micro flow into jacked flow. To help understand more what it feels like to be in flow, visualize yourself when you have been in flow. Here are some exercises to help you understand more about flow and to visualize yourself when you have been in flow.

1. Ask yourself: When have hours passed by without you realizing it? Perhaps you were so engrossed with painting or dancing that you didn't hear your phone or, like me, you were working on a PowerPoint presentation so intently that you lost track of time. Think of a time when you were doing an activity and you felt this way. What activity were you doing?

2. Ask yourself: When have you felt like things just clicked into place, when what you were doing seemed to be effortless and

you felt a sense of ease? Perhaps you spent the whole morning phoning clients and it just seemed so easy and effortless as you were engaging with them and building connections. Think of a time when you were doing an activity and you felt this way. What activity were you doing?

3.  Observe yourself: With an understanding of what it feels like to be in flow, for the next two weeks, notice when you feel this way – when what you are doing seems effortless and that time passes without you realizing it. What kinds of activities are you doing when this happens? This is your flow state and you can get yourself into it with different activities.

### The Neuroscience of Flow

In flow, as our attention heightens, the slower and energy-intensive extrinsic system (conscious processing) is traded off for the far faster and more efficient processing of the subconscious, intrinsic system. According to Arne Dietrich, a neuroscientist at the American University in Beirut, "It's an efficiency exchange. We're trading energy usually used for higher cognitive functions for heightened attention and awareness."[2] This is why it feels effortless. Because it's an efficiency exchange of the energy in our brain – trading the energy we normally use for resource-intensive conscious thinking activity for (resource-efficient) heightened attention and awareness. The technical term for this exchange is "transient hypofrontality."

There are also changes in our brainwaves. When we are in flow, we transition from the faster-moving beta waves of normal waking consciousness to the slower, deeper alpha waves and even borderline with the theta waves. Alpha waves are like a day-dreaming mode – when our mind goes from idea to idea smoothly without friction. Theta waves are the ones that we experience during REM or just before we fall asleep, in that transitional state between awake and asleep, where ideas combine in amazing and unique ways. This change in brainwaves helps us in idea generation and decision-making.[3]

This is just like when we are dragon boating (I am also a dragon boater), which is a competitive canoeing sport with 20 paddlers and a coxswain. The paddlers paddle and the coxswain is in command of and steers the boat. The world around us is the fast-moving beta waves.

Then, the coxswain will say, "Heads in the boat!" And then we suddenly filter out the outside world and enter the mindset of complete focus and slower alpha-theta waves, which rides us into flow.

There is also the neurochemistry of flow. Neuroscientists at Bonn University,[4] as well as other researchers, have determined that endorphins, norepinephrine, dopamine, anandamide and serotonin are all part of flow's cocktail of neurochemicals. All five of these are pleasure-inducing, performance-enhancing neurochemicals that increase muscle reaction times, attention, pattern recognition and lateral thinking – all of which will aid us in quick problem-solving. And very few activities except flow can produce all five of these neurochemicals.

### The Benefits of Flow

There are many benefits of flow. Our self-consciousness disappears (that inner Woody Allan); we keep calmer. Creativity and performance go up. Linking ideas and problem-solving go up. We are happier. It truly is peak performance.

In a ten-year McKinsey study, top executives reported being five times more productive in flow.[5] This means, if you spend Monday in flow, you can actually take the rest of the week off and still get more done than your steady-working peers. Most of us spend less than 5% of our work life in flow; however, according to that same McKinsey study, if we increase that number up closer to 20%, overall workplace productivity would almost double.

Flow also helps us learn faster than ever. Recent research has put this number somewhere between 400% and 500% faster. According to research by Advanced Brain Monitoring and DARPA, subjects had a 490% increase in skill acquisition in the state of flow.[6]

Flow also enhances creativity and problem-solving. When researchers at The University of Sydney tested flow's impact on creative problem-solving abilities with a very tricky mental puzzle, none of the participants could solve the problem normally. But when flow was induced artificially 40% of them could solve the puzzle. The same researchers also found that in a flow state, creative problem-solving increases by 430%.[7]

Csikszentmihalyi also found, through his research, that the people who have the most flow in their lives are the happiest people on Earth.[8] One interesting dimension of flow is that, while we are in flow, we are able to forget all the unpleasant aspects of life. Our self-consciousness disappears (that inner Woody Allan). This feature of flow is an important by-product of the fact that enjoyable activities require our complete focus of attention on the task we are doing, thus leaving no room in the mind for irrelevant information.

Flow is important because it makes our life in the moment more enjoyable, and because it builds the self-confidence that allows us to develop skills and make significant contributions to ourselves and the world. In flow, we are challenged to do our best and must constantly improve our skills. When we are in flow, we don't have the time to reflect on what this means in terms of ourself. But afterward, when the activity is over and our self-consciousness has had a chance to resume, our self is now enriched with new skills and achievements and is not the same self that existed before the flow experience.

Following a flow experience, the organization of ourself is more complex than it had been before. Because it is becoming increasingly complex, our self grows and becomes more than it was before.

Flow helps to integrate ourself because in this state of deep concentration, our consciousness is unusually well ordered. Our thoughts, intentions, feelings and all our senses are focused on the same goal – they are in harmony. And when the flow episode is over, we feel more "together" than before, not only internally but also with respect to other people and to the world in general. This is an amazing benefit of flow.

### The Conditions and Triggers for *Flow*

Flow is not something that simply happens. There are conditions and triggers for flow to occur. We can divide these into the psychological conditions/triggers and the environmental conditions/triggers. Both are necessary for us to ride into *jacked* flow.

### Psychological Conditions/Triggers for Flow:

1. **Complete concentration** on the task – no distractions, no multitasking, singular tasks, solitude, laser-focused attention.
2. **Clarity of goals and reward** in mind – this helps us to stay focused and motivates us to perform and achieve something meaningful.
3. **Immediate feedback** – measuring our progress and knowing how to improve performance in real-time means that our mind stays present and propels us to perform even better.

4. **Transformation of time** – time may feel that it is speeding up or slowing down or that it is standing still, or that we lose track of the time because we are so absorbed in the task at hand.

5. The experience is **intrinsically rewarding** – we get an immediate rush of joy and pleasure from the activity we are doing while we are in *flow*.

6. It feels **effortlessness** – as mentioned earlier, we are using a resource-efficient part of our brain and therefore it feels easy and effortless.

7. There is a **balance between challenge and skills** – the task or goal is challenging, but manageable; it is stretching, but not straining; we feel our skills and knowledge are being challenged and stretched; we experience a feeling of "being on the edge," of having the right balance between challenge and skills.

8. **Actions and awareness are merged** – because of the intense concentration and laser-focus on the task and goal, we eliminate the state of our self-conscious rumination.

9. There is a feeling of **control** over the task – we feel a sense of autonomy and executive control in what we are doing.

**Environmental Conditions/Triggers for Flow:**

1. **High consequences** – an elevated level of risk keeps us focused; this could be because it's an extreme sport, a performance for an audience, a looming deadline, etc.

2. **Rich environment** – an environment with lots of novelty, unpredictability and complexity can focus our attention; not knowing what is coming next can activate *flow*.

For example, this morning when I woke up, I knew I was going to spend all day working on this book. There is a clear deadline and it will be published for the world to read. So, there are clearly high consequences. We are living through the COVID pandemic, the world is changing rapidly and I am surrounded by interesting and successful people. So, the environment is quite rich indeed.

With these clear goals and rewards in mind, I am able to completely absorb myself in writing with laser-focused attention and concentration, which transforms time, and makes it feel easy and effortless. I reread what I write and talk to others about it and, therefore, can get immediate feedback. I feel that I am in control, that actions and awareness merge and it's intrinsically rewarding – so much so, that slowing down or getting distracted feels painful. And finally, I feel that I am at the edge of my capabilities and skills, without going over – I feel challenged and stretched, but it is manageable and not straining.

Now, to help me prepare to get into flow, there are some exercises that I do which allow my brain to create the conditions and triggers to ride myself into *jacked flow*. Below are the exercises, and I invite you to do them as well too.

---

**Exercise**

**The Conditions and Triggers for Flow**
To help activate the conditions or triggers for flow, here are three exercises to help stimulate your brain into this state. Do them in this order as they build on each other.

1. Mindful breathing (or any other *PQ Reps* from Chapter Four: *Mindfulness*). This is to filter out distractions and help you take executive control of your attention.

2. Focus on the words of your goal or task (e.g., for me: the goal could be "Create PowerPoint slides" [this is easy to reach at one time]; a task could be "write book" [this cannot be completed at one time, but rather it is part of a bigger goal; it can also be made into a goal, e.g., "Finish making notes for and structuring this chapter."]). So, focus on the words of your goal or task. This will help trigger your brain into an "alpha state," where ideas will start to come together.

3. Visualize what "being on the edge" looks and feels like to you. Maybe this could be riding the edge of a wave on a surfboard. Or lining up at the start of a race. Or maybe it's the feeling of stretching an elastic to the maximum and maintaining that stretch. Maybe it's the feeling of being at the top of the mountain, at the edge between land and air. Think first then, what does "being on the edge" look and feel like to you? Then hold this image in your mind, visualize it and feel the rush of "being on the edge." This will help ride your brain into complete focus and *jacked flow*.

---

### How to Get Into and Increase *Flow*

There is a process that can get us into flow and even the simplest physical or mental acts can become enjoyable when they are transformed to produce flow. The essential steps in this process are:

a. Set an overall goal, and as many subgoals as are realistically feasible.
b. Find ways of measuring progress in terms of the goals chosen.
c. Keep concentrating on what you are doing, and keep making finer and finer distinctions in the challenges involved in the activity.
d. Develop the skills necessary to interact with the opportunities available.
e. Keep raising the stakes if the activity becomes boring.[9]

#### *Flow* Through Physical Movement

We can get into flow through activities that involve physical movement. This is what athletes call "the zone." Dancers get into this when they are in the moment of moving their bodies with the music. Musicians and painters get into it as well with the movement of their crafts. Musicians call it "being in the pocket" or "being in the groove." It could also be doing yoga, going for run, a hike or a bicycle ride; or doing physical labor like construction, carpentry or working on a factory line; or cooking or cleaning – any activity that involves physical movement that challenges us to the edge of our capabilities.

For me, I get into this kind of flow when I dragon boat. As mentioned before, when the coxswain says, "Heads in the boat!," everyone focuses in. I focus in. And with complete concentration, we hit that first stroke of the race. And we don't give up until we hit the finish line. Each one of us is in flow and together we are all in flow.

Also, for me, when I play drums, I get my mind "in the pocket" or in flow, feeling the physical movement of my hands and arms as well as the sounds being produced. And I sustain this through the entire piece of music, until the very last sound.

I get into this while I'm cooking too, with such concentration that it is fast and seems effortless.

What physical activities do you do that challenge you and your capabilities – that allow you to concentrate and sustain that concentration until the end? Perhaps, it is yoga, running or hiking. Perhaps, dancing, painting or music. Maybe it's an extreme sport like snowboarding or mountain climbing. Or perhaps not so extreme like soccer or basketball.

Maybe it's cooking or sewing; or doing some kind of manual labor. What physical activity do you do that allows you to get into flow? The next time you do this, feel yourself getting into flow as you are doing it.

*Flow* Through Mental Stimulation

We can also get into flow through mental stimulation. This could be through brainstorming and solving complex problems, or focusing on achieving work-related goals like designing a deck of PowerPoint slides, drafting a proposal, solving a technical issue, planning a production schedule or executing a solution – any activity that involves mental stimulation that challenges us to the edge of our capabilities.

For example, this is exactly how I feel right now as I am completely focused on writing this book, and writing this chapter on flow. I myself am in flow, completely absorbed in what I am doing. With a goal of completing this book and completing this chapter, being able to measure my progress to that goal by finishing each section in the chapter, and pushing myself to the edge of my capabilities by stretching and challenging my brain through mental stimulation.

It is also the same, as I mentioned before, when I design a deck of PowerPoint slides. First, having the idea. Then, storyboarding it with pencil and paper. Then, using templates from past presentation decks. Then, making the new slides I need. Finally, checking and revising the slides, looking out for any gaps or omissions that need filling in. Then, bang, I'm done. And all of this will take about half a day, and it just feels effortless – challenging my brain through mental stimulation, yet feeling effortless.

**Exercise**

**Flow Through Mental Stimulation**

We're going to use this exercise to ride ourselves into *jacked* flow. This will help you to 5× your productivity and accomplish more with less effort. To do this, allow yourself 90 minutes to focus on a goal and tasks that are very important to you right now.

Think of something you are working on now. What is the goal? This could be to "finish a deck of slides," "design a proposal for a client," "troubleshoot a client's issue," "write computer code," "phone clients to make sales," "complete a process or admin work," "plan a production schedule," etc. Choose something that you need to do yourself, through your own efforts and time, even if it's "your part" of a bigger project. In other words, choose something that you need to do yourself, without other people.

Then, prime your brain for flow:

1. Do some mindful breathing (or any other PQ Reps from Chapter Four: Mindfulness). This is to filter out distractions and help you take executive control of your attention.
2. Focus on the words of your goal. What are you aiming to achieve? Why? What is the benefit? What tasks will you need to do?
3. Visualize what "being on the edge" looks and feels like to you. Visualize yourself at the edge of your capabilities, using your skills and knowledge to push and challenge yourself.

Now focus your mind on that goal and the tasks you need to do. Keep your "head in the boat," feeling complete concentration and control over the tasks you are doing. Do not stop or let up until you have completed it. If 90 minutes have passed, take a ten-minute break or so to relax and clear your mind. Have some downtime to switch off. Then, get back into it, by priming your brain for flow and then again complete concentration on what you are doing.

Use this exercise every time you want to get yourself into flow with all your work-related activities that require your mental capabilities. This will help 5× your productivity and make it feel effortless.

## NOTES

1 Csikszentmihalyi, M. *Flow*. New York, NY: HarperCollins. 1990. (p. 53).

2 Dietrich, A. "Neurocognitive mechanisms underlying the experience of flow." *Consciousness and Cognition*, 13(4), 746–61. December 2004.

3 Sacchet, M. D., LaPlante, R. A., Wan, Q. Pritchett, D. L., Lee, A. K. C., Hämäläinen, M., Moore, C. I., Kerr, C. E. and Jones, S. R. "Attention drives synchronization of alpha and beta rhythms between right inferior frontal and primary sensory neocortex." *Journal of Neuroscience*, 35(5), 2074–82. February 4, 2015.

4 University of Bonn. "Runners' high demonstrated: brain imaging shows release of endorphins in brain." *ScienceDaily*. March 6, 2008.

5 Cranston, S. and Keller, S. "Increasing the 'meaning quotient' of work." *McKinsey Quarterly*. January 1, 2013.

6 Berka, C., Levendowski, D. J., Cvetinovic, M. M., Petrovic, M., Davis, G., Lumicao, M. N., Zivkovic, T., Popovic, M. V. and Olmstead, R. E. "Real-time analysis of EEG indexes of alertness, cognition, and memory acquired with a wireless EEG headset." *International Journal of Human–Computer Interaction*. 17(2), 151–70. June 9, 2010.

7 Chi, R. P. and Snyder, A. W. "Facilitate insight by non-invasive brain stimulation." *Plos One*. 6(2), e16655. February 2, 2011.

8 Csikszentmihalyi, M. *Flow*. New York, NY: HarperCollins. 1990.

9 Csikszentmihalyi, M. *Flow*. New York, NY: HarperCollins. 1990. (p. 97).

**COMPANION WORKBOOK**

As you may have noticed, each chapter has exercises and reflection activities. If you would like to keep a record of your journey all in one place and have a working tool that you can go back to, there is a Companion Workbook. This is a free interactive pdf that you can save as you go along. To access it, go to the following URL or scan the QR code below.

www.selfleadershipassessment.com/workbook/

# Six

In 1943, Abraham Maslow created *Maslow's Hierarchy of Needs*, which represents human needs as a pyramid with the more basic needs at the bottom, and the higher-level psychological needs at the top. At the very bottom are the physiological needs (food, water, warmth, rest, oxygen). These needs are not only for our survival, they are also, as modern neuroscience has shown us, necessary for higher cognitive functions and regulating our stress.

This chapter focuses on the impact of physical health on cognitive behavior – how our physiological needs for food, water, warmth, rest and oxygen can help or hinder our thinking, decision-making, processing of information, regulating our emotions, managing ourselves through change, building relationships with others and all other higher cognitive functions.

The ideas in this chapter are suggestions and not meant to be a definitive list for everyone. I would like to advise all readers to find what works for you at your level (the local level), whether that be consulting with a dietician or nutritionist about food, a sports trainer who can help you adapt exercise, a doctor or counselor, or any other person or way to find what works best for you.

This is a very complex topic, which is compounded by structural inequalities and inherent risk factors. The ideas in this chapter are meant as suggestions and examples. Please substitute with similar or equivalent ideas that are more familiar or more accessible to you, wherever you are located; and adapt these suggestions and ideas to fit what's best for you.

### Food

What are you eating? And what is it doing to your brain?

There are many foods that have a positive effect on our brains to help us concentrate, think better, regulate our emotions and make better decisions. In general, we want a wide variety of foods including fish and

DOI: 10.4324/9781003127000-6

meat (for those who eat it) and a wide range of colors for the vegetables and fruits that we eat.

Below is a list of some of the top foods for our brain and the effects that they have. Some of these may be more readily available than others and some people may have specific dietary needs. So, please do exercise caution, choose what works best for you and consult a dietician or nutritionist if you like.

### Fatty Fish

Fatty fish includes salmon, trout and sardines, which are all rich sources of omega-3 fatty acids. About 60% of our brain is made of fat, and half of that fat is the omega-3 kind. Our brain uses omega-3s to build brain and nerve cells, which are essential for learning, memory and decision-making.

### Coffee

Coffee can help boost alertness, improve mood and sharpen concentration because of the caffeine and antioxidants.

### Blueberries

Blueberries are packed with antioxidants and flavonoids that improve memory and retention.

### Pumpkin Seeds

Pumpkin seeds are an excellent source of magnesium, iron, zinc and copper, which boost learning, memory and cognitive functioning, as well as enhancing our mood.

### Green Tea

Green tea contains caffeine and an amino acid called L-theanine. These improve alertness, performance, memory and focus. L-theanine also increases the frequency of alpha waves in the brain, which helps us relax without making us feel tired.

### Broccoli and Kale (and Other Green Vegetables)

Broccoli and kale are rich in compounds called glucosinolates. When the body breaks these down, they produce isothiocyanates, which can help lower stress and improve our mood.

### Oranges

Oranges contain vitamin C, which is useful in managing anxiety and stress.

### Beets

Beets contain betaine, which supports serotonin (a mood stabilizer) production in the brain. Beets also have a potent dose of folic acid in them, which stabilizes emotional and mental health.

### Wholegrains

Wholegrains have a low glycemic index, which means they release their energy slowly into the bloodstream, keeping us mentally alert throughout the day and improving concentration and focus.

Other foods, which contain vitamins, antioxidants and other nutrients that are good for our brain, include turmeric, dark chocolate, nuts (especially walnuts), dried fruit, avocados, eggs, soybean products, beans, tomatoes and spinach.

And, of course, there are foods that have a negative effect on our brain like carbonated soft drinks, red meat, fried foods, alcohol and junk food. These should be avoided or minimized.

Having a balanced diet that includes all of this will boost our cognitive functioning, increase alertness and concentration, lower our stress, help regulate our emotions and enhance our learning and memory. This will help us make better decisions and lead ourself and others more effectively.

So, what are you eating? What choices of foods could you make to help you improve your brain and cognitive functioning? Do an audit of your food intake and make some healthier choices. Consult a dietician or nutritionist, if you like, to choose what works best for you.

## Water

I used to go get a glass of water when I felt I needed it. However, I realized that when I am in flow and focused on my work, that I would often forget this. As a result, at times, I would go a long time without getting another glass of water. Therefore, I decided to keep my sports water bottle with me at all times so that I don't need to get up to go get water.

So then, how does water affect our brain?

Dehydration leads to a loss of concentration and negatively affects our cognitive performance. Studies have shown that dehydration can affect our motor skills, awareness and even our mood. It causes our brain to not run at full speed. Some of the mental symptoms of dehydration include brain fog, afternoon fatigue, focus issues, depression, anger, exhaustion, headaches, sleep issues, stress and a lack of mental clarity and acuity.

Have you ever found yourself feeling this way? Are you drinking enough water?

Our brain is about 75% water. When our brain is functioning on a full reserve of water, we will be able to think faster, be more focused and experience greater clarity and creativity. Water is also essential for delivering nutrients to our brain and for removing toxins. When our brain is fully hydrated, the exchange of nutrients and toxins will be more efficient – thus ensuring better concentration and mental alertness.

Since our brain is mostly water, drinking it helps us in a number of ways, including:

- Improving concentration and cognition.
- Helping to balance our mood and emotions.
- Maintaining memory function.
- Boosting our brain's reaction time.
- Increasing blood flow and oxygen to our brain.
- Preventing and relieving headaches.
- Reducing stress.

Since everybody is unique, everyone needs a different amount of water per day. The amount of water we need is based on many factors including our gender, height, weight and activity level. On average, an adequate intake for men is roughly about 3 liters (100 fluid ounces) a day; for women it is about 2.2 liters (74 fluid ounces) a day.

The color of our urine can help us determine our hydration level. If our urine is very light yellow (like lemonade) and has little odor, we're well hydrated. The darker and more aromatic our urine, the more dehydrated we are.

How much water are you drinking? Are you getting the right amount for your gender and size? Do you have water with you when you need it? Decide what works best for you and consult your doctor or other professional for advice if you like.

### Temperature

Our body needs warmth to survive; we need to maintain a normal temperature between 36.5°C (97.7°F) and 37.5°C (99.5°F). Dropping below will give us a cold; going above will give us a fever. But what is the effect of temperature on our brain? For example, I like air conditioning when I work because it keeps me alert and stimulates my thinking; others prefer natural outdoor air to facilitate their cognitive functions.

Scientific studies indicate that weather conditions such as high temperature and humidity can impair mental performance and cause cognitive impairment, and that complex tasks are impaired more than simple tasks.

In a study by Harvard University,[1] researchers found that extreme heat makes it harder to think. In the study, the researchers tracked 44 students living in college dorm rooms during the summer of 2016. About half of the students lived in air-conditioned buildings, while the rest lived without air conditioning. Over 12 days, including a five-day heat wave, students took two tests each morning just after waking up. One test measured students' cognition and their ability to focus. The second test measured how quickly students processed and memorized information. The findings showed that during the heat wave, students who lived in the heat performed significantly worse than those who lived in air-conditioned dorms. The overheated students experienced decreased test scores across five measures, including reaction times and memory. Students in air-conditioned rooms were not just faster, but also more accurate.

#### What About Cold Weather?

One of the body's most important tasks is temperature regulation. When the environmental temperature is unusually hot or unusually cold, we must use energy – in the form of glucose – to maintain a healthy internal temperature; we shiver to avoid hypothermia and sweat to avoid heat exhaustion. These two processes, however, are not equally taxing. Cooling the body down requires more energy than warming it up.[2]

Warm temperatures, then, are more likely to deplete our resources as our bodies work to maintain a healthy internal temperature. This then uses up resources that would otherwise be available for mental processes. As a result, it reduces our capacity for cognitive functioning and we are less able to make complex decisions – we give up early, make more mistakes, and make poorer decisions.

These results do not mean, however, that people in warmer climates are more prone to impaired cognitive functioning and making poorer decisions than those in cooler environments. Human beings are remarkably adaptive; we automatically acclimatize to the environmental temperature where we live. What it does suggest, however, is that slight deviations in temperature from an expected norm do make a difference – what feels hot to me based in Singapore is different than what feels hot to someone in New York. It is the relative feeling compared to the expected norm that makes a difference in our cognitive functioning.

### What About Air Conditioning?

There have been studies also on different temperatures of air conditioning and the effect this has on cognitive functioning.[3] The results indicate that unfavorable air temperatures, whether too cold or too hot (i.e., 18°C or 30°C [64.4°F and 86.0°F)), considerably affect cognitive functions among indoor employees. The results of this study indicate that participants have better performance (accuracy) in 22°C (71.6°F) compared to 30°C and 18°C. In other words, the air temperature was more pleasant in the neutral air temperature range (22°C) and the participants had a good thermal comfort at these air temperatures, so their performance was significantly better. Many studies have shown that an increase of 1°C (1.8°F) leads to a decrease in performance by 2% compared to a neutral air temperature range of 22°C (71.6°F).

These results indicate that thermal comfort improves work performance, as well as the efficiency and quality of work, especially in controlled rooms, offices and other similar environments.

Each individual, of course, has their own preferences and optimal temperature, depending on where we are in the world, our gender, height, weight and other factors. Therefore, we should optimize the temperature for our peak performance and decide whether we perform better with air conditioning or natural air.

What is your preference? What temperature do you perform best at? How can you keep that optimal temperature while you are working? Decide what works best for you and consult your doctor or other professional for advice if you like.

### Sleep

Do you feel tired today? Did you not get enough sleep last night? If yes, or when this has happened, how does it make you feel the next day? Does it impact your behavior, your thinking, your concentration? Chances are, you could answer this with a resounding, "yes!" Our mental states vary over the course of the day, and sleep plays a major role in our alertness levels. If we have difficulty getting sleep due to our work or the demands of day-to-day life, we accumulate a sleep debt. The consequences of this include decreased levels of alertness and mental efficiency. While there is variation in our sleep needs, most adults require 7–9 hours per night.

Let's now look more at the effects of sleep on our brain and cognitive function.

First of all, sleep deprivation causes many issues:

- It leaves our brain exhausted. It can compromise our concentration, creativity, problem-solving skills and decision-making processes.
- It can slow down our reaction time.
- It can make us moody, emotional and quick-tempered, and lead to anxiety or depression.
- It makes us forgetful and get distracted more easily.
- It can negatively impact both our short- and long-term memory.
- It can impair learning.
- It can cause brain fog and cause us to make dumb mistakes.

On the positive side, sleep has many restorative functions for our brain. During sleep, our body heals itself and restores its chemical balance. Our brain forms new thought connections, helps process new information learned and helps memory retention. We even use the phrase, "Let me sleep on," to indicate this. This then frees up space for taking in new information the next day. Sleep also allows new ideas to form in our brain by connecting ideas together. These are those light bulb "aha" moments or *insights* (we deep dive more into insights in Chapter Seven: Insight). Sleep also plays a housekeeping role that removes toxins in our brain that build up while we are awake.

The benefits of adequate sleep include:

- Higher concentration and focus.
- Faster thinking and response time.
- Fewer mistakes.
- Regulating emotions; more positive mood; less stress.
- Enhanced memory.

- More creativity and better decision-making.

So how can we help ourselves have a better sleep? Here are some tips for getting a good night's sleep:

- Set a schedule – go to bed and wake up at the same time each day.
- Exercise regularly, but not in the evening hours close to bedtime.
- Stick to your bedtime schedule during weekends and holidays.
- Avoid caffeine and nicotine late in the day and alcoholic drinks before bed.
- Avoid heavy meals within a few hours before bedtime.
- Relax before bed – try a warm bath, reading or another relaxing routine.
- Create a comfortable room for sleep – avoid bright lights and loud sounds, keep the room at a comfortable temperature, and don't watch TV or have a computer in your bedroom.
- Refrain from using electronic devices right before bed.
- Don't lie in bed awake. If you can't get to sleep, do something else, like reading or listening to music, until you feel tired.
- See a doctor if you have a problem sleeping or if you feel unusually tired during the day. Most sleep disorders can be treated effectively.

### Power Naps

Sometimes we need that extra boost during the day. A power nap is great for this as it will increase our energy level. We can get incredible benefits from a 15- to 20-minute nap. We reset the system and get a burst of alertness and increased motor performance. This is what most people really need to stave off sleepiness and get an energy boost.

It can also enhance our memory, cognitive skills and creativity. After learning something, have a nap and we will remember and retain it more. In between major tasks, have a nap and it will ignite our cognitive skills and creativity. This is because a power nap will clear our brain's inbox and migrate short-term ideas and memories into our longer-term storage, freeing up our mind for new ideas.

How are you sleeping? Are you getting enough? Do you take power naps during the day? Are you able to keep your mental alertness and concentration all day? Decide what works best for you and consult your doctor or other professional for advice if you like.

In Chapter Eleven: *Time Management*, moreover, we dive into "*circadian rhythms*" and how sleep and power naps can match our natural cycles. If this resonates with you, and you haven't read this yet, perhaps read this next.

---

**Reflection**

**Food, Water, Temperature, Sleep**

1. Reflect on the kinds of foods you are eating (or maybe not eating), the amount of water you drink, the temperature of your environment, and the amount and quality of sleep you are getting. Thinking about what works best for you, what new habits could you start that would have a positive impact on your brain, emotions and thinking? (*Make a note here*).

   _____

   _____

   _____

   _____

   _____

---

**Breathing**

"Take a deep breath."

We often say this to people when they are stressed or feeling tense – and there is a good reason. Breathing has a major impact on our feelings, thinking and how our brains function.

You may also have noticed that when you are surprised at something, you take a sharp inhalation; and when you feel frustrated, you sigh it out.

So, what does all this mean, and how can we use our breathing to enhance our emotional and cognitive abilities?

Again, the ideas in this section are suggestions and examples. I would like to advise all readers to find what works for you at your level and adapt and modify any of these suggestions to your needs. And please consult a doctor, counselor, sports trainer or any other person who might advise you to find what works best for you.

### Controlling Our Breathing Calms Our Brain

While yoga and meditation have used breathing to calm the brain for ages, only recently has science started uncovering how it works. A 2016 study[4] accidentally stumbled upon the neural circuit in the brainstem that seems to play the key role in the breathing-brain control connection. Slow, controlled breathing decreases arousal and activity in the circuit; fast, erratic breathing increases arousal and activity. This, in turn, influences our emotional states. Simple controlled breathing exercises can regulate this circuit.

Moreover, inhaling deeply may not always calm us down. Taking a deep breath in is actually linked to the sympathetic nervous system, which controls the fight-or-flight response. But exhaling is linked to the parasympathetic nervous system, which influences our body's ability to relax and calm down. So, exhaling will calm us down more than inhaling.

### Breathing Modulates Emotional Recognition and Memory

Breathing also helps in emotional recognition and memory recall, with both processes being more accurate during breathing in, compared to breathing out. When we breathe in, we stimulate the neurons all across the limbic system, which are used for emotions and memory; and with mindful or focused breathing, we can synchronize the activity in this region. Moreover, inhaling through the nose stimulates the brain, whereas through the mouth causes little stimulation.

Also, when we are in a panic state, our breathing rhythm becomes faster. As a result, we'll spend more time inhaling than when in a calm state. Therefore, our body's innate response to fear with faster breathing could have a positive impact on brain function and result in faster response times to stimuli in our environment.

### Breathing Increases Arousal and Concentration

It turns out the yoga masters were right – breathing properly really can improve our attention span and help us focus better.

Researchers at Trinity College Institute of Neuroscience and the Global Brain Health Institute found that focused breathing affects levels of noradrenaline, a natural chemical in our brain.[5] Noradrenaline gets released into the bloodstream when we are curious, focused or emotionally aroused and enhances our attention to detail and concentration.

When we are stressed, we produce too much noradrenaline, making it difficult to focus. When we are feeling lethargic, we produce too little of it, which also makes it hard to focus.

Our attention and concentration are influenced by our breath, and it rises and falls with our cycle of breathing. It is possible, therefore, to optimize our attention level by focusing on and regulating our breathing.

There are two types of breathing practices that lead to greater concentration, depending on what it is that we want to improve.

If we are easily distracted and therefore can't concentrate, mindfulness breathing will help us focus better. Mindfulness breathing brings our attention to the present moment as we simply observe our breathing without attempting to control our breath.

If our level of arousal (feeling too stressed or too lethargic) is affecting our ability to focus, controlled breathing like *pranayama* can help by calming our nervous system. *Pranayama* breathing, also known as belly breathing, is a breathing technique that helps us to breathe with our lower abdomen and diaphragm for low deep breathing.

Mindfulness breathing: step-by-step guide:

1. Sit in a comfortable cross-legged position, upright in a chair or lie down if that's more comfortable.
2. Close your eyes.
3. Center yourself on your breath – just observe its natural rhythm without making an effort to adjust it.
4. Focus on the rise and fall of your chest, the sensation in your nostrils, and the sound the breath makes in your throat.

*Pranayama* breathing: step-by-step guide:

1. Inhale one continuous, long breath.
2. Pause and hold before exhaling without moving your muscles.
3. Exhale in a controlled, relaxed and continuous fashion.
4. Pause after exhaling, just as you did for the first pause.
5. Repeat this cycle.

Another technique we might want to use from time to time to shake up our thinking is *Alternate Nostrils* breathing. With this type of breathing, breathe in slowly through one nostril, holding the other one closed using your finger; then switch and hold the other nostril closed and breathe out. Breathe in through this nostril; then switch and breathe out through the other nostril. Continue this pattern. As this is not the usual way we breathe, it will shake up our mind a little.

So, to summarize the key takeaways from breathing:

1. Inhaling increases alertness; exhaling decreases stress.
2. If you have anxiety or are stressed, consciously and deliberately slow your breathing, with an emphasis on exhaling. This will calm your emotions.
3. If you are distracted and can't concentrate, try mindfulness breathing. This will increase your focus for deep thinking.
4. If your level of arousal is low (or too high) and you can't concentrate, try pranayama breathing. This will increase your focus for deep thinking.
5. If you are calm and want to increase your attention and response time of your brain, slightly speed up your breathing, but keep it deep and long. This might be useful for rapid thinking like brainstorming.
6. If you want to shake your thinking up, try alternate nostril breathing for a couple of minutes, then get back to thinking.

---

**Exercise**

**Breathing**

1. Practice these breathing techniques depending on the purpose you are aiming for. Try each one of them and notice the impact that it has on your brain, emotions and thinking. Note which ones work best for you and continue to practice these every day.

---

### Physical Fitness

Physical fitness is not only good for our body, it's good for our brain too. This includes sports, hiking, dancing, walking, biking, running, swimming, yoga, weight lifting, aerobic movement, zumba, stretching, tai chi and any other kind of physical fitness that gets our body moving and/or our heart and our sweat glands pumping.

The ideas in this section are meant as suggestions and examples of what physical fitness can do to our cognitive functioning. It is not meant to be a definitive list for everyone. I would again like to advise all readers to exercise caution and find what works for you and consult a doctor or sports trainer if you want help with your needs.

This is a very complex topic, which is compounded by structural inequalities and inherent risk factors. Please substitute with similar or equivalent ideas that match your needs, and adapt these suggestions and ideas to fit what's best for you.

### Exercise Boosts Our Mood and Reduces Stress

When we exercise, our body releases chemicals such as dopamine and endorphins in our brain that make us feel happy. Not only is our brain dumping out feel-good chemicals, but exercise also helps our brain get rid of chemicals that make us feel stressed and anxious, lowering our cortisol level. People who exercise tend to be happier and less stressed than those who don't exercise. Regular exercise can also help us control our emotions when we do feel angry or upset.

### Exercise Improves Memory and Thinking

Exercise increases the size of the hippocampus, the brain area involved in verbal memory, learning and thinking. This can then improve our long-term and short-term memory, as well as sharpen our cognitive functioning. Exercise also increases the blood flow and oxygen to the brain areas (e.g., prefrontal cortex) associated with rational and analytical thinking to facilitate and improve thinking ability.

### Exercise Improves Sleeping

Being active gives us more energy during the day and helps us sleep better at night. In turn, better sleep improves creativity and brain function.

### Exercise Regulates Breathing

I noticed when I go hiking, I inhale for three steps, then exhale for three steps. It creates a nice pulse and rhythm within us, walking at the same pace, regulating our breathing. When I go running, it's every four steps.

And, as we indicated earlier, breathing has a whole range of positive effects on our brain.

So, there are many great benefits of staying active and engaging in regular physical fitness.

What do you do to stay active and physically fit? This could be running, swimming, yoga, tai chi, zumba, stretching, weight lifting, playing sports, etc. What works best for you? How does it make you feel during and after?

### Massage

We get sore muscles from sports or working out, or from mental stress or tension. When we get a massage, it relaxes our muscles, aligning our muscles and putting them back into place where they should be, relieving our tension and stress.

Massage has a direct impact on lowering the levels of stress hormones that create the fight-or-flight response by lowering our cortisol level and can boost "feel-good" neurotransmitters like dopamine, serotonin, endorphins and oxytocin.

Massage also promotes efficient thinking and improves memory. Tight neck and shoulder muscles often limit the circulation to the brain, which then suppresses memory and concentration. When massage relaxes tense muscles, it eases stress, which then benefits thinking, memory and work efficiency.

And again, decide what works for you, consulting your doctor, sports trainer or any other person to match your needs.

**Reflection**

*Physical Fitness, Muscles, Massage*

1.  Reflect on the kinds of and amount of physical fitness that you engage in. Thinking about your needs, are you doing it regularly? Are you engaging your muscles and getting your heart rate up to have an impact on, not only your body, but also your brain? How might massage help you to improve your brain and cognitive functioning? Thinking about what works best for you and your needs, what new habits could you start

that would have a positive impact on your brain, emotions and thinking? (*Make a note here*).

_____

_____

_____

_____

_____

## NOTES

1  Cedeño-Laurent, J. G., Williams, A., Oulhote, Y., Zanobetti, A., Allen, J. G. and Spengler, J. D. "Reduced cognitive function during a heat wave among residents of non-air-conditioned buildings: an observational study of young adults in the summer of 2016." *PLOS Medicine*. e1002605. July 10, 2018.

2  Cheema, A. and Patrick, V. M. "Influence of warm versus cool temperatures on consumer choice: a resource depletion account." *Journal of Marketing Research*. 49(6), 984–95. December 1, 2012.

3  Abbasi, A. M., Motamedzade H., Aliabadi, M., Golmohammadi, R. and Tapak, L. "The impact of indoor air temperature on the executive functions of human brain and the physiological responses of body." *Health Promotion Perspectives*. 9(1), 55–64. January 23, 2019.

4  Yackle, K., Schwarz, L. A., Kam, K., Sorokin, J. M., Huguenard, J. R., Feldman, J. L., Luo, L. and Krasnow, M. A. "Breathing control center neurons that promote arousal in mice." *Science*, 355(6332), 1411–15. March 31, 2017.

5  Melnychuk, M. C., Dockree, P. M., O'Connell, R. G., Murphy, P. R., Balsters, J. H. and Robertson, I. H. "Coupling of respiration and attention via the locus coeruleus: effects of meditation and pranayama." *Psychophysiology*, e13091. 2018.

# Seven

Some four million babies around the world die within a month of their birth, according to the World Health Organization. But as many as 1.8 million of those infants might be saved if they could spend a week in an incubator. The problem is that incubators are expensive, require electricity and need expertise to maintain. This is a real issue for developing countries.

Now, we could take an analytical approach to solving this: what is the root cause of the problem? how can we solve this? Or, we could take a more diffuse approach. An analytical approach is good when there is one clear solution. For example, a math problem, the shortest route to our destination, or creating a part of a product smaller. However, when we have problems that don't have one clear solution, for example, creating renewable energy, motivating someone in our team, or writing a book, a diffuse approach can help us.

One organization, Design That Matters, tackled this issue with a diffuse approach.[1] Instead of asking, "How can we get more incubators to places that need it?," they asked the question, "Of the places that need it, what are the available material and human resources that could be used to address this issue?" What they had noticed is that in most of these areas, there are cars, specifically Toyota cars, and that most towns had garages with skilled mechanics. So Design That Matters built an incubator made mostly out of car parts: a motorcycle battery as backup power in case the lights go out; car headlights to generate heat; an HVAC (heating, ventilation and air-conditioning) fan that blows the heat around; an engine-intake filter to remove dust, bugs and pathogens; BMX tires to help maneuver the incubator over rough floors; and turn signals to function as visual alarms if the baby is in trouble. Taking a diffuse approach, they generated insight.

So how can we have this kind of thinking to come up with such brilliant insight? What are the conditions to generate insight?

DOI: 10.4324/9781003127000-7

First, however, let's take a poll:

Question: Where do you have your best ideas?

a.  In the shower
b.  While exercising
c.  At your desk doing work
d.  Just before falling asleep or after waking up
e.  While going for a walk or hike
f.  While talking with a friend

Insight is really about connecting "weak signals" together, different ideas in our mind that may not seem to go together, to make new connections in our mind. Although we think insight is like an "a-ha" moment that suddenly happens, it is in fact a process with conditions that can lead to insight. And we have more control over our insight than we think we do.

First, if we focus too much directly on the problem (i.e., being too analytical), we create too strong of a signal in our mind. Therefore, weak signals won't be able to take over, we won't be able to make new connections and, as a result, won't generate insight. So, in order for us to have insight we first need to have a quiet mind (or a "resting prefrontal cortex"). In the poll, most people do not select "at your desk doing work" because there we are focused on our work, thinking analytically. Analysis is linear, using the rational, conscious part of our brain (the "prefrontal cortex"); insight, by contrast, relies on nonconscious parts of our brain. There is an increase in alpha activity just before the insight; then suddenly the alpha activity drops off and the gamma activity shoots up at the moment of insight. If we can influence the alpha and gamma activity, then we can lead to more, better and more frequent insight. By activating certain parts of our brain, we can create more gamma activity. The first step, therefore, is to quiet our mind, to let it drift and wander, to put our mind in a more alpha state, which will then lead to the gamma state. In Chapter Four: Mindfulness and Chapter Five: Flow, we dive into this also. If you haven't read these yet, and this resonates with you, perhaps read these next.

We also need to focus inward, freeing our mind of distractions, gating sensory input, not allowing too much external information in. This will allow the weak signals to take over and decrease the competition for conscious awareness. This will also allow our minds to have more "pattern completion" as opposed to "pattern separation." In neuroscience, pattern separation is defined as the process by which overlapping or similar inputs (ideas, thoughts) are transformed into less similar outputs; in other words, we separate them to categorize or make them distinct (an analytical process). Pattern completion, by contrast, is the process of transforming or reconstructing partial inputs (ideas, thoughts) into complete representations (new ideas); or in other words, forming new connections. So, we need to focus inward, and not allow too much external information in, so the weak signals can take over, decrease the competition for conscious awareness and allow new connections to form.

Finally, a positive mood also facilitates more insight; when our mood is anxious, we tend to solve problems in a more analytical way and focus more on external activity. A positive mood frees our mind to wander, thinking more diffusely, and therefore generate more insight.

Quieting the mind and letting it drift, having a positive mood, being open to pattern completion and allowing new connections to form, and not directly focusing on the problem – these then are the conditions for insight to happen. Moreover, if we release the constraints on one problem, it will loosen the constraints on other problems we have. This then leads to more insight in other complex problems we are facing. This is what Design That Matters did; and this is what you can do too. And the best and most efficient way to create more insight is to practice creating the conditions for insight, focusing on these four conditions:

1. Quietening the mind and letting it drift.
2. Having a positive mood.
3. Being open to pattern completion, allowing new connections to form.
4. Not directly focusing on the problem.

---

### Exercise

#### Practicing the Conditions for Insight
A paper clip is normally used to clip paper together. What other uses are there?

Quiet your mind, and let it to drift and wander.

Be open to new patterns of thinking and new connections.

Allow your mind to think freely.

1. What other uses of a paper clip can you think of? Try to come up with at least 10. (*Make a note here*).

_____

_____

_____

_____

_____

_____

_____

_____

_____

_____

2. What new insights or connections are forming in your brain? (*Make a note here*).

_____

_____

_____

_____

_____

### Developing Insights to Solve Our Own Challenges

I applied this to my own situation to solve one of my challenges.

Besides writing books and developing leaders, I am also a musician, composer and producer. More specifically, I play drums and write the music by developing interesting syncopated and polyrhythmic drum patterns, then structuring the music around this. After the song has been structured, I then give it to my cowriting partner to add the melodies on top of it. The end result is a very rhythmic dance music.

However, for over a year, after moving to Singapore (from Japan, where I had spent 17 years), I had not been able to write anything new. We played some good shows and released a new CD; however, I had not been able to write anything new. This then led me to the challenge.

So, the challenge is: how can I write new music?

As a complex problem, with no one clear solution, linear analytical thinking may not be the best approach; opting for a more diffuse approach will lead to new connections and insight. So, I tried that.

The first question I asked was: *"What is it similar to in my life?"* This question helps to activate diffuse pattern recognition, allowing us to not think about the problem directly. I thought it is similar to developing my YES brand. YES is the HR consulting company I started. How? You need to create an image (positioning), create value for the end user, have a concept, tell a story, create deliverables and execute with best practices. It is a whole value chain, as is writing music. Perhaps we can borrow something from the branding value chain to apply here; perhaps something where the bottleneck is (e.g., How to position our music? What value does it create for the end user? What value does it create for other stakeholders? What is the theme/story? How do we create the deliverables? What best practices are there to execute?).

I then reflected on the question: *"What am I considering already to solve this?"* This question leads us to go inward rather than focusing outward; and it takes us off the problem, and not thinking about it directly.

Here were the ideas that I thought:

i.   Considering now: structuring the songs with a theme, studying darbuka.

ii.  Did before: studied new drum patterns for inspiration, practiced the rhythms to see what would come of them.

iii. New idea (insight) that was formed through thinking of this question: the main song I am trying to write now is called *Goddess Song*; so I will research the term *"goddess rhythm"* on the internet for drum rhythms that will influence and inspire me; then I will practice those rhythms, molding them into the unique style of drumming I created.

This last idea was most interesting. Although I started with the question: *"What am I considering already to solve this?,"* I ended with a deep insight about a new idea. A new connection was formed between structuring songs with a theme and what I did before that was successful (practicing new drum patterns to see what would come of them). This also then ties in with the first question: *"How is it similar to my YES brand? Where is the bottleneck in the value chain?"* Positioning the music, the value and the themes were all okay. Perhaps creating deliverables? But the biggest bottleneck is the last question: *"What best practices are there to execute?"* I seem to have lost sight of this, looking for a new way to write songs. So, yet another connection was formed tying it all together: research the theme's "rhythm" for influence and inspiration; using best practices to execute, practice the new drum patterns to see what would come of them; and then structure the song from there. And I could do this with each of the new songs I am trying to write.

And so, these were the insights I had, by creating the conditions for insight.

And there are many examples of this in the world.

### The Dyson Vacuum

In 1978, James Dyson became frustrated with his vacuum cleaner's diminishing performance. Taking it apart, he discovered that its bag was clogging with dust, causing the suction to drop. A few years before that, he had designed and built an industrial cyclone tower for a factory that separated paint particles from the air using centrifugal force (a "weak" signal still in his mind, i.e., not directly connected with a vacuum cleaner). And he thought: could the same principle work in a vacuum cleaner? So, he set to work. And five years and 5,127 prototypes later, he invented the world's first bagless vacuum cleaner. Making associations and new connections between these "weak diffuse signals," he had an insight. And the rest is history.

### 3M Post It Notes

In 1968, Dr. Spencer Silver, a chemist at 3M Company, was trying to create a new super-strong adhesive for envelopes. Instead, however, he inadvertently invented a unique, low-tack adhesive that would stick to things but also could be repositioned multiple times. Instead of rejecting the idea as a failure because it could not be used for envelopes, he spent the next five years promoting his invention within 3M. Finally, after five years, someone thought it could be used as a bookmark or for writing memos on it. 3M launched the product and it was very successful. Had he taken an analytical approach and discarded the idea because it couldn't be used for envelopes (the goal he was aiming for), we never would have had Post It Notes. But by adopting a diffuse approach and asking the question: What *can* this be used for?, the use was found, and now Post It Notes are used every day around the world.

### The Invention of Velcro®

VELCRO® (hook and loop fastener) was invented by a man named George de Mestral in the 1940s while hunting in the Jura mountains in Switzerland. Mr. de Mestral, a Swiss engineer, realized that the tiny hooks of the cockle-burs were stuck on his pants and in his dog's fur and wondered how they attached themselves. Under the scrutiny of a microscope, he observed the hooks engaging the loops in the fabric of his pants. He duplicated mother nature's hook and loop fastener in a manufacturing plant. The result was VELCRO®, which comes from the French words for velvet "velour," and hook, "crochet." Having a problem of cockle-burs on his socks and pants, rather than just take them off, he thought "aha ... this can be used like a zipper to join things together" – an insight created by connecting two weak signals together.

### The Great Ormond Street Hospital

The Great Ormond Street Hospital is one of the largest children's hospitals in the UK, treating around 100,000 kids per year who suffer from various heart diseases. In 1994, studies found that the handover of patients from the surgical unit to the intensive care unit was at a high risk. There was a lack of coordination in the surgical team and small mistakes made by the team, which often went unnoticed, added up strongly to produce bad outcomes. This prompted the doctors to look hard on their teamwork and how they transferred patients from the surgical unit to the intensive care unit to overcome this threat to the life of the patients.

Two such doctors, Drs. Allan Goldman and Martin Elliot, fans of Formula 1 motor racing, found striking similarities between the Ferrari's pit crew and the handover procedures in the hospital. The "lollipop man" ushers the car into a halt and the crew changes the tires, replaces the damaged parts and clears the air vents and in a staggering 4–7 seconds the car is good to go back onto the track. In the hospital, the patient comes in, they are operated on by the group of surgeons and nurses and then handed over to the Intensive Care Unit. Drs. Goldman and Elliot then recruited the Ferrari's pit crew, technicians and racers as consultants to help them streamline the handover. After adopting the new method, technical errors caused during the handover dropped by 42%, and more lives were saved as a result. By borrowing from another process or area that was similar, they generated deep insights they would not have otherwise had and created amazing innovative ideas.

---

**Exercise**

**Developing Insights to Solve Your Own Challenge**

Get yourself in the mindset/conditions for insight:

- Quiet your mind, allowing it to drift and wander.
- Have a positive mood, with no anxiety.

- Focus inward, freeing your mind of distractions, gating sensory input, not allowing too much external information in.
- Focus not directly on the problem, but allow new connections to form.

Then answer the following questions about your situation.

1. What challenge or dilemma are you facing that does not have one clear solution? (Make a note here).

   _____

   _____

   _____

2. What situation or aspect in your life is it similar to? How is it similar to that? (Make a note here).

   _____

   _____

   _____

3. What are you considering already to solve this? (Make a note here).

   _____

   _____

   _____

4. What new connections or ideas came to you as a result of thinking of this? (Make a note here).

   _____

   _____

   _____

Use this exercise every time you have a dilemma or challenge. This will help you to have more and deeper insights. And the more you practice this, the more natural it'll become, forming a habit that will help you with your biggest challenges and dilemmas.

## NOTE

1  Drexler, M. "Looking under the hood and seeing an incubator." *The New York Times*. December 15, 2008.

# Eight

"What did you expect?"

We often use this phrase when we are disappointed because we didn't get what we wanted. Reality and expectations are not always the same. Expectations often contradict reality.

But what are expectations? Expectations are beliefs about what will happen in the future. Everything and every person we encounter, we assign meaning to and set expectations of them, whether conscious or unconscious. These expectations, moreover, come from our emotions, not from assessing the situation logically; they are what we feel or hope to get. These expectations then alter our perception and we behave and act based on our expectations.

For example, in a wine tasting experiment (Hilke Plassmann et.al., 2008), participants were presented with two wines, one was described as costing $45 a bottle, the other $5 a bottle. They were then assessed on their liking of the wines, as well as measuring the neuro activity in their brains. This experiment was repeated several times with different wines. In all cases, participants preferred the more expensive bottle of wine and had increased neuro activity in their brains. However, for each pairing of wines, the wine was exactly the same. The expectation was that the more expensive wine is better, and therefore it was perceived, and triggered in the brain, that it is better. I'm sure many of us have felt something similar: it's more expensive, and therefore we expect it to be better.

Or when we go to the doctor, they speak professionally with gentle body language, wear a white coat (rather than a suit), a medical degree is hung on the wall, a clean, well-lit doctor's office and soft music playing in the background. This makes us feel less anxious, that our pain will go away, and that we are being cared for. And even more so if the doctor was recommended by a close friend. So, the social context and credibility of

DOI: 10.4324/9781003127000-8

the person will influence our expectations. Contrast this with the feeling you might get if a junior nurse is going to attend to you.

And yet another example is with airline service. When we fly first class, we expect champagne, preferential treatment and more amenities. However, when we fly on a low-cost carrier, perhaps a smile and politeness may be enough. And so, we set a higher expectation with first class, and a lower one with a low-cost carrier.

I'm sure all these examples, and more, are familiar with all of us in our daily lives. We constantly set expectations of the situations we are in, of ourselves, and of the people we meet.

For myself, at the time of writing this book, I started again a process of choosing seven roles that I will do during the week and setting for each of them realistic and achievable goals for the week. One of the goals was creating a proposal for three events. Part of the proposal included creating a stage plan. I had never done it before so I researched what others had done, found some best practices and added my own ideas. The end result was something that was BTE (better than expected). I felt a rush in my brain and a reward sensation. It felt good.

In the past, by contrast, when I hadn't set goals for myself, it created a downward spiral because things weren't happening the way I wanted them to, and therefore, my expectations were definitely unmet.

Another example:

In 2015, on a sunny day, I moved to Singapore (from Japan, where I had spent 17 years). I started a company in Singapore for leadership development. I was excited to embark on a new journey; and I was excited to have coworkers, from a partner company, that I could socialize and go drinking with. I had expected us to be friends; however, their expectation was very different. They wanted/expected just to be coworkers, keeping more distance, and interact only on a professional level when there was a project to work on. Expecting to be friends and building a social relationship, my expectation was not met, and it created a strong threat response, a feeling of disengagement and distance.

In neuroscience, dopamine is the neurochemical in our brain that makes us feel good and is associated with feelings of euphoria, bliss, motivation, concentration and reward. If we meet our expectations, then it generates a slight increase in dopamine, and a slight reward response. If we exceed our expectations, it generates a strong increase in dopamine, and a strong reward response. And if our expectations are unmet, it generates a large drop in dopamine, and a strong threat response.

Expectations are the feeling of a "possible" reward, not the "actual" reward itself. This affects our emotions, motivations and changes the way we function (think, act and feel). Because of this, it can be overwhelming, as it could set us up for massive success or massive failure. Expectations are central in the creation of upward and downward spirals in the brain. They can take you to the peak of performance or to the depths of despair. Figure 8.1 shows the pattern of an upward spiral; Figure 8.2 shows the pattern of a downward spiral.

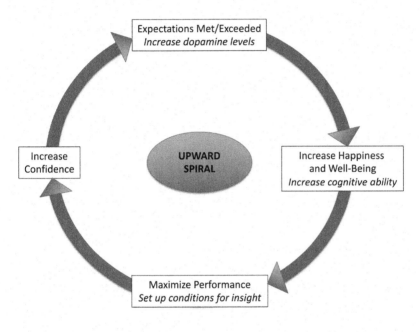

**Figure 8.1** Upward Spiral

If our expectations are met or exceeded, it increases our dopamine levels, which leads to increased happiness and well-being, which helps maximize our performance by setting up the conditions for flow and insight, which leads to more productivity and increased confidence. If our expectations are not met, however, then it dramatically decreases our dopamine levels, we feel disappointment and stress, resulting in poor performance and decreased confidence. And if a person doesn't meet our expectations, then we are disappointed in them.

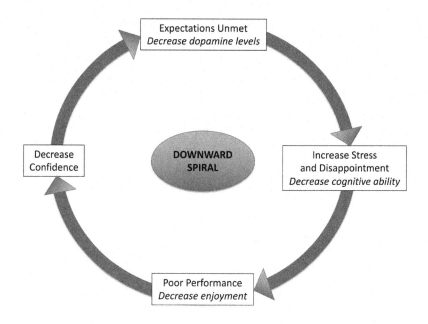

**Figure 8.2** Downward Spiral

**Exercise**

**Expectations, Upward and Downward Spirals**

Quiet your mind and reflect on your expectations: expectations of yourself, of others and of the situations you are in.

Then answer the following questions:

1. Thinking about the situations you are in now, what do you expect for yourself? What do you expect from the situation? What do you expect from others? What do they expect from you? (*Make a note here*).

   _____
   _____
   _____

2. Think of a time when your expectations were not met. How did it make you feel? (*Make a note here*).

_____

_____

_____

3. Think of a time when someone exceeded your expectation of them; how did it make you feel? (*Make a note here*).

_____

_____

_____

4. Think of a time when you achieved something that exceeded your expectations; how did it make you feel? (*Make a note here*).

_____

_____

_____

### Managing Our Expectations

Influencing our own, and other people's, expectations can have a remarkable effect on our perception or theirs. In addition, by delivering higher than expected, we can affect people's perception, which in turn influences what they think, feel and do. To do this, it requires a strong executive control and a strong director of our own brain. In neuroscientific terms, this comes from the front part of our brain called the prefrontal cortex (or PFC). When we go through change or experience disappointment, we feel unfairness or disgust because of mismanaged expectations. When we expect the worst or our expectations are violated, two other parts of our brain – the amygdala and the insula – get upset. The amygdala is responsible for our initial reaction: fight, flight or freeze; the insula is responsible for our feeling of disgust or unfairness. When we are in these situations, the amygdala and insula are screaming and overpower the PFC, not allowing it to take executive control for self-regulation and self-control.

To help us reduce future bursts of arousal, we can manage our expectations by being aware of what they are and choosing new expectations in their place. We can also preempt these bursts so that they don't happen at all. Each of the following techniques is even more effective if you have a strong director of your brain, and each of them builds your director further as you execute them.

### Strategies to Manage Expectations

#### Set the Expectations High to Create a "Placebo" Effect

Recall the example at the beginning, with a doctor wearing a white coat (rather than a suit), gentle voice, good environment, light music; we feel more confident with this person and trust/expect more positive as a result. This is okay, if it is to put people at ease, not to manipulate/deceive them. It can be something very beneficial and can help to influence the expectations and perceptions of others. This can also be applied in a corporate environment; for example, the way that a Manager communicates and relates to Team Members. On an organizational level, we can think of Google or Apple; we think "oh wow, look how cool it is to work here."

In psychology and neuroscience, a "placebo" effect is a beneficial effect produced, which cannot be attributed to the properties of the placebo itself, and must therefore be due to the person's belief in that placebo. This is often found in medicine or treatment research with patients, where they believe that the placebo, which has no inherent therapeutic value, makes them feel better. There have been decades of research on this that show that belief in the placebo has a very positive impact on people's brains, affecting their perception, feelings and actions.

In the example above, if the same doctor were wearing shorts and a t-shirt, and their office was dimly lit and unclean, although it's the same doctor, it would create a different perception for us.

I have also applied this for myself with clients and partners I work with. By looking and dressing professionally, walking the talk, listening with intent and adopting a consultative approach, it increases my credibility to deliver on what I say, builds trust and develops the relationship, creating even better outcomes for all parties involved, and increasing the overall value.

#### Set the Expectations Low, then Deliver High

Years ago, I used to have a phrase in my head: "Expect nothing and get everything in return." By setting expectations low, we will not be disappointed. If a bad outcome occurs, then we are not affected; if a good outcome occurs, then we think "wow, I didn't expect that." Even more so, if we set expectations low and then deliver high, we can dramatically influence the perceptions of others, in turn influencing their feelings, thoughts and actions.

Some of you may recall this. On April 11, 2009, Scottish singer Susan Boyle made an appearance as a contestant on the TV program *Britain's Got Talent*. She came out looking awkward and frumpy; not so attractive, as our magazine and pop star image might dictate; spoke in a very rough, inelegant way; and said, "I want to be a singer!" The camera then panned to the judges and the audience, who rolled their eyes and laughed to themselves. Well, for those of you who saw it, you know what happened. She began singing I *Dreamed a Dream* from the musical *Les Misérables*. And she was brilliant. The judges and audience stopped rolling their eyes and laughing; they felt her power, her energy and her emotions as she smashed it. We were all with her, every word, every sound that came out of her voice. And by the end of her performance, the audience was standing with tears in their eyes. She set the expectation very low, and she delivered on a level that was beyond imagination; and as a result, she became one of the most successful artists that have ever been on that show and launched an impressive singing career.

### Focus on Things Getting a Little Bit Better, Even at Times to the Contrary

I had a colleague once that used to say, "I like to think of a holiday coming up, even if it's months away, to help me be positive. If I focus on this, though it's not logical, I have learned this helps when times are not always great." Choosing to focus on things always getting a little bit better, even at times that may be contrary to this, helps us maintain a good level of dopamine. This, in turn, helps us to create more of an upward spiral.

What is it that you can think of to focus on things getting a little bit better? This could be a holiday coming up, a goal that you might have set for yourself, an important meeting with a client with whom you have a great relationship, an interview with your dream company, giving a talk at a networking event or any other activity you can think of to help you focus on things getting a little bit better.

### Do Positive Things That Are Unexpected

Unexpected rewards release more dopamine than expected ones. For example, the surprise bonus at work, even a small one, can positively impact our brain more than an expected pay raise. However, if we're expecting a reward and we don't get it, dopamine levels fall steeply. This feeling is not pleasant; it feels a lot like pain and disgust.

With this strategy in mind, think of some of the positive things you can do for others that they don't expect. This could be introducing them to someone who can help them, sharing knowledge with them with no expectation of something in return, listening to them when they need an ear to listen, inviting them to your private event, giving them a unique thoughtful gift, helping them to see things in a different way, or any other positive thing you can think of that they don't expect. This will give them a big hit of dopamine and create an upward spiral for them.

So, these are some of the techniques you can use to manage your expectations, create an upward spiral and increase the reward sensations of achieving or exceeding expectations.

---

**Exercise**

*Managing Expectations and Increasing the Reward Sensations*

1.  Reflecting on the strategies mentioned, how can you control or manage your expectations? (*Make a note here*).

    _____

    _____

    _____

2.  What actions can you take to promote an upward spiral? (*Make a note here*).

    _____

    _____

    _____

3.  What can you do to exceed others' expectations of you? (*Make a note here*).

    _____

    _____

    _____

# Nine

Imagine going for a peaceful hike, walking through the forest or along a mountain path. Then suddenly, "Rooooaaarrrrr ..." – a bear comes right in front of your face. How do you feel? What happens to you? Your senses register the stimuli: sharp teeth, growl, feral smell. Your autonomic nervous system takes over: heart races, adrenalin rush, sweating, increased breathing. The limbic system of your brain, where you feel instincts and impulses, bypasses the prefrontal cortex (PFC), where rational thinking occurs; and you feel fear. In essence, your body reacts before your mind even knows what happened.

Neuroscience has now shown us that the exact same feelings we get from a physical threat also occur with social or emotional threats.[1] The rest of this chapter will focus on how we can understand and deal with situations that we appraise, or interpret, as socially or emotionally threatening, and ways to handle these situations more effectively.

As an example, we all probably know the movie *Star Wars*, directed and written by George Lucas. In 1975, when he first proposed it to the studios, they loved it, but wanted to have control over it. How did this make him feel? Discomfort at a gut sense level, frustrated, powerless. One pathway he could have taken is to think, "Everybody in the film business agrees I should take the deal," and accept the offer. The result of this might have been the death of the most successful movie in history. Another pathway, and the one he took, is to think, "They are going to butcher my work, so I should say 'no'," decline the offer and make the film himself. This is what he did. The result: well, we know ... the greatest film franchise in movie history.

Let's look at another example, one that we all might be able to relate to:

You have a disagreement or argument with your boss, for example, about a task or piece of work you did. He or she blames you and gets angry. However, it wasn't because of you; it was because of something else, like you didn't have the data you needed. But they are still angry and blame you.

DOI: 10.4324/9781003127000-9

If this happened to you, what would you do?

A.  Avoid your boss.
B.  Don't listen to him or her.
C.  Focus on certain elements to listen to; filter out the rest.
D.  Reframe the meaning of what he or she is saying.
E.  Suppress your emotions.
F.  Moderate your emotional response.

Now, before we dig into each of these strategies, let's look at how the brain processes this situation.

### Cognitive Appraisal

Figure 9.1 shows how our brain processes any situation we encounter. The situation happens. This then causes feelings in us (initial unconscious reactions), which then lead to our conscious thoughts. Based on this, we then interpret or give meaning to the whole situation (i.e., is it threatening or rewarding?). This then, in turn, will influence the responses we have, the actions we take and the results of those responses and actions. Emotion is a process (how our brain responds to a situation), which then influences our behavior and actions.

How we appraise the situation is important. This varies across time (immediate vs longer term) and varies across individuals (some individuals interpret more negatively; some individuals interpret more positively).

After we appraise the situation, if it is something rewarding, we will pursue it, much as we would our goals. However, if we appraise the situation as something threatening or creating negative emotions in us, then we will need other strategies to help us.

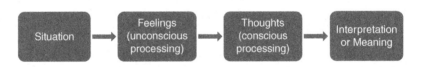

**Figure 9.1** Cognitive Appraisal

**Reflection**

*Cognitive Appraisal*

1. Thinking about your own situations you are in or have been in recently, how have you appraised them? (*Make a note here*).

   _____

   _____

   _____

2. Which ones are rewarding? (*Make a note here*).

   _____

   _____

   _____

3. Which ones are threatening or create negative emotions in you? (*Make a note here*).

   _____

   _____

   _____

### Ways to Regulate Emotions

Let's now look at the different ways to regulate emotions. Figure 9.2 shows different strategies to regulate our emotions.

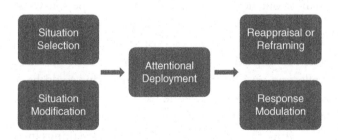

**Figure 9.2** Ways to Regulate Emotions

### Situation Selection

This is about choosing the situation you want to start with. In the example above, when you disagree with your boss, this would be "A. Avoid your boss," or even more extreme, quit the job. This is one option, but may not necessarily be the best one. For example, if George Lucas chose this, then we would not have *Star Wars*.

### Situation Modification

This is about modifying the situation you are in to make it more comfortable or bearable. For example, "B. Don't listen to your boss," or sit far away from them during team meetings. This is something we may choose, but may not have long-term lasting results.

### Attentional Deployment

This is where it becomes really important: where we deploy or focus our attention. If we focus on the threatening or emotional aspects, it will bring/drive us into a downward spiral. However, if we focus on the nonemotional aspects or distance ourselves, this is the start to creating an upward spiral. The more we sustain our focus on something, the denser our attention gets and the more hard-wired that habit or interpretation will become.

When faced with an emotional situation, one typical strategy for attentional deployment is *distraction*: shifting our attention away from the situation. This can have a temporary effect, but will not last because the situation is still there, and our attention will come back to it. But, at times, this will be effective for temporary relief. This could be, for example, thinking about lunch or our next vacation, rather than the person we should be listening to. So, we distract ourselves from the emotional situation.

A second strategy is *distancing ourselves*: seeing the situation or stimuli as a detached, impartial objective observer, seeing it from a third person, reflecting on it from their perspective. This could be hypothetical or through the eyes of someone we know, or a famous person. Or, imagining that the situation or stimuli occurred far away or a long time ago, seeing it from that angle. This can help us to see things in a different light. This could be, for example, thinking about our situation from our boss's perspective, as our best friend might see it, or how we might see it from ten years in the future.

And a third strategy is *concentration*: selecting certain aspects of the current situation and filtering out others; or focusing on elements tangently related to the situation to contextualize it in "the bigger picture" (expanding the situation, as it were). Deploying attention on elements tangently related can help us to reframe/reappraise the meaning (e.g., someone fears networking because it's awkward and makes them nervous, then ask them "Do you like having a chat with a friend over coffee?" "Yes" – it's the same; or another example, someone gets nervous making a presentation, and then they think "Well, the last presentation I made was successful" – this could help the person to bring up their confidence for this one. Expanding the pie, looking at "the bigger picture," then looking at how we might want to cut it to get the best piece we can. Other examples might include focusing on the aspects of our job we like best, or seeing our current situation in the context of our larger career.

One important skill of attentional deployment is *labeling*: being able to self-reflect and verbalize all the different range of ideas and feelings we have clearly in words. Mindfulness (being aware of ourselves, others and the environment around us) can help us with this. This has been shown to lower stress and create new connections in our brain. In Chapter Four: *Mindfulness*, we deep dive into this. If you'd like to develop this more and haven't read it yet, perhaps read this chapter next. We can then use this to reframe our thoughts or create implementation intentions: "If ..., then ..." statements to help us plan for and mitigate various future scenarios. For example, "If my boss gets angry with me for something that was a misunderstanding, I will breathe deeply and reflect on what I can do to make things better."

So, attentional deployment and labeling help us with, and are necessary for, cognitive reappraisal (reframing the meaning). However, it is not a linear process, but rather an iterative one, where we can go back and forth through these elements as we regulate our emotion: deploy attention, label, reframe, label, reframe, deploy attention, label, reframe, etc. And to take this a step further still, neuroscience research has shown us that attentional deployment and labeling use far less cognitive resources than reappraisal.[2] Therefore, spending time up front deploying attention and labeling will help us regulate our emotions most efficiently and most effectively. It's like filling your car up with gas before your trip, so everything runs more smoothly.

Many people find themselves stuck in "the old groove," repeating particular interpretational and behavioral patterns that are less useful, drain their resourcefulness and undermine their relationships and results. The way forward lies in selective attention and willful activation of one circuit over another, allowing the brain to form new connections. This is exactly what George Lucas did. And you can too deploy your attention willfully and create an upward spiral.

---

**Reflection**

*Attentional Deployment*
Think of a situation you are in now that is causing you some negative feelings.

1.  First, label the emotions, feelings and ideas that you are having. (*Make a note here*).

    _____
    _____
    _____

2.  What can you do to distract you from this to give you some temporary relief? (*Make a note here*).

    _____
    _____
    _____

3.  How can you distance yourself from it? This could be seeing it through someone else's eyes (e.g., a famous person or someone you know) or seeing it from your future self. (*Make a note here*).

    _____
    _____
    _____

4.  How can you concentrate on certain aspects of the situation and filter out others (e.g., the aspects most connected with your goals or that energize you)? (*Make a note here*).

    _____
    _____
    _____

### Reappraisal or Reframing

This is about changing the way we think of something, reappraising or reframing it in a different more positive or effective way. After deploying our attention and labeling our thoughts and emotions, we can then reframe or reappraise them. There are many different types and ways to do this, as we will see later. Mindfulness (being aware of ourselves, others and the environment around us, in a more passive-reception, observational way, as compared to laser-focused attention like we might have in flow) can help us with this. Mindfulness can help us take a step back, lower anxiety, bring attention to the moment, become less judgmental about what is happening, help the brain to not attach meaning to the emotions and be open to new meaning and new connections.

Reappraisal or reframing involves conscious, deliberate and effortful attempts to change our thoughts and feelings by accepting the anxiety, distancing ourself and reframing what happened. We can think of this as "going to the balcony." Down below is the dance floor where all the action takes place, where our situation is, where all our situations are. Reappraisal or reframing allows us to take a step back, go to the balcony, to get that bird's eye perspective, distancing ourselves. This not only will affect the actions and behavior that result, it often alters the context that gave rise to the emotion in the first place.

We can also make a distinction between "antecedent-focused regulation," which helps us prepare for a future situation so that we are able to act with the utmost resourcefulness and able to respond effectively; and "response-focused regulation," which takes place once we have experienced emotional arousal and need to downregulate these negative emotions. A response-focused regulation is like mopping up our emotions after they've spilled; an antecedent-focused regulation keeps them from spilling in the first place. The strategy we will look at in a moment can help us with both. Moreover, just like the scenarios above, with you and your boss, or George Lucas and the studio, a response-focused regulation can pave the way for an antecedent-focused regulation for future.

Finally, this strategy can be done on our own, with our own self-reflection; or it can be done in a coaching session or a conversation with a friend, where the other person asks us certain questions to help our thinking, as well as help come up with different ways of reframing.

There are three parts to the strategy:

1. Ask/explore the current appraisal.
2. Begin reframing in many different ways.
3. Choose your best reframings.

### Ask/Explore the Current Appraisal
*Reflect on the following questions:*

- What is my current framing (of the situation/person)?
- Which emotions and emotional effects does this create in me?
- What thoughts do I have?
- What actions do I take as a result? What are the results of those actions?
- Is this appraisal helping me get closer to any of my goals? (Yes/No)

### Begin Reframing in Many Different Ways

Keep it light-hearted and playful; nurture the creative processes involved in brainstorming, allowing the slower verbal system of the brain to work, as well as the faster visual system, being challenged and creative at the same time. Positive, optimistic humor is a more effective coping strategy than being solemn and cynical. Therefore, the more lightness, playfulness and constructive quirkiness that can be put into it, the better. This will force a change of perspective and energy, allowing the mind to relax and generate many new ideas, connections and insights. At this point, quantity and diversity is important; come up with 30 different ways to reframe. Later, you can then choose the ones that are most effective.

Some questions you might use for reframing:

- How might a person who loves this situation (or finds it easy) frame it?
- What benefits or positive side effects does this situation give you/others?
- What advice would you give if your friend/child were in a similar situation?
- How might it sound if you were to reframe the situation in a humorous way?

- From the other's/someone else's point of view, what does this situation look like?
- How could you frame the situation, so that you would not want to miss out on it?
- How would a fictional character view the situation (Mickey Mouse/Harry Potter/Yoda)?
- How would a wise person (such as one of your personal role models) view the situation?
- Which mottos/sayings may be helpful?
- If we go to the world of music or sports: How might a professional singer (football player) view such a situation?
- Which metaphors can help you make new connections?
- Which of your values (or skills) are strengthened through this?
- What may be your constructive learning looking back at the situation 10 or 20 years from now?
- Which aspects of the situation could you pay attention to that you seem to overlook today?

### Choose Your Best Reframings

Read your alternative framings and "taste" their effects. Choose one or two that make you resourceful and that you would like to try out as an experiment. This is what George Lucas did when he reframed his feelings of frustration to anger and power, and thought, "They are going to butcher my work, so I will say 'no'."

If we apply this to the example with our boss, we may come up with a list like this to choose from:

- My boss is under stress and pressure from head office.
- I haven't been as diligent with my work as I could have been.
- To achieve my career goals, I should be more proactive and exceed people's expectations.
- This is a chance for me to learn and grow.
- Motto: "if you don't brand yourself, others will brand you."
- Preventing this will make other things in future smoother too.
- Metaphor: a luxury car that looks and performs on a high level.

### Response Modulation

Once the emotion has taken hold, is it better to suppress it or acknowledge it? When the emotion is too strong and feels like a tsunami flooding us, it is better to suppress the emotions; however, when we feel strong, clear-headed and have executive control, it is better to acknowledge the emotion so we can regulate it. People prefer reappraisal to suppression when emotion intensity is low, but prefer suppression to reappraisal when emotion intensity is high because at high-intensity levels, reappraisal is often not effective.

Expressive suppression means pushing down the emotions, hiding the emotions from showing, suppressing negative expressions and enhancing positive expressions. The emotion is still there, but we modulate the expression of it (change the expression of emotion). This may provide temporary relief, but in the long term, it takes away cognitive resources, which can affect our focus and performance; amps up the affective arousal because we failed to respond appropriately to the situation; and we could rebound, experiencing this feeling again more intensely.

Emotional introspection, by contrast, allows us to reflect on our emotions, leads to decreased levels of negative emotional experience and increased positive emotional experience and leads to lesser activation in emotion-generative brain regions such as the amygdala. Therefore, if we are in the right state of mind (relaxed, mindful; not flooded), then emotional introspection is best. Think of this as being like moving flowing water in a river, or a wave for surfing, as compared to a tsunami. This will help us deal with our emotions in the most positive way, so we can regulate them. This will then, in turn, help us with "response-focused regulation." As Jon Kabat-Zinn said, "You can't stop the wave, but you can learn to surf."

More interesting, when we have dealt with our emotion by regulating or modulating it, we feel better, and it may seem that the emotion has disappeared. However, really in the brain the connection is still there, but we form new inhibitory connections, which will then inhibit this emotion. We don't unlearn it, but rather we build nuance, new connections, to help us modulate it. The original connection is still there, and we can relearn/reactivate the emotion again very easily. We are, however, wiser because of this nuance. George Lucas still felt frustrated and powerless, but by regulating this emotion, he turned it into a new connection that became more salient, and he became wiser as a result.

So, the next time your boss gets angry with you, take a step back, go to the balcony and reflect how you will deal with this.

**My Example**

In Chapter Eight: *Expectations*, I shared the following situation and looked at how we dealt with the "expectations" piece of it. Now we will explore the emotion regulation piece of it.

> In 2015, on a sunny day, I moved to Singapore (from Japan, where I had spent 17 years). I started a company in Singapore for leadership development. I was excited to embark on a new journey; and I was excited to have coworkers, from a partner company, that I could socialize and go drinking with. I had expected us to be friends; however, their expectation was very different. They wanted/expected just to be coworkers, keeping more distance, and interact only on a professional level when there was a project to work on. Expecting to be friends and building a social relationship, my expectation was not met, and it created a strong threat response, a feeling of disengagement and distance.

With this situation, I could:

1. Select the situation (avoid it, choose something else, end the relationship).
2. Modify the situation (don't listen to them; avoid these people).

Because the relationship is very important, I didn't select either of these. Also, since the emotions were not that strong, I didn't need to suppress them. I did, however, regulate my emotional response (i.e., my behavior) to always appear in the most positive light.

But really, I focused on deploying my attention and reframing the meaning.

First, I explored the current appraisal:

- I wanted to be friends; they wanted a professional relationship.
- Feeling disengaged and distance.
- Thinking: there will be fewer projects because the relationship is not "friendly."
- Actions: freeze, do nothing.
- Is this appraisal helping me get closer to my goal? No.

Then, I used deploying attention, labeling and reappraisal to reframe the situation as many different ways as I could. Here is what I came up with:

- Deploy attention: focus on the elements that they are saying about business and work, as they are in line with what I want for myself too regarding creating a "professional brand."
- Labeling: creating a "professional brand" also means looking professional. So, I will get new suits and hairstyle; it is a makeover, it's fun, I will look more handsome. On a relationship level, people judge and create perceptions of others. These perceptions will lead people to make decisions. These perceptions are controllable. Perceptions of a person are the same as "branding" (i.e., the image people have of perceived value).
- Reappraisal:
    ◇ Keeping a professional distance is important for creating perception and branding.
    ◇ If you do not brand yourself, others will brand you.
    ◇ Trust takes time to build and can be added to with every interaction.
    ◇ People have biases, but these biases can be overcome/mitigated through future interactions that show results and build credibility.
    ◇ This is a virtuous circle, an upward spiral, that will create more reward and achieve the branding goals.
    ◇ Learn from previous experience to apply for future.
    ◇ You win some, you lose some.
    ◇ I have a better relationship with some people higher up in the organization.
    ◇ Being professional only is not a bad thing.

And so, having reappraised the meaning of the situation, I changed my response to the situation and the actions I took. I thought of myself as a brand, and what I wanted to be known and remembered for (knowledgeable, credible, delivering results); then responded and took actions to show this. The results of this enhanced the perceptions others had of me, and I got even more projects because of it.

And so, this then is one example of how we can apply this to regulate our emotions and develop better work relationships.

### Public Speaking Example

How many of you get nervous speaking in front of a group? I am sure many of us do. People cite fear of public speaking as the number one fear, even more than the fear of dying. As American comedian Jerry Seinfeld once joked, "At a funeral, we'd rather be the one in the casket than the one giving the eulogy."

So, what can we do?

**Situation selection:** meet one-on-one instead; put it in writing; delegate someone else to speak.

**Situation modification:** research the audience; familiarize yourself with the room; practice in front of a friend.

**Attentional deployment:** focus on past presentations when it did go well; imagine you are speaking to your friends.

**Reappraisal:** the audience will receive my presentation well; there is value for them.

**Response modulation:** suppress negative emotions; enhance positive expressions.

### Performance Review Example

Or maybe it is time for your performance review. Always a time for heightened arousal and emotional effects.

**Situation selection:** don't go (although maybe not possible).

**Situation modification:** prepare for the discussion; talk to a friend about it.

**Attentional deployment:** think of all the things that went well and the results of those; think about what you would like to do to become even better.

**Reappraisal:** my performance was better than expected so the review will be good; the purpose of the performance review is to highlight what was done well and identify ways to become even better; ultimately it is good for me.

**Response modulation:** suppress negative emotions; enhance positive expressions.

All of these are professional examples. We could equally apply this to our personal life and our interpersonal relationships as well.

**Exercise**

*Mapping Our Appraisal and Reframing*

Think of a situation that happened recently or is happening at the moment, where there was/is emotional tension or a possible (or real) threat. This could be a performance review, public speaking, work relationship or any other challenging situation you recently or currently are facing.

1. Map out your current appraisal: What is your current framing (of the situation/person)? Which emotions and emotional effects does this create in you? What thoughts do you have? Is this appraisal helping you get closer to any of your goals? (Yes/No) (*Make a note here*).

   _____

   _____

   _____

2. Reframe the situation in as many different ways as you can. Go for quantity and diversity of ideas, using the questions mentioned earlier to help you. Try to come up with 7~10 different ways of reframing. Keep it light, have fun.
   (*Make a note here*).

   _____

   _____

   _____

   _____

   _____

   _____

   _____

   _____

   _____

3. Choose your best reframings.

4.  What actions would you take because of these new reframings?
    What will be the results of those actions?
    (*Make a note here*).

    _____

    _____

    _____

## NOTES

1 Steimer, T. "The biology of fear- and anxiety-related behaviors." *Dialogues in Clinical Neuroscience*, 4(3), 231–49. September 2002.

2 Ochsner, K. N. and Gross, J. J. "Cognitive emotion regulation: insights from social cognitive and affective neuroscience." *Current Directions in Psychological Science*, 17(1), 153–8. 2008.

# Ten

Imagine the following scenarios. Think about them one at a time. What would you do?

- One of your colleagues has a pen that you would like to have. How do you persuade them to give it to you?
- You would like to have a promotion 6–8 months from now. How do you influence your Line Manager over the next 6–8 months so that you will get the promotion that you want?
- You want your client to buy now. How do you persuade them to do it?
- You want all of your clients to buy more and grow your sales over the next year. How do you influence them to do that?

What is the difference between these scenarios? What is the difference between *persuade* and *influence*? Think back on these; how would you describe the difference?

*Persuade* we can think of as quick, more direct, more for short-term or immediate gain. *Influence*, on the other hand, is softer, more subtle, more for longer-term and lasting gain. *Persuasion* is perhaps more tactical, whereas *influence* is more strategic.

### Persuasion Tactics

Persuasion has been around for thousands of years. The early Greek philosophers used it in their debates; and Aristotle wrote about the "modes of persuasion." He said there are three modes of persuasion: *logos*, *pathos* and *ethos*. *Logos* is about logic and reason; it is in the words or argument itself. *Pathos* is about emotion and inspiration; it is the feelings in the listener or audience. And *ethos* is about the speaker's own character and credibility.

We will talk about the speaker's character and credibility later. Let's first, however, look at logic/reason and inspiration/emotion.

DOI: 10.4324/9781003127000-10

Which is more important or influential: logic and reason, or inspiration and emotion? Now, we can probably debate this forever and still not have a decisive conclusion. Because it depends on the situation. For example, if we are giving a talk about artificial intelligence, then logic and reason may be more important to influence or persuade the listener because it is something more distant from their experience, more unknown. If, on the other hand, we are giving a talk about relationships (in business or personal), then inspiration and emotion may be more effective influencing or persuading the listener because they can easily relate to it on an emotional or inspirational level. Understanding your audience, the situation and the nature of the topic, therefore, is important to get the right balance between logic and reason, and inspiration and emotion.

Notice, in the above paragraph, we said influence or persuade, because logic and emotion are important for both, whether we are persuading someone now for immediate or short-term gain, or whether we are influencing people for more longer-term and lasting gain.

There are also a whole host of other tactics we can incorporate to strengthen our persuasive approach:

- Asking our audience questions to lead them to ideas or actions we would like them to have or do, thus giving them a sense of ownership.
- Making our audience feel good by praising them genuinely to build the relationship, putting them in more of a mood or mindset to be persuaded.
- Making an exchange or deal with them; or if they are a close relationship, just asking them for a favor.
- Appealing to other similar success stories for third-party endorsement ("others are doing it, so you should too!") – think YouTube views, Facebook likes or TripAdvisor rankings; testimonials or feedback from clients; company case studies; consumer behavior ("over 2 billion customers served" or "75% of customers like you helped the environment").
- Using our authority or threat to persuade someone. For example, a parent says to their child, "Because I'm your Father, that's why!" or "If you don't eat your vegetables, then there is no dessert!" Or in business, someone may say, "As the Project Leader, I have decided to

delay the launch" or "If you don't improve your performance, then we may have to escalate this to HR." This tactic is used as a last resort, if nothing else has worked, and we really need to happen what we want to happen. However, as you can imagine, people may do things because they have to, not because they really want to.

We then want to combine these tactics together, with logic and emotion, to create the most persuasive communication we can. For example, if we are trying to persuade our client to buy now, we might ask them questions to lead them to uncover what they really want, then use logic to show them how what we offer will help them get that; tell a story of how wonderful life is of someone using our product to elicit emotions in them; and maybe even appealing to other success stories of other companies using it for third-party endorsement. Or if we are trying to persuade our colleague to give us their pen, we might share our genuine feelings of how we enjoy working with them, tell a story to elicit emotion, ask questions about their pen and make an exchange or deal with them for something they value.

And this will all be enhanced through our character and credibility, which we will talk about later.

---

**Exercise**

**Persuasion**

1. Think of someone you would like to persuade to think, feel or do something in the short term and fill in the blanks: I would like to persuade _____ to _____

   _____

2. Now think about what is important to them: their goals, concerns, passions, values and list it up: (*Make a note here*).

   _____

   _____

   _____

3. Review the tactics and plan your persuasive communication:

| Mode: | What to Say: |
| --- | --- |
| Logic | e.g., how to meet their objectives |
| Emotion | e.g., tell a story |
| **Tactics:** | |
| 1. | |
| 2. | |
| 3. | |

## Influence

All of what was said above about *persuasion* can apply to *influence* as well. We will now, however, contextualize *influence* on a deeper level and on a broader scope.

Let's use the example of Paul Revere, whom some of you may have heard of.

This story takes place in the United States during the American Revolution in 1775. When people learned that the British were about to launch an attack outside Boston, resistance leaders sent two riders to warn the towns and villages along the way and to let militia members know that the fight was coming to them. Of the two riders, history remembers one – Paul Revere – because his ride was so much more successful.

On April 18, 1775, Paul Revere and William Dawes rode to the towns and villages to warn them. Revere and Dawes, both skilled riders, set off to deliver the same message, but took different routes. Their journeys were designed to be closely similar in terms of distance and towns covered. Those familiar with American colonial history will know the story of one of these riders, because his message spread rapidly through the communities he visited, reaching local militia leaders and many others. The other rider also delivered his message to communities, but on his route the message sometimes failed to get to militia leaders and often stopped with the person he spoke with (rather than being carried forward and passed along).

Why was one rider so much more effective than the other? Evidence suggests that Paul Revere was connected to an extensive network of strategic relationships and had significant credibility and social capital with them, whereas William Dawes's connections were less useful. Paul Revere knew everybody and was well respected by these people. When he came upon a town, he would have known exactly whose door to knock on, who the local militia leader was, who the key players in town were. Not only did Revere alert whole towns to the looming threat, but also the leaders in these towns themselves sent riders to alert the surrounding areas. Dawes's message failed to spread through the network, whereas Revere's message spread quickly throughout the area, ultimately covering a 750 square mile area (1942 km$^2$). Historians tell us that Dawes was unfamiliar with the anti-British opinion leaders in his territory, so rather than stopping at the homes of key people in the underground, Dawes simply knocked on random doors. Many people simply went back to bed without taking the news further.

The two men had the same resources (a fast horse), and neither had direct or positional authority over the people they sought to influence (i.e., they weren't members of any militia or government officials), but their ability to influence was different. The key difference was that Revere had a broad network of strategic relationships; knew who to influence to influence others; had credibility and personal relationship or social capital; and was able to gain commitment to action.

This is where *ethos* comes in: our credibility and character. This is the perception that others have of us, how others see us. This also includes personal relationship or social capital: what we bring to the table of value to others.

There are several ways to build and demonstrate our credibility and social capital:

1. **Be genuinely likeable**: being courteous, respectful and patient when interacting with others, acknowledging others and approaching them as equals, and highlighting similarities between ourself and them.
2. **Focus on unique benefits for others**: knowing what others personally value individually and connecting the unique personal benefit of our request to what an individual values.
3. **Reciprocate**: building and maintaining relationships of reciprocity and trust and contributing proactively to the priorities of those around us.

4. **Use our "currency:"** identifying our own unique abilities, resources, information and expertise, and communicating with others in specific ways we can help achieve their objectives.

One of the key and most powerful concepts, in order to influence people effectively, is *reciprocity*, which we will now take a deep dive into and explore more.

### Reciprocity

Reciprocity is the practice of exchanging things with others for mutual benefit. This can be simultaneous or a delayed exchange.

For example, in one psychology experiment (Cialdini, 2009), Joe, a Middle Manager, wanted to sell raffle tickets to his colleagues. In the morning, when he was saying "Hi" to his colleagues, half the time he would say "Hi" empty-handed. On the other half of the occasions, he would have two cans of Coke and offer his colleague one of the cans, saying, "I got this for you." Later in the afternoon when Joe came around to sell raffle tickets, the colleagues who got a can of Coke bought twice as many raffle tickets as the others, whether or not they liked Joe, which worked out as a 500% return on investment.

Another example that Dale Carnegie shared in *How to Win Friends and Influence People* (1936), one of the most powerful books on influence ever written:

Andrew Carnegie, the poverty-stricken Scotch lad who started to work at two cents an hour and finally gave away $365 million, learned early in life that the only way to influence people is to talk in terms of what the other person wants. He attended school only four years; yet he learned how to handle people. For example, his sister-in-law was worried sick over her two boys. They were at Yale, and they were so busy with their own affairs that they neglected to write home and paid no attention to their mother's frantic letters. Then Carnegie offered to wager a hundred dollars that he could get an answer by return mail, without even asking for it. Someone called his bet; so, he wrote his nephews a chatty letter, mentioning casually in a post-script that he was sending each one a five-dollar bill. He neglected, however, to enclose the money. Back came replies by return mail thanking "Dear Uncle Andrew" for his kind note and—you can finish the sentence yourself.[1]

And in the hotel industry, have you ever stayed in a hotel and seen those little signs in the bathroom saying:

Dear Guest,
Everyday millions of litres of water are used to wash towels that have only been used once. You make the difference. If you do not need your towel washed, please leave it hanging on the towel rack.
   Thank you for helping us conserve the Earth's vital resources.

I am sure many of us have seen these. In an experiment by Robert Cialdini (2008), he experimented with the wording to see what would be most influential. At the Holiday Inn in Tempe, Arizona, they randomly placed cards with conceptually different recycling appeals in its 190 rooms. The cards were identical in two respects. First, on the front, they informed guests that they could participate in the program by placing their used towels on the bathroom towel rack or curtain rod. Second, on the back, the cards provided information regarding the amount of energy that could be saved if most guests participated in the program. They differed, however, in terms of the message.

In some rooms, the following (environmental protection) message was placed:

HELP SAVE THE ENVIRONMENT.
You can show your respect for nature and help save the environment by reusing your towels during your stay.

In others, this (reciprocity) message was placed:

WE'RE DOING OUR PART FOR THE ENVIRONMENT. CAN WE COUNT ON YOU?
Because we are committed to preserving the environment, we have made a financial contribution to a nonprofit environmental protection organization on behalf of the hotel and its guests. If you would like to help us in recovering the expense, while conserving natural resources, please reuse your towels during your stay.

Of those who received the first message, 38% reused their towel. Of those who received the second message, 47% reused their towel. Reciprocity has a powerful effect, even when it is for a common cause rather than personal.

In the same experiment, they tested "social norms" as well, appealing to what others have done in the same situation as a third-party endorsement ("others are doing it, so you should too!")

This sign read:

JOIN YOUR FELLOW GUESTS IN HELPING TO SAVE THE ENVIRONMENT
Almost 75% of guests who are asked to participate in our new resource savings program do help by using their towels more than once. You can join your fellow guests to help save the environment by reusing your towels during your stay.

Of those who received this message, 48% reused their towel, showing the influential power of social norms.

So, using reciprocity, social norms and our own personal relationship or social capital, we can influence people more effectively and gain commitment to action. Couple this with knowing who to influence to influence others and having a broad network of strategic relationships, and this gives us a great recipe for influencing others.

### What Is Your Intention?
On a final note, we also have to look at what your intention is.

All of these tactics and strategies can be used for ill-intentions to take advantage of people or manipulate them. This, however, lowers credibility and character; and once uncovered, will backfire, lower our personal or social capital, and not only have a negative consequence now, but for future as well. Having genuine good intentions will not only increase our personal or social capital, it will also be much more effective influencing people now and in the future and demonstrate our *ethos* or character.

**Exercise**

**Influence**

1.  Think of a bigger project you are working on and what you aim to accomplish. (*Make a note here*).

    _____

    _____

    _____

2.  List up all the people connected to this project and all the people in your extended network who could possibly help:

    _____

    _____

    _____

3.  For each of these people, list up what is important for them (independent of your project and what you want):

    _____

    _____

    _____

4.  Reflect on your own personal relationship or social capital (what you bring to the table of value to them), and think of ways that you can use reciprocity and your own social capital to help them get what they want, so you can get what you want:

    _____

    _____

    _____

## NOTE

1 Carnegie, D. *How to Win Friends and Influence People*. New Delhi: Digital Fire. 1936. Chapter 3.1.

# Eleven

There have been lots written about time management and dozens of time management seminars. But what exactly do we mean by *time management* and *managing time?*

### Managing Ourself Through Time

It is not so much about managing time, but rather managing ourself through time and managing our energy through time. While we can't create more time, we can generate something of greater value: more energy. If we bring sufficient energy to whatever we do, we will have both greater impact and "extra" time.

How many of you make a task list? I used to be notorious for my task lists. In fact, I would wake up in the morning and the first thing I would write on my task list is "1. Wake up," then cross it off my list because I already did it. I kid you not. I really did this. And I would continue to make a task list of 50 or more tasks – every single small task that I could think of that I needed to do.

Then I discovered a different technique, a different approach to thinking about time. Having read several of Stephen Covey's books (namely, *First Things First* and *The 7 Habits of Highly Effective People*), which influenced me and changed the way I thought about time, I then created my own "7 Roles Planning Sheet" (see Figure 11.1).

With this method of planning, instead of writing a long task list with all the tasks and micro-tasks we need to do for each day, we plan for the whole week, by deciding seven roles in our life for that week and creating a weekly goal for each of those roles. These roles, moreover, are from our professional, as well as personal, life. For example, for a consultant, this could include knowledge expert, rapport builder, competent salesperson, collaborative team member, wife, mother, tennis player. And then for each of these roles, identify a weekly goal that is challenging and achievable (see Figure 11.2 for an example).

DOI: 10.4324/9781003127000-11

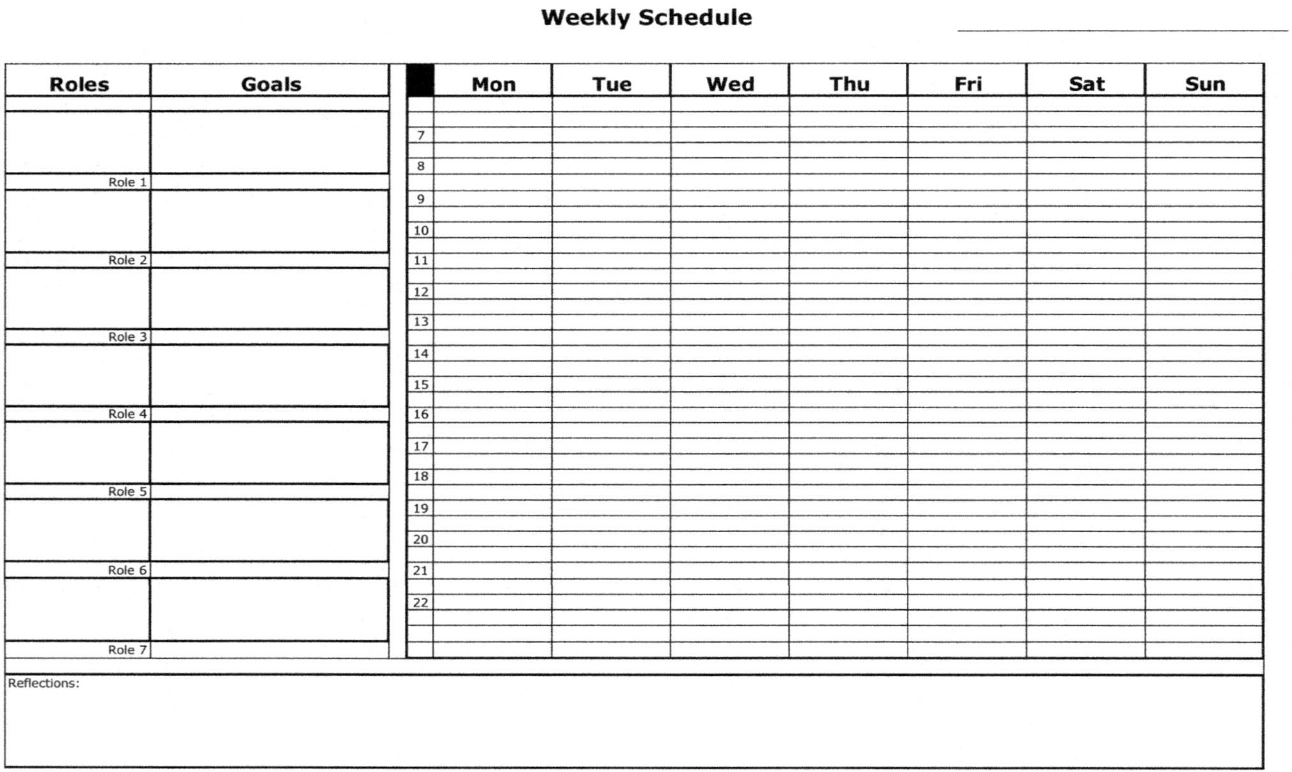

**Weekly Schedule**

| Roles | Goals | | Mon | Tue | Wed | Thu | Fri | Sat | Sun |
|---|---|---|---|---|---|---|---|---|---|
| | | 7 | | | | | | | |
| Role 1 | | 8 | | | | | | | |
| | | 9 | | | | | | | |
| | | 10 | | | | | | | |
| Role 2 | | 11 | | | | | | | |
| | | 12 | | | | | | | |
| Role 3 | | 13 | | | | | | | |
| | | 14 | | | | | | | |
| | | 15 | | | | | | | |
| Role 4 | | 16 | | | | | | | |
| | | 17 | | | | | | | |
| Role 5 | | 18 | | | | | | | |
| | | 19 | | | | | | | |
| Role 6 | | 20 | | | | | | | |
| | | 21 | | | | | | | |
| | | 22 | | | | | | | |
| Role 7 | | | | | | | | | |

Reflections:

**Figure 11.1** 7 Roles Planning Sheet

| Roles | Goals | | Mo |
|---|---|---|---|
| **Knowledge Expert** | Learn more about Design Thinking | 7 | |
| | | 8 | |
| Role 1 | | | |
| **Rapport Builder** | Develop rapport with my three new clients: ABC, DEF and GHI Companies | 9 | |
| | | 10 | |
| Role 2 | | 11 | |
| **Competent Saleperson** | Complete the proposal for XYZ Company | 12 | |
| | | 13 | |
| Role 3 | | | |
| **Collaborative Team Member** | Listen more to other people's ideas and proactively build on them, paraphrasing them and adding to it | 14 | |
| | | 15 | |
| Role 4 | | 16 | |
| **Wife** | Make my husband smile everyday | 17 | |
| | | 18 | |
| Role 5 | | | |
| **Mother** | Make my children feel that they can come to me for advice or help them anytime | 19 | |
| | | 20 | |
| Role 6 | | 21 | |
| **Tennis Player** | To serve more accurately at 5% faster speed | 22 | |
| Role 7 | | | |

Reflections:

**Figure 11.2** 7 Roles Planning Sheet (Example)

This allows us to visualize the goal and "see" all the tasks and micro-tasks that need to be done without having to write them all out. For example, if our goal for "competent salesperson" is "to complete the proposal for XYZ company," we know that we need to do research, understand the client's needs from the meetings with them, innovate ideas, socialize those ideas to get feedback and soundcheck them, and craft and design the proposal.

This planning sheet also has space to schedule our time-bound activities (e.g., meetings) to allow us to see where our blocks of non-time-bound activities can be done. There is also space at the bottom to reflect on the week at the end of each week.

I did this planning process for three years very diligently. It was not only extremely productive in managing myself with time, it actually changed the way I thought about planning and productivity. My brain started intuitively to visualize goals and align the tasks necessary to achieve them. Doing this planning process each week over a period of time can change the way our brain thinks and help us to be more productive in achieving our goals.

---

**Exercise**

*7 Roles – 7 Goals Planning Sheet*

1. Decide seven roles for you this week (4–5 professional, 2–3 personal). Write them in Figure 11.1 or make your own similar planning spreadsheet to use each week.

2. For each role, identify a weekly goal that is challenging and achievable and write it in your planning sheet.

3. At the end of the week reflect on it. Did you accomplish all the goals? If not, which ones and why? Were the goals the right level of stretch? Or were they too easy or too straining?

4. Do this each week over a period of time. Look for patterns and observe and reflect on how it changes your thinking of time and managing yourself in time.

Another useful exercise, and this could be done as part of your weekly reflection, is to look at your current tasks and short-term (weekly) goals in the context of the bigger picture of your long-term and mid-term goals. In Chapter Two, we looked at goal setting and goal getting. Whether you have read Chapter Two: *Goals* or not, take a few moments now to reflect on your long-term and mid-term goals, and how your current tasks and short-term goals align with this.

---

**Exercise**

**Current Tasks and Long-Term Goals Alignment**

1. What are your long-term and mid-term goals? (Write them on the timeline in Figure 11.3).

2. How do your current tasks and short-term goals align with your mid-term and long-term goals?

3. If they are not aligned:
   a. How could they align?

   b. Are there any changes you need to make or anything you need to do differently to get more alignment?

---

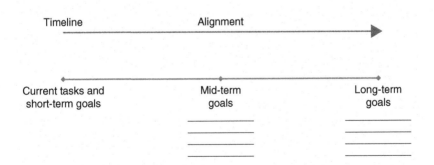

**Figure 11.3** Current Tasks and Long-Term Goals

**Managing Our Energy**

Once we have decided our short-term (weekly) goals and tasks, the next step is to sort and prioritize them based on necessity to do, amount of time needed, importance and urgency. The first question we need to ask is, "Is it necessary for me to do it myself?" If the answer is "no," we can either delete it or delegate it. For example, *"respond to webinar invite"* – if it's something we are not interested in, we can delete or ignore it. Or *"do final check of proposal"* – perhaps we can delegate this to a colleague to get some fresh eyes on it; likewise, they may do the same for us for their proposal.

If the answer is "yes, I need to do it myself," we then want to consider the amount of time needed. If it is a simple task that can be done in two minutes or less, do it now. For example, *"respond to client's email about time of meeting."* If it's a task that will take more time, we can then ask ourselves, "Can we defer it to another day or later in the day?" For example, *"follow up with Finance about new procedure."* We can also ask ourselves, "Can we diminish the amount of effort or time required to do it?" For example, using templates from previous proposals to make a new proposal, or using slides from a previous presentation to include in a new presentation.

And finally, if it's a task or goal that would take several (e.g., ten or more) hours to do, we want to then ask ourselves, "How can we divide this up?" For example, *"make proposal for new innovative ideas."* We might then divide this up into two hours brainstorm on one day, two hours assess and shortlist ideas on another day, two hours expand on shortlisted ideas on yet another day, and then spend four hours on another day putting the proposal together.

The following matrix illustrates all of these different techniques and strategies:

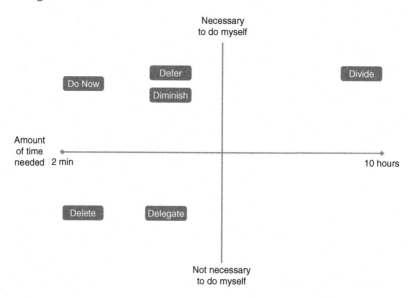

**Figure 11.4** Sort and Prioritize Matrix

The next question we want to ask ourselves is, "How urgent and important are these tasks?" If it is urgent and important, we definitely have to prioritize it. If it is urgent, but not important, we have to prioritize it and do it based on the time constraint. If it is important, but not urgent (e.g., goal setting or planning), we have to be careful that we don't procrastinate or ignore this, as it is important and, therefore, deserves our time and attention. And if it is not urgent and not important, perhaps we can delete or delegate it.

Sometimes, also, we may get sudden tasks that come up. One strategy to help us with this is to allocate only 80%–90% of our time to allow "extra time" for these sudden tasks. Also, follow the same strategies above with these tasks as well, deciding how you will sort and prioritize them in this matrix.

---

**Exercise**

**Sort and Prioritize**

1. List up all the tasks you need to do this week.

2. Ask yourself the following questions and sort the tasks accordingly:
   a. Is it necessary for me to do the task? If "no," then delete or delegate it. If "yes," then consider the other questions.
   b. Can it be done in less than two minutes? If "yes," then do it now. If "no," then ask yourself the next questions.
   c. Can I defer it to another day or later in the day? When exactly will I do it?
   d. Can I diminish the amount of effort or time required to do it? How? In what ways?
   e. How urgent and important is it? Urgent and important? Urgent but not important? Important but not urgent? Not urgent and not important? Based on this, how will I sort and prioritize them?

3. Plot your tasks on the matrix (Figure 11.4).

Allow 10%–20% "extra time" for sudden tasks that may come up and/or time to check tasks where diligence and accuracy is important.

### "Circadian" Rhythms of Life

Are you a morning person or a night person? Do you think best early morning when the sun rises? Or in the twilight just before sleeping? Perhaps you are most alert in the middle of the afternoon or just before eating. Biology, psychology and neuroscience have studied circadian rhythms for hundreds of years. We will focus here on the applied psychology and neuroscience of it and the practical use of our natural circadian rhythms.

Circadian rhythms are physical, mental and behavioral changes that follow a daily cycle. The term comes from the Latin *circa*, meaning "around" (or "approximately"), and *diem*, meaning "day." They respond primarily to light and darkness in our environment. Sleeping at night and being awake during the day is an example of a light-related circadian rhythm. They are governed by a master clock, a group of neurons called the suprachiasmatic nucleus, located in a region of the brain called the hypothalamus. This master clock translates cues from the environment into directives for the body, which help determine whether we feel energized or exhausted at different times of the day. By understanding the natural rhythm of our brain and what drains our energy, we can have more energy and be more efficient and effective. This will help us lead ourselves and others better.

Do you feel tired today? Did you not get enough sleep last night? If yes, or when this has happened, how does it make you feel the next day? Does it impact your behavior, your thinking, your concentration? Chances are, you could answer this with a resounding, "yes!" Our mental states vary over the course of the day, and sleep plays a major role in our alertness levels. If we have difficulty getting sleep due to our work or the demands of day-to-day life, we accumulate a sleep debt. The consequences of this include decreased levels of alertness and mental efficiency. While there is variation in our sleep needs, most adults require 7–9 hours per night. In Chapter Six: *Physical Health*, we talk more about sleep and the effects of this on our brain and cognitive function. If you do have difficulty sleeping enough and you have not read this chapter yet, perhaps this is one to read as well.

Now, assuming we have sufficient sleep, let's look at some different examples of circadian rhythms and mental functioning.

For me, I work and think best in the morning. So, creative, thinking and planning activities are done then. I then do my administrative tasks like email, invoicing, etc. in the afternoon, as well as schedule meetings, insofar as I can choose this.

Another consultant I know, Mark, wakes up at 6 am every day when his small child wakes up. He then takes him to the park to play. This is when his peak time for work (creative, innovation, planning) is done. Then, his child has nap time at noon, and so does he. In the afternoon, he does his administrative work and meets clients. So, we may also take a power nap during the day to refresh ourselves and clear our mind.

A designer I know, Nik, has two children in school. He finds that his best thinking time is late at night after his children have gone to bed (from 10 pm to 2 am). Then he will sleep, wake up to get his children off to school, then go back to sleep for a couple of more hours. In the late morning, he will do his administrative work and schedule his meetings for the afternoon.

Another business person I know, Rachel, a senior leader in regulatory affairs for a retail brand, told me,

> I think best at night. I like when I work without pressure, when everyone else is off. And I know I have several hours ahead of me until I need to deliver or discuss something. I can work at my own pace, as long as I want and without any disruption. And sunshine always makes me want to be outside to do other things. Not concentrate on work.

With more people working from home now, we have much more freedom in how we allocate our time and how we manage our energy. If you work from home, when is your best time for thinking? When are you most alert? If it is the morning, is checking your email first thing the best thing to do? Or can it be deferred until later in the day? Is your best thinking at night or in the afternoon? Think about when you are at your peak energy and peak mental alertness; schedule your thinking, planning or design activities then, and schedule the administrative tasks, where less cognitive functions are needed, around that.

Now what about those of us who go to the office? Some of our time will be scheduled by others (e.g., meetings), which are time-bound. The time around that, however, we have more control over. We could adjust our time and tasks accordingly, if you do not have choice over when the meetings are, or voice your thoughts to others when is best for you to have meetings. One Analyst I know in the Financial Services industry told the Sales People that there are certain times that she would like to be scheduled for meetings, and other times when she does not.

For those of you who lead others understand the circadian rhythms of your team members and schedule meetings accordingly. For example, if people think more creatively in the morning, hold your brainstorming sessions then, and schedule catchups or routine meetings for an afternoon rather than the morning.

And if you have several meetings in the same day, we could all learn from Rachel, the senior leader in regulatory affairs for a retail brand I mentioned before. Sometimes she could have seven meetings in a day. The night before, she prepares herself mentally for this. Then in the morning she gets her energy up and plans in between her meetings to stretch or go for a little walk in order to reenergize and rejuvenate herself.

Find what works for you.

---

**Exercise**

**Circadian Rhythms of Life**

1. Think about when you are at your peak energy and peak mental alertness: early morning, late morning, after lunch, evening, nighttime.

2. What activities would you do at this time? Planning? Doing research? Writing a report? Creating a presentation? Schedule and write these on your "7 Roles Planning Sheet" (Figure 11.1 or your own similar planning spreadsheet to use each week). Having it all on one page helps us to make the connection with our goals and visualize how we will budget our time and energy.

3. Then schedule your administrative tasks, where less cognitive functions are needed, around this.

---

**Time Traps and How to Overcome Them**

Let's now look at some of the traps that drain our energy and our time and may stop or hinder us from managing ourselves and our energy most effectively; and what we can do to help us manage or overcome these traps.

### Procrastination

Procrastination is the avoidance of doing a task that needs to be accomplished by a certain deadline. But why exactly do we procrastinate? Behavioral psychology research has revealed a phenomenon called "time inconsistency," which helps explain why procrastination seems to pull us in despite our good intentions. Time inconsistency refers to the tendency of the human brain to value immediate rewards more highly than future rewards.

We can understand this better by imagining that we have two selves: our Present Self and our Future Self. When we set goals for ourself – like losing weight or writing a book – we are actually making plans for our Future Self. We are envisioning what we want our life to be like in the future. The research has found that when we think about our Future Self, it is quite easy for our brain to see the value in taking actions with long-term benefits. The Future Self values long-term rewards.

However, while the Future Self can set goals, only the Present Self can take action. When the time comes to make a decision, we are no longer making a choice for our Future Self. Now we are in the present moment, and our brain is thinking about the Present Self. And the research has found that the Present Self really likes instant gratification, not long-term payoff.

Jamie, a Sales Person I know in the Financial Services industry, had to make a deck of slides for her performance review. She woke up and planned to do it (thinking about her Future Self). Then, she spent the entire morning cleaning up her desk, checking emails, sweeping the floor and cleaning the kitchen. Her Present Self took over for the instant gratification of completing these simple tasks.

Now, how do we overcome procrastination? We cannot rely on long-term rewards or consequences to motivate our Present Self. Rather, we need to find a way to move these future rewards, consequences or punishments into the present, and regulate the negative emotions associated with procrastinating.

Here are some tactics we can use to do this:

- **Forgive Yourself for Procrastinating**
  - In our example, Jamie could have relieved some of the stress, guilt and anxiety caused by procrastinating by forgiving herself. Stress, guilt and anxiety are one of the main triggers of procrastination. Forgiving ourselves for this will regulate these feelings and lower the tendency to procrastinate.

- *Make the Rewards of Taking Action More Immediate*
  - In our example, Jamie could have bundled a behavior that is good for her in the long run (creating her deck of slides) with a behavior that feels good in the short run (cleaning the kitchen). So, while cleaning the kitchen, she could visualize what she wants in the slides.
- *Make the Consequences of Procrastination More Immediate*
  - In our example, Jamie could have told her best friend that for every minute she procrastinates, she will pay her best friend $1. With an immediate consequence like this, surely the procrastination would be much less.
- *Design Your Future Actions*
  - In our example, Jamie could have taken a piece of paper the night before, drew a circle in the middle and wrote in the circle "My Performance." Then left the paper and a pencil on her desk before going to sleep, ready for the next morning.
- *Make the Task More Achievable*
  - In our example, Jamie could have broken the larger goal into manageable smaller tasks: brainstorm points, cluster themes, organize ideas, then transfer to the slides. Psychologically, by completing the first task quickly, moreover, it would develop her day with an attitude of productivity and effectiveness.

So, these are some tactics that you could use as well to help you overcome procrastination.

We will briefly now take a look at four other time traps we find ourselves falling into as we take on and perform our tasks, and what we can do about them.

### Saying "Yes" to Everything

When people come to us with tasks or extra tasks, some of us may find ourselves saying things like:

"I can do it; it will only take five minutes."
"I don't like saying no – it projects the wrong image."
"I am an optimist who is up for any challenge."

Here are some tactics we can use to help deal with or overcome this trap:

- Compare it with your own goals and use this to decide whether to say yes.
- Estimate exactly how long it will take to do the task before saying yes.
- Figure out if and where in your schedule you can fit this in. If there is no time, let them know and the reason behind it.
- Reframe what you are saying yes to, and possibly only take on part of it.
- Suggest other alternatives.

### Compulsive Concern

Sometimes and/or some of us may find ourselves compulsively concerned about everything that is going on. We might be thinking:

"I'm so curious."
"Others need me."
"I always want to help."

Here are some tactics we can use to help deal with or overcome this trap:

- Identify your own goals and focus your concerns around this.
- Schedule an hour block of your time twice a week when people can come to you.
- Let others know what you are focusing on and ask them to help you keep that focus.
- When you start a project, clarify who is responsible for what and when is best for them to consult or inform you.
- Help people to help themselves.
- Turn off notifications and check email only every hour.

### Busy Bee

Some of us may also find that we want to be "busy" all the time. We might think:

"I like doing lots of things."
"If I'm not busy then I feel I am not doing my job."
"I like the intensity of things going on around me."

Here are some tactics we can use to help deal with or overcome this trap:

- Clarify for yourself and others what is your focus.
- Pause and reflect: do I need to be doing this? Can it be deleted or delegated? Is it urgent or can it be delayed? Can the task be diminished to make it simpler and less time consuming?
- Budget your time based on your own natural circadian rhythm.
- Stay calm where you usually might rush in.
- Respect and value time by yourself.

### Perfectionist

And finally, some of us may be perfectionists, always wanting to spend more and more time to make sure we get it right and the best possible ever. We might be saying to ourselves:

"Everything always has to be perfect."
"I need more time to do it as I want to do it."
"I can't stop until it is the best."

Here are some tactics we can use to help deal with or overcome this trap:

- Set your one highest priority and focus around this.
- Focus on the "need to have" items, leaving the "nice to have" items until later.
- Applying Pareto's Principle, 20% of your work will produce 80% of the value; focus on this.
- Discuss expectations and standards with others in your team to give them what they expect or slightly more, without overdoing it.
- Schedule "down time" in your week to refresh and recover.

---

### Exercise

#### Time Traps and How to Overcome Them

1. Think about a time when you procrastinated, or perhaps you are doing it now, when you avoid doing a task that must be completed by a certain deadline. Which tactic will help you

overcome this procrastination the most and how will you apply it for your own situation? (*Make a note here.*)

---

---

---

---

---

2. Which of the other four time traps are you most likely to fall into, whether that is to a large extent or a small extent? Which tactics will help you overcome this the most and how will you apply them for your own situation? (*Make a note here.*)

---

---

---

---

---

Change

# Twelve

Imagine going for a walk in the woods, enjoying nature to the fullest, then you come to an opening with the most beautiful breathtaking view, how do you feel?

Now imagine, going for a walk in the woods, enjoying nature to the fullest, and all of a sudden, a large bear appears in front of you, how do you feel?

Imagine you have been working hard and there is an opening for a dream position, and you get the promotion, how do you feel?

Now, imagine you have been working hard and there is an opening for a dream position, and you don't get the promotion, another person gets it, how do you feel?

With the breathtaking view or getting the promotion, we feel like we got a reward. It's a rush. We get a sensation in our brain and a hit of the big neurochemicals: dopamine, serotonin, oxytocin, norepinephrine, adrenaline.

With the bear in the woods or being overlooked for the promotion, we feel like it is a threat. We feel tense, stressed, pressure, disgust, repulsed, frustrated. Our body physically feels it. Neuroscience has shown us, moreover, that the feeling we get from a social or emotional threat is the same as the feeling we get from a physical threat, and that the negative (threat) response is stronger than the positive (reward) response.[1]

Everything and everyone we meet we interpret as a reward or threat, and then based on this, our body reacts, our brain and mind think and feel what they do, and this leads to the decisions, behavior and actions we make.

### A Brief History of Needs

To help us understand this and what happens in our brains and minds, let's take a deep dive into our human needs.

DOI: 10.4324/9781003127000-12

### Maslow's Hierarchy of Needs

In 1943, psychologist Abraham Maslow created the hierarchy of needs, which has had a huge impact on humans and the field of psychology. There are five levels of needs, according to this line of thought. At the bottom are our physiological needs (food, water, shelter); then safety needs (health, emotional security, financial security). These bottom two levels are our survival needs. The top three levels are our psychological needs: the need for social belonging (friendship, love, intimacy); the need for self-esteem (confidence, recognition, respect); and the need for self-actualization (pursuing a goal, seeking happiness).

### Self-Determination Theory

For years and decades after Maslow, psychologists explored and developed our understanding of our psychological needs. In 2000, Edward Deci and Richard Ryan reviewed three decades of research and, based on this, created "self-determination theory," which posits that there are three psychological needs: the need for Competence (feeling valued for our knowledge, skills and experience), the need for Relatedness (collaborating, connecting or serving others) and the need for Autonomy (exercising self-regulation, within guidelines, to achieve our goals).

### ACRES Model of Needs

Others have expanded on this, calling it different names. I call it the "ACRES" model of needs, which outlines five psychological needs: Autonomy (a feeling of control and choice), Competence (feeling valued and respected for our contribution), Relatedness (a fundamental need to belong and be accepted, to have social connections), Equity (perceiving decisions and actions as fair) and Sureness (predicting what's going to happen moment to moment).

### Why We Resist or Block Change

With a deeper understanding of our needs and the appraisal system in our brain (whether we appraise something as a reward or a threat), we can understand better why we resist or block change, whether it is intentional or unconscious.

If all of our ACRES needs are met, it will put us in a "toward state" and we will fully embrace everything ahead of us; however, if our ACRES needs are threatened, it will put us in an "away state" and we will then resist or block things ahead of us. Moreover, as stated earlier, the negative (threat) response is stronger than the positive (reward) response. Therefore, if one of our ACRES needs is threatened (even if the other four are met), we will still resist or block the change. Impulsively, the "fight or flight" response kicks in and our body prepares for the threat. This is like the bear in the woods: our body feels it before our mind even knows what happened.

For example, in 2015, on a sunny day, I moved to Singapore (from Japan, where I had spent 17 years). I started a company in Singapore for leadership development and was excited to embark on a new journey. However, at the same time, I was also concerned and anxious about this change in my life.

So, let's look at what happened when I relocated …

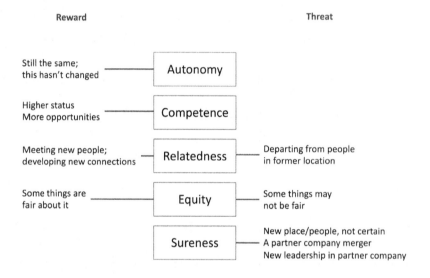

**Figure 12.1** ACRES Relocation Example

For me, I was excited about the higher status and more opportunities; meeting new people and developing new connections. However, at the same time, there was the threat of departing from people in the former location, and perhaps some things which may not be fair, as well as a partner company merger and new leadership in that company. This was the state of my mind going through this change.

So, what happens when our mind feels threatened?

When threatened, the increased overall activation in the brain inhibits us from perceiving the more subtle signals required for solving nonlinear problems, involved in insight or an "aha!" experience (Subramaniam *et al.*, 2007). This could help explain the lack of creativity I had during this period, and perhaps not joining all the dots in the best way I possibly could.

Also, when threatened, the tendency is to generalize more, which increases the likelihood of unintentional connections; a tendency to err on the safe side, shrinking from opportunities, as they are perceived to be more dangerous; and people become more likely to react defensively to stimuli (small stressors become more likely to be perceived as large stressors) (Phelps, 2006). I am sure I felt this too.

Another interesting phenomenon is "The Multiplier Effect," where a threat in one domain augments the threat in other domains; likewise, a reward in one can augment rewards in others. For example, I felt this with the reward of "higher status and more opportunities," augmenting the reward of "meeting new people and developing new connections." I also felt it with the company merger, augmenting that some things may not be fair.

And yet another interesting phenomenon is "The Offsetting Effect," where one or two of these domains are in the positive to balance out the threats. We can see in Figure 12.1 that this is the case. I also felt this myself within my own brain.

As another example, with the COVID-19 pandemic in 2020, for many people working from home brought on a reward for autonomy as they have more freedom in how they do their work. However, at the same time, the lack of being able to physically meet with people and the uncertainty of the pandemic itself and what the future might look like was, and is, a big threat for many of us.

---

**Exercise**

*Analysis of Change Situation*
Let's take a moment to analyze a change situation that you are going through right now.

1.  What change are you going through right now at the moment? (*Make a note here.*)

    _____

    _____

    _____

2. Do an ACRES analysis: Which of your needs are being met? Which of your needs are or may be threatened?

**Reward**                                                    **Threat**

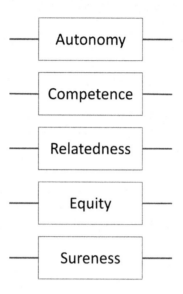

3. How is this impacting your thinking? For example, do you feel any inhibitions, generalizations, multiplier or offsetting effects? (*Make a note here.*)

_____

_____

_____

_____

_____

This is a great tool to help us analyze a change that we are going through to understand more of the impact it is having on us.

### Change Responses

Now that we understand more about our psychological needs and how change might reward or threaten them, let's look at how this is going to play out in our behavior and responses. Figure 12.2 shows "The Change

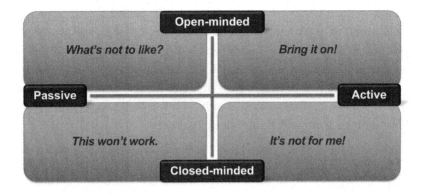

**Figure 12.2** Change Responses

Response Grid" created by Michael Mahoney,[2] inspired by his work as a psychotherapist.

The open-minded/closed-minded dimension relates to the degree of mental openness to the environment and our level of curiosity. Open-minded represents the level of reward that we perceive, and closed-minded represents the level of threat that we perceive. The dimension of passive/active relates to how we may feel and our behavior during a specific event or aspect of a specific event. With a passive mindset, we will either subtly support or subtly oppose the change; with an active mindset, we will either overtly support or overtly reject the change. Throughout our lives and with the different changes that we experience, we "oscillate" between these different mental states and degrees of activity, which impacts our feelings, thinking, behavior and actions. Overall, our goal is to spend more of our time in the open-minded, active state in order to embrace the positive aspects of the change and the benefits it can bring.

For example, when I moved to Singapore, the excitement about more opportunities and meeting new people put me in an open-minded, active state, seeking out all the possible opportunities. However, the company merger and new leadership brought my mind into a closed-minded, passive state. I then oscillated between these two states. This impacted how I felt and thought, and my behavior and actions. For example, I was very social and enthusiastic meeting new people, perhaps even, on occasion, a little too much so. I was also very skeptical, which inhibited my thinking, and made me reserved and self-conscious about my interactions with certain people.

During the COVID-19 pandemic in 2020, perhaps several people were excited to work from home to have more freedom and work in a comfortable environment. But then, as it didn't go away, they got into a closed-minded passive or active state. It's like holding a glass of water. If someone asks you to hold a glass of water for five minutes, it's not so difficult. However, if they ask you to hold it for 24 hours, after a couple of hours, your hand will surely start to get tired.

### Triggers

So, what triggers a threat or perceived threat? There are several catalysts that could trigger a threat response. Here is a list of a few:

- **Historical personal relationship with that particular change or change in general** – Differences exist in people's overall tolerance for change. Some people enjoy change because it provides them with an opportunity to learn new things and grow personally and professionally. Others dislike change because they prefer a set routine – these are usually the people who become suspicious of change and are more likely to resist it.
- **Fear of loss or difficulty** – Fear of loss creates insecurity and unsureness.
- **Fear of the unknown** – People will only take active steps toward the unknown if they genuinely believe and, perhaps more importantly, feel that the risks of standing still are greater than those of moving forward in a new direction.
- **Lack of a plan** – It's common for us to want to be prepared and have a plan. It creates a feeling of security or sureness.
- **Sense of destabilization** – Some people may feel that changes are forced upon them for no particular reason other than to inconvenience them.
- **Ignorance** – Lack of knowledge or understanding of what's happening can make us feel threatened.
- **Personality** – Some personality factors might make people naturally more prone to worry, be moody and have anxiety. Other factors make it easier for us to embrace change more easily.
- **Values** – Research into change and individual differences shows that if security values are more important to you than social values, you're more likely to see change as a threat.
- **Fear of giving up freedom** – With a change, we feel we may lose some of our freedom.

**Reflection**

*Change Responses*

1. Thinking about the change you are going through right now, where would you place yourself on The Change Response Grid? Are you oscillating between different states? What is it in the environment and your feelings that would lead you to place yourself there? (*Make a note here.*)

   _____

   _____

   _____

   _____

   _____

2. What is your level of tolerance for change? What is it that might be triggering a threat or perceived threat for you? (*Make a note here.*)

   _____

   _____

   _____

   _____

   _____

### Build a Positive Change Network

When we face change, we don't need to take it all on ourselves, and we are probably not alone in the change we face. So, build a positive change network. This will help us deal with the change we are facing.

We can divide this into two groups: our social ties and our instrumental ties. Social ties are people who have a similar point of view or values as us, or with whom we have a shared experience. They can provide emotional support, help us make sense of the situation and build our confidence. Instrumental ties are people who may hold a position of power or have the knowledge we need. They can provide technical or knowledge support, help us act practically in situations and minimize the challenges we face.

For example, when I moved to Singapore, I met several other people who also just moved here, so we could share our experiences. I also joined a dragon boat team to connect with other expats and local Singaporeans and had great conversations with a close friend of mine from Japan about it. In business, I went to many networking events to get knowledge and practical advice about living and doing business in this new country.

I recall also, in July 2020, when my cousin passed away, all of us cousins bounded together to support each other. He was the first of our generation to pass away from a very large and close family. My father has 10 brothers and sisters and there are 25 of our generation. We connected via email, zoom, letters and photos to support each other during this time.

With the COVID-19 pandemic in 2020, people reached out to each other to offer support and solidarity. Physical distancing did not mean social distancing, and people connected via zoom, phone, email, WhatsApp, Facebook and Instagram to share information, practical tips and emotional support during this time; and relationships deepened as a result.

**Reflection**

*Build a Positive Change Network*

1. Thinking of the change you are going through right now, what social ties do you have that you can reach out to? What kind of support would you like or need from them? How will this help you with the change you are going through, mitigate or minimize any threats and increase the positive rewards? How will you connect with them? (*Make a note here.*)

_____

_____

_____

_____

_____

2. What instrumental ties do you have that you can reach out to? What kind of support would you like or need from them? How will this help you with the change you are going through, mitigate or minimize any threats and increase the positive rewards? How will you connect with them? (*Make a note here.*)

_____

_____

_____

_____

_____

In the next two chapters, we will look at Agility and Resilience. With agility, how we can have the mental strength in the moment to deal with the changes we face, pivot and see the opportunities on the other side. With resilience, how we can build up the mindset and ability to sustain peak performance during and through whatever changes or adversities we may face. If these chapters resonate with you, and you haven't read them yet, perhaps explore them now.

## NOTES

1 Beaumeister, R., Bratslavsky, E., Finkenauer, F. and Vohs, K. D. "Bad is stronger than good." *Review of General Psychology.* 5(4), 323–70. 2001.

2 Mahoney, M. J. *Human Change Processes: The Scientific Foundations of Psychotherapy.* New York, NY: Basic Books.. 1991.

**COMPANION WORKBOOK**

As you may have noticed, each chapter has exercises and reflection activities. If you would like to keep a record of your journey all in one place and have a working tool that you can go back to, there is a Companion Workbook. This is a free interactive pdf that you can save as you go along. To access it, go to the following URL or scan the QR code below.

www.selfleadershipassessment.com/workbook/

# **Thirteen**

Every day, in every part of our lives, we are faced with multiple changes, big and small, quick or long-lasting. We all respond differently to each change; however, some individuals are able to cope better with the uncertainty of it, and so adapt and thrive through these changes more effectively than others. We can describe these people as being agile. Agility is not necessarily about the speed of response to a change, but more the proactive ability to adapt and thrive in the moment in the face of change. And this can be learned and developed.

As I am writing this chapter and reflecting on what agility is, basketball came to mind. Imagine a basketball player coming down the court toward the other team's basket. Then, a player from the opposing team stands right in front of them to block and defend. That first basketball player needs to be agile in order to be successful. That player stops suddenly in the face of this opposing player, sizes up this obstacle, looks around for an open teammate, pivots on one foot, then delivers a bounce pass with the proper velocity and accuracy, and their teammate scores.

In basketball, a pivot is when a player maintains one foot having contact with the ground without changing its position on the floor and utilizes the other foot to rotate their body to improve position while in possession of the basketball. In life and business, when we are faced with a change or challenge immediately in front of our face, it is the same. We need to be agile and pivot in order to be successful.

Let's break this down into its components. In basketball, to be agile and pivot, a player needs to be physically fit and have strong ankles; otherwise, they may injure themselves or trip in the moment of stopping suddenly. They need to be able to see the obstacles around them that are preventing them from moving forward in their course of action; for example, the big opponent in front of them trying to block them or steal the ball from them. They also need to be able to see the opportunities on the other side; for example, looking through the obstacle (beyond their

DOI: 10.4324/9781003127000-13

opponent) and seeing a teammate open in front of the basket. Then, they need to pivot in the moment to improve their position. And then execute their strategy and action; for example, a bounce pass around the obstacle to their open teammate.

This is the same, in business or life, when we are faced with a challenge or change that makes us stop suddenly in our course of action. At that moment, we need to have mental agility to be strong in that moment of suddenly stopping or it may be too overwhelming and derail us. We need to be able to size up the obstacle in front of us that is preventing us from moving forward, see the opportunities on the other side, pivot to improve our position, then execute our strategy and action to break through and be successful.

For example, a few years ago, I was the Team Manager of an amateur sports team and the former Team Manager tried to defame me. Out of jealousy or ego or whatever reason, he started spreading lies about me and wrote a three-page document of lies that he distributed to all of the other leaders on the team, in an attempt to discredit my character and defame me. It was very erratic behavior and caused tension for everyone. This was one of the biggest stressors of my life, as no one had ever treated me this way before, nor did I know anyone personally who had gone through this either. At first, it was overwhelming and derailed me. Then, after regulating my own emotions and putting it into perspective, I built up the mental agility to overcome this obstacle. I saw the opportunities on the other side and that this person was irrelevant. I pivoted around it, grew and, as a result, came out on the other side stronger and more successful.

We will face stressors and challenges in our life. We need to push through, adapt and thrive in the moment, so that we can pivot, see the opportunities and come out even stronger on the other side.

### Stressors and Triggers

First, let's look at the various stressors or triggers that may cause us to suddenly stop our course of action. Then, we will deep dive into ways to improve our mental agility and ability to pivot.

A *trigger* is an event that is the cause of a particular action, process or situation. A *stressor* is something that causes a state of strain or tension. We are not focusing on the distinction between the two, but rather combining them, focusing on events or situations that cause us strain or tension and, as a direct result, lead us to take particular actions or strategies.

The following provides us a list of some of the stressors we may face in the workplace and in our personal lives:

**Table 13.1** Stressors and Triggers

| Stressors in the Workplace | Stressors in Our Personal Lives |
|---|---|
| • Workload | • The death of a spouse |
| • Unrealistic demands | • Filing for divorce |
| • Organizational change | • Losing contact with loved ones |
| • Career and job ambiguity | • The death of a family member |
| • Lack of recognition | • Hospitalization (oneself or a family |
| • Harassment | member) |
| • Organizational culture | • Injury or illness (oneself or a family |
| • Bad management practices | member) |
| • Job content and demands | • Being abused or neglected |
| • Physical work environment | • Separation from a spouse or |
| • Relationships at work | committed relationship partner |
| • Change management | • Conflict in interpersonal relationships |
| • Lack of support | • Bankruptcy/money problems |
| • Role conflict | • Unemployment |
| • Lack of time or perceived lack of time | • Children's problems at school |
| • Too many open folders | • Legal problems |
| • Lack of clarity | • A global pandemic |
| • Tentative status/indecision | |
| • Lack of knowledge | Daily "stress" events |
| • Change | • Traffic |
| • Worrying about events that have not | • Lost keys, wallet, mobile phone |
| happened yet | • Quality and quantity of physical |
| • Lack of control | activity |
| • Job insecurity | • Gaining weight |
| • Poor communication | • Sleep problems |
| • No reviews | |
| • Poor equipment | |
| • Unable to climb | |
| • Workplace violence | |
| • Random interruptions | |
| • Unclear policies and no sense | |
| of direction | |
| • Conflicts with teammates and | |
| supervisors | |
| • Inadequate authority necessary to | |
| carry out tasks | |
| • Lack of training necessary to do the job | |
| • Making presentations in front of | |
| colleagues or clients | |
| • Unproductive and time-consuming | |
| meetings | |
| • Commuting and travel schedules | |

The magnitude and frequency of stressors matter. We tend to do better with acute rather than chronic stressors, particularly when they are followed by sufficient time for recovery. For example, experiencing an intense emotional shock from having a colleague made redundant with an increase in workload for us, followed by a period of reflection and recovery long enough for us to regain control of our emotions, would be beneficial for our health and allow us to move forward positively. This is what I did, a few years ago, when the former Team Manager tried to defame me. In Chapter Nine: *Emotion Regulation*, we deep dive into *emotion regulation*. If you haven't yet read this, and you're looking for strategies to do this, perhaps read this chapter next.

With higher magnitude or chronic stressors, like the death of a spouse or loved one or the loss of your job, it is obviously much harder but still possible. One colleague of mine, who is a 9/11 survivor, told me a story of her house burning down in 2018, then three months later her mother passed away, then three months after that her mother-in-law passed away. She decided then to quit her job to give herself space and time to recover.

Frequency is also a factor, even with acute stressors. If, for example, we have stressor after stressor after stressor, even if they are acute, without such periods of recovery, they are harmful for us. It would be like the so-called Chinese water torture: a drop continuously hitting the same spot on your head, never letting you recover.

When a random event happens, it is already too late to react, so we need to be prepared to withstand the shock. Recovery after, no matter how fast, is always after the event. Therefore, we need to have mental strength to withstand the event or stressor in the first place, just like the basketball player needs to have physical strength to withstand the sudden stop or risk breaking their ankle.

Psychiatry talks about *post-traumatic stress*, the stress that people get after experiencing a particularly traumatic event or events, like my colleague above experienced. There is also, however, the concept of *post-traumatic growth*, the ability to grow as a result of experiencing such events. What doesn't kill us, makes us stronger. This is what we will focus on in this chapter.

### The Antifragile

In his book, *Antifragile*, Nassim N. Taleb talks about three types of systems, organizations or people[1]:

- **The fragile** – which is like an egg and breaks easily under stress.
- **The robust** – which is like a phoenix, when destroyed comes back exactly as it was before.
- **The antifragile** – which gets stronger from uncertainty – like the Hydra from the Greek myth where when you cut off one head, two grow back in its place. It gets stronger from the volatility.

When we face challenges, changes and stressors, we need to become antifragile. Like the Hydra growing two more heads, we need to focus on how we can grow from this and get stronger. So, the opposite of *fragile* is not *robust*, where something stays the same; but rather the opposite of *fragile* is antifragile, where it gets stronger as a result of the stress. This is what *post-traumatic growth* is all about. In Chapter Fourteen: *Resilience*, we dive more into this and how we can grow from change or adversity, and sustain peak performance, no matter what life throws at us.

We introduce the idea of *antifragile* here in this chapter, however, so we can first look at ways to train our brain to be *antifragile* in order to be more agile in the moment when we face challenges or stressors. *Agility* is the ability to adapt and thrive in the moment of change, when the change first happens; *resilience* is the ability to grow and sustain peak performance during the change. Training our brain to be *antifragile* will not only help us be more *resilient* for the long term, but also more *agile* in the very moment when we face the change. That's why we introduce it here.

I recall, several years ago, I designed and facilitated a communication training program for commercial airline pilots for emergency situations when emotions and stress are high. The pilots told me that, with modern commercial aircrafts, every part of flying can be done automatically, on autopilot: auto takeoff, auto cruise and auto landing. They said they will always use autopilot when they reach cruising altitude. However, they do not like it for takeoff and landing, although it is possible. The reason they said is because it will weaken their skills at this, they will become *fragile* and, as a result, especially in emergency situations, it could be costly.

I recall also, about two years ago, a friend of mine over coffee once, introduced me to the term "Strawberry Generation," a term that originated from Taiwan and has spread elsewhere in Asia. It refers to people born between 1981 and 1991 who grew up being overprotected by their parents and in an environment of economic prosperity and, therefore, "bruise easily" like strawberries and have difficulty with social pressure, challenges and stress, in a similar manner to how strawberries are grown in protected greenhouses because of their fragility.

Now, certainly, we are not characterizing *all* people this age like this. However, growing up being overprotected and in an environment of economic prosperity can increase the *fragility* of people's minds and make them less agile, much in the same way as pilots can become more *fragile* by relying on autopilot and automated flying. It makes it more difficult to handle stressors in the workplace or personal life.

In the next section, we will look at specific strategies and exercises that can help us build our mental strength and agility, which will help us handle stressors more effectively and help us to pivot in the moment when we face such challenging situations. But first, let's reflect on our own situation and how we might become less *fragile*.

**Reflection**

*Fragile, Robust and Antifragile*

1. Think about your current situation and the stressors that you are facing.

2. What aspects of your life or situation might cause you to feel *fragile?* This could be about comfort, overprotection, prosperity, systems, processes, resources or any other aspect that might hinder your ability to handle and grow from the stressors that you are facing right now. (*Make a note here.*)

   _____

   _____

   _____

   _____

   _____

3. How can you be more *antifragile* to grow as a result of the stressors or volatility you face? (*Make a note here.*)

   _____

   _____

   _____

   _____

   _____

## Adapting and Managing Ourselves Through Change

Let's now look at some strategies to adapt and manage ourselves through change. There are three strategies that we will explore: Mental and Physical Strength; Mental Self-Talk; and Anticipate the Future.

### Mental and Physical Strength

As we mentioned earlier, when a random event happens, it is already too late to react, so we need to be prepared to withstand the shock. Therefore, we need to have mental strength to withstand the event or stressor in the first place, just like a basketball player needs to have physical strength to withstand the sudden stop, when faced with an opposing player blocking them, or risk breaking their ankle.

A great example of mental and physical strength is Dana Glowacka. On May 18, 2019, Dana Glowacka, a Canadian athlete from Montreal, Canada, held plank for a record 4 hours and 20 minutes to set a new women's world record for the longest plank held. Clearly, this takes not only an enormous amount of physical strength but also an enormous amount of mental strength to push through and endure.

I recall another example as well. About ten years ago, when I was snowboarding with friends, I created a concept called "snoga," which is yoga for snowboarders. It was a series of specific yoga stretches that targeted the exact muscles needed for snowboarding. As a result, this would not only prevent injuries but also allow people to jump higher, carve deeper, pivot sharper and overall enjoy snowboarding more, giving them the physical and mental strength to push through and endure.

So, what can we do to improve our mental and physical strength? First of all, maintain a healthy life and lifestyle, with proper amounts of sleep, food, water and physical fitness. This will increase your energy and mental alertness. In Chapter Six: *Physical Health*, we look in detail about the neurological effects of physical health on our brains. If you haven't yet read this and feel that you could improve your physical and mental health, perhaps read this one next.

It is also important to take time to renew and recover. This could be going for a walk, practicing yoga or meditating. It also includes taking regular breaks while working to allow our brains to decompress from the heavy thinking and focus we use while we work. In Chapter Four: *Mindfulness*, we look in more detail about mindfulness meditation and the benefits of this. If this resonates with you, and you haven't yet read this, perhaps read this next. Renew and recover also includes allowing time for the things that make us feel relaxed. This could be our hobbies, sports, reading books, watching movies, cooking or any other activity that makes us feel relaxed.

And yet another way to improve our mental well-being and strength is to find meaning in what we do. This practice involves understanding what our personal values are and the bigger purpose of our life, and then exploring the links between this and what we are doing and the situation we are facing. By aligning personal meaning and doing what matters most, we will create a focus and a source of energy that can help us cut through a lot of the chaos. We talk more about this in Chapter Two: *Goals* and Chapter Three: *Inspiration and Motivation*. Perhaps read these too, if you haven't already.

### Overshooting

As a subset of mental and physical strength, we can also look at *overshooting*. In weight training, *overshooting* is a method that consists of short episodes in the gym in which you focus solely on improving your past maximum, the heaviest weight you could possibly lift, in a single lift. This workout is limited to trying to exceed that mark once or twice, rather than spending time on repetitions. As a result, the body overshoots in response and prepares (up to the point of biological limit of course). This is how the body builds muscle and gets stronger. As you are *overshooting* past your maximum, it is important to have a "spotter" – someone who can spot the weights for you in case your muscles give in. Training in this technique is dangerous to do by yourself.

We can use this same technique to help build our minds to be stronger and increase our agility and ability to adapt in the moment to stressors – to help us to grow and become mentally stronger. Intentionally introducing small stressors will make us more *antifragile* and build agility.

For example, one of my hobbies is dragon boating, which is a competitive boat racing sport where teams of 10 or 20 paddlers compete on speed. Such races are usually 200 m or 500 m. When our team trains for these races, we will *overshoot* these marks in order to build the mental strength and agility to compete more effectively. We will practice 250 m for a 200 m race and 600 m for a 500 m race. This will allow us to have the mindset and agility to paddle harder and get a faster time in the race.

For pilots, this is also the reason that they undergo very strict and diligent simulation training. In fact, such simulation training *overshoots* the real possibilities to build the mental strength, agility and skills in case they were to face the real situation. Moreover, they don't do the simulation training alone. Rather, they have an instructor or coach to guide and support them.

With my own example, a few years ago, when that person tried to defame me, I *overshot* in order to build up my own mental agility and strength. At one point after it happened, I took it all on myself and what my behavior could have done to lead someone to do this. Although being defamed by someone and them telling lies is clearly their problem, I wanted to build up my own agility, so I took it all upon myself to *overshoot* my mind. As an exercise, this helped me to build up more mental strength and agility to not only handle this stressor but others in future as well.

As we mentioned before, *overshooting* in weight training is dangerous to do by yourself in case your muscles give in. Likewise, *overshooting* mental stressors is dangerous to do by yourself in case your mind gives in. So, while doing this process or exercise of *overshooting*, I had friends to support me and help me so that my mind would not be in danger and they could pull me back if necessary.

### Mental Self-Talk

Have you ever had bad service in a restaurant? I have. Four years ago, I remember, at a restaurant I went to with some work colleagues after work, I experienced this. First, the waiter reached over my plate to serve dishes and clear the table. Then, he even poured the beer over top of my bag, which was on a chair beside me. When I asked if he minded not doing that, he said, "you can move your bag."

Boom … red card!!! My first thought was; what?! Did I just hear you correctly? Are you really that bad? Do you not know anything about service?

Instead of confronting him, however, I decided to let it slide. I noticed also though that there was another waitress who had overheard all of this. She then came over and said, "oh I can pour that for you." And then she intentionally poured it away from my bag, and we both smiled.

And so, my initial mental self-talk could have led me down a path to get upset and complain about it. However, after taking a deep breath and pausing, I looked at what was in my own control (my own thoughts, how I react to this, my emotions), how can I take ownership (I could talk to a Manager about this, I could use other servers only), what is the scope of this (it only impacts this situation and nothing else in my life), and what is the time span (it is only impacting right now).

When we are faced with stressors, we may react with negative self-talk. This could be anger or frustration, like in the example above. It could also take the form of blaming others or the situation ("It's not my fault, it's everyone else."); pessimism ("I've already tried that, it didn't work; why do anything at all?"); or an aversion to change ("I'd rather not change in case I risk losing something."). All of this negative self-talk will lead us to ruminate about the stress and negativity of our situation and lead us into a negative downward spiral.

In his book, *Learned Optimism*,[2] Martin Seligman makes a distinction between *learned optimism* and *learned helplessness* (stemming from pessimism). An optimist will think of negative events as temporary and specific, and positive events as permanent and universal. In other words, they will compartmentalize the negative event as happening now and for this occasion only, and it will not last forever and affect other parts of their life. They also believe that positive events will have longer lasting impact and brighten every part of their lives, not just in this particular situation. A pessimist, however, will think the opposite. They believe that negative events are permanent and universal impacting their whole life and lasting forever, and that positive events are temporary and specific only creating joy at this moment and in this situation.

This is one way, then, to have more positive self-talk: to compartmentalize the stressor or negative event as temporary and specific. This will help us, like in my restaurant example, to manage the scope and time span of the situation.

Two other aspects we want to look at are control and ownership. With the situations and stressors we face, we may not have control over every part of it (higher workload, a global pandemic, the loss of a loved one). We do, however, have control over certain parts of it. We can control where we deploy our attention, whether we ruminate about the negative aspects only or mentally introspect to regulate our emotions in affirming ways. In Chapter Nine: *Emotion Regulation*, we look at this in detail. We also have control over our reactions to the event or stressor. We could react impulsively, like a knee-jerk reaction when the doctor hits our knee with a little hammer, or we could take a pause to reflect and then respond in a more controlled way.

We also want to look at ways to empower ourselves and take ownership of the situation. Rather than wasting time blaming or complaining, we want to exercise personal responsibility and accountability. When a negative event happens, stop and ask yourself, "What can I personally do to overcome this?" Ownership requires feeling accountable for improving things and doing what we can to fix them. This will empower us and increase our sense of ownership and control.

Learned optimism (managing the scope and time span of the situation) and exercising control and ownership will help us size up the stressors and obstacles, like the basketball player sizing up the opposing player in front of them. This will create the mental space and mental agility to decide what we need to do in the face of such stressors and obstacles.

When we face stressors or obstacles, there is a lot of uncertainty and ambiguity. Each of us has a different tolerance for ambiguity that we can absorb. The higher our threshold, the more we can tolerate or absorb. Think of this like spicy food – the higher your threshold for spiciness, the more of it you can tolerate. Everything has a breaking point, at which point, we cannot take it anymore. Even a metal bar has a breaking point. Expanding out ambiguity threshold will help us to tolerate and absorb more of the uncertainty and ambiguity we face from the stressors or obstacles.

Some of us may say, "I am not comfortable with not knowing." This will increase the stress and anxiety we feel when we are faced with such changes and challenges. There are ways, however, that we can expand our ambiguity threshold to cope better with the uncertainty of it and adapt and thrive through these situations.

First of all, be curious. Open up the range of sources of information, ideas, people and opportunities that we entertain. This will train ourselves to look for what is interesting and relevant in the usual and mundane, and also what is new and different. Building this desire to learn about the unknown will help us deal more effectively with ambiguity and uncertainty. Venture beyond the boundaries of information and ideas to satisfy more than your immediate needs. Know what your scope of expertise is, then make opportunities to work at the edge of it, so that you need to learn more about other things. Expand your repertoire of personal experience. Undertake a study of an entirely new domain, try a different way of doing things to test yourself or your ideas, meet and talk to a wide range of different people, or take a field trip to other organizations or other industries to find out what they are doing.

Also, look beyond the immediate situation and spot connections and opportunities. Just like the basketball player who is going to be looking down the court for an open teammate to pass the ball to, we also need to look beyond the immediate situation and find the opportunities.

A couple of days ago, before writing this section, I was going for a bike ride, one of my hobbies. As I was riding, I was reflecting on this very topic. I was looking beyond what was immediately in front of me and looking out into the distance at other people walking or riding, dogs, children and elderly. And as I was riding, I was planning my best route and course of action to get me around all of these obstacles to where I want to go. And by seeing this, even in the moment, we can react quickly to course-correct if necessary. It's like the Jedi knights from *Star Wars* with their "jedi reflexes" to immediately respond to things in the moment if they happen.

Wayne Gretzky, the greatest ice hockey player in history, once said, "I don't go to where the puck is; I go to where the puck will be." And that's what we need to think in order to get through these stressors or obstacles and find the opportunities on the other side.

In our own lives, both in business and in our personal lives, we can build our knowledge about the future by reading books and articles about our industry or situation or about the future, reading as broad a range of information, news, events and concepts as we can. Meet a wide range of different people from different organizations and industries, different backgrounds and experiences and talk to them about the future, sharing our ideas and listening to theirs. And then think about how these ideas relate to each other, linking together even apparently unconnected ideas, and how these may affect us and our future. This will help us spot the opportunities and go beyond our immediate situation.

Steve Jobs provides a great story for us as well. Steve Jobs cofounded Apple at the age of 21. At 23 he was a multimillionaire, and by 30 his whole world came crashing down as he was fired from the revolutionary company he helped create. He described the next few months of his life as brutal. "*I really didn't know what to do for a few months,*" he admitted. "*I felt that I had let the previous generation of entrepreneurs down, that I had dropped the baton as it was being passed to me. I just wanted to run away from Silicon Valley forever.*" It's fair to say that Steve Job's removal from Apple was traumatizing. However, instead of sinking deeper and deeper into his misery, he chose to look at his failure in a different way: as an opportunity to grow. In 1985 he called a former colleague and launched the new computer company, NeXT. He founded Pixar Animation Studios, now one of the most successful film animation companies in the world. Ultimately, he returned to lead Apple, with a renewed focus on helping to bring cutting edge technology to the masses. This new perspective led to the iMac, iPod, iPad and iPhone revolution that's still alive today. He later had the following reflection on his fall from grace:

> I didn't see it then, but it turned out that getting fired from Apple was the best thing that could have ever happened to me. The heaviness of being successful was replaced by the lightness of being a beginner again, less sure about everything. It freed me to enter into one of the most creative periods of my life.

Steve Jobs's story is a remarkable one. Faced with unbelievable trauma, he chose to pivot, and ultimately use it to grow in his gifts and help millions of people around the world. He focused, not on the trauma he went through, but on what he did about it, and how he created new beliefs to lead him toward growth. When adversity strikes, no matter how big or how small, we can do this too and seek *post-traumatic growth*.

---

**Reflection**

*Adapting and Managing Yourself Through Change*

1. What can you do to build up the necessary mental and physical strength to push through and endure the stressors and obstacles you face? (*Make a note here.*)

   _____

   _____

   _____

   _____

   _____

2. How will you *overshoot* to strengthen this mental muscle to endure even more? Who will you turn to support you through this? (*Make a note here.*)

   _____

   _____

   _____

   _____

   _____

3. How can you manage your mental self-talk by developing more learned optimism (managing the scope and time span of your situation) and exercise control and ownership to size up the stressors and obstacles to decide what you need to do in the face of such stressors and obstacles? (*Make a note here.*)

   _____

   _____

   _____

   _____

   _____

4. How can you expand your ambiguity threshold and anticipate the future? What will you read and who will you speak to help you with this? What are the possible implications, consequences and results of this for you? What opportunities are there? (*Make a note here.*)

_____

_____

_____

_____

_____

## NOTES

1 Talib, N. M. *Antifragile*. New York, NY: Random House. 2012.
2 Seligman, M. *Learned Optimism*. New York, NY: Vintage Press. 1990.

# Fourteen

### The Farmer and the Donkey

One day a farmer was walking with his donkey. As they were walking, the donkey fell down into a well. The animal was shocked and cried for hours as the farmer tried to figure out what to do. Finally, he decided the animal was old, and the well needed to be covered up anyway and it just wasn't worth it to save the donkey. So, he invited all of his neighbors to come over and help him. They all grabbed shovels and began to shovel dirt into the well. At first, the donkey was shocked as dirt was being shoveled onto his back and he cried horribly. Then, to everyone's amazement, he quieted down. A few shovel-loads later, the farmer looked down the well. He was amazed at what he saw. With each shovel of dirt that hit the donkey's back, he would shake it off and take a step up. As the farmer and his neighbors continued to shovel dirt on top of the donkey, he would shake it off and take a step up. Pretty soon, the donkey was at the top of the well and he stepped up over the edge and happily trotted off!

Life is going to shovel dirt on us, all kinds of dirt. We can either get buried in the dirt or shake it off and take a step up. Each adversity we face is a stepping stone, and we can get out of the deepest wells by shaking off the dirt and taking a step up.

### What Is Resilience?

We often face adversity in our personal and professional lives. This could be a disagreement with someone that causes the end of a friendship, a break up in a relationship or a pandemic that has affected the entire world. At work, it could be an organizational restructuring, a company losing money and going into the red, a disagreement with our boss or an organization being acquired by another. This causes a lot of stress for us, affects our emotional, mental and physical well-being, and hinders our behavior and performance.

DOI: 10.4324/9781003127000-14

Some say that resilience is the ability to bounce back from adversity, just like the donkey in the story, and get us back to where we were before. What if, however, we could not only bounce back but also take that adversity and make our situation even better?

### A Carrot, an Egg and a Cup of Coffee

A young woman, working for a consulting company, went to her mother one day and told her about her life and how things were so hard for her. She did not know what to do and wanted to give up. She was tired of fighting and struggling. It seemed that as one problem was solved, a new one arose. She was frustrated, affecting her emotionally, mentally and physically.

Her mother then took her into the kitchen. She filled three pots with water and placed each on the stove and turned on the elements. Soon the pots came to a boil. In the first she placed carrots, in the second she placed eggs and in the third she placed ground coffee beans. She let them sit and boil, without saying a word.

In about 20 minutes, she turned off the burners. She took the carrots out and placed them in a bowl. She scooped the eggs out and placed them in a bowl. Then she poured the coffee out and placed it in a bowl.

She then turned to her daughter and asked, "Tell me, what do you see?" "Carrots, eggs and coffee," the young woman replied. Her mother brought her closer and asked her to feel the carrots. She did and noted that they were soft. The mother then asked her to take an egg and break it. After peeling off the shell, she observed the hard-boiled egg. Finally, the mother asked her to sip the coffee. The daughter smiled as she tasted its rich aroma. The daughter then asked, "What does this mean?"

Her mother explained that each of these objects had faced the same adversity – boiling water. Each reacted differently. The carrot went in strong, hard and unrelenting. However, after being subjected to the boiling water, it softened and became weak. The egg was fragile. The shell protected its liquid interior, but after being in the boiling water, its inside became hardened. The ground coffee beans were unique, however. After being in the boiling water, they changed the water.

"Which are you?" she asked the young woman. "When adversity faces you, how do you respond? Are you a carrot, an egg or a coffee bean?"

And so, reader, which are you? Are you the carrot that seems strong, but with pain and adversity wilt and become soft and lose your strength?

Are you the egg that starts with a soft heart, but hardens with the heat? Or are you like the coffee bean that actually changes the hot water, the very circumstance that brings the pain?

### Terry Fox

Terry Fox was a distance runner from British Columbia, Canada, having won several competitions both at the high school and university level. In 1977, at the age of 19, he was diagnosed with osteosarcoma or, simply, bone cancer. He was frustrated and angry, saying, "How can this happen to me? I am healthy and an athlete. How can this happen to me?"

As a result, he had to have his right leg amputated and replaced with an artificial leg. Rather than give up or give in, rather than become hard or soft, he changed the situation. In 1980, he decided to run across Canada to raise money for cancer research, an 8,000-kilometer distance. He said, "We have to try." This was called the Marathon of Hope.

Running the equivalent of a full marathon every day, he was determined to beat cancer and raise $24 million Canadian dollars for cancer research to match the 24 million population of Canada at that time. After nine months of running, the cancer spread and forced him to end his quest after 143 days and 5,373 kilometers and ultimately cost him his life. His efforts, however, made him a hero around the world and resulted in a lasting, worldwide legacy. The annual Terry Fox Run, first held in 1981, has grown to involve millions of participants in over 60 countries and is now the world's largest one-day fundraiser for cancer research, with over $750 million Canadian dollars raised in his name.

### Kawhi Leonard

Kawhi Leonard is a professional basketball player with the National Basketball Association (NBA). When he was 17 years old, his father, Mark Leonard, was shot and killed on January 18, 2008 at the Compton car wash he owned. Still in high school, Leonard insisted on playing the next evening and broke down emotionally after the game. The murder of his father, at such a young age, was heavy in his heart and mind.

Rather than give up or give in, rather than become hard or soft, he changed the situation. With a laser-focus on practicing basketball and improving himself to be the best, it helped him regulate his emotions and be resilient.

After being drafted to the NBA, he won an NBA championship in 2014 with the San Antonio Spurs, where he was named the Finals Most Valuable

Player. After seven seasons with the Spurs, he was traded to the Toronto Raptors in 2018, and in 2019, he led the Raptors to their first NBA championship in franchise history and won his second Finals MVP award. He is a four-time All-Star with two All-NBA First Team selections, has earned five All-Defensive Team selections, won Defensive Player of the Year honors in 2015 and 2016 and is one of the greatest basketball players of all time.

And so, resilience is not only about bouncing back from adversity, but rather it is about surviving and thriving through the stress caused by the adversity, and changing our situation to make it even better.

---

### Reflection

#### Changing Your Situation of Adversity

1. Think of an adverse situation you have been in in the past.

2. How did you go into it and how did you come out? Like the carrots? Like the eggs? Like the coffee?

3. What can you do to overcome adversity more and change the water into coffee in order to grow and make your situation even better? (*Make a note here.*)

   _____

   _____

   _____

   _____

   _____

---

### Changes Aren't Permanent, But Change Is

Change is happening all the time. It's not like things are normal, then suddenly there is a change, and then suddenly we are back to normal. Change is constant. We live and operate in a *VUCA* world: it's volatile, uncertain, complex and ambiguous; and it is more *VUCA* than ever before. The rate, amount and magnitude of change can vary drastically at short notice. Issues, situations and events are unpredictable. There is an overwhelming dependency and connection of multiple factors. And information and events can be interpreted in multiple ways.

All of this can lead to stress, anxiety and disengagement. To be successful in this environment, we must be highly resilient. Resilience isn't about bouncing back from change or adversity, but rather it is about sustaining peak performance regardless of whatever situation we face, even during turbulent times. It is about surviving and thriving despite stressful circumstances – and to think and act constructively when stressful circumstances occur.

### What Derails People During Adverse Times?

We are going to focus on three areas that derail us the most during adverse times, and what we can do to make things better:

1. Stress
2. Unclear Expectations
3. Dysfunctional Teams

### The Two Wolves

In North America, a First Nations Chief of the Ojibwe Tribe was teaching his grandchildren about life. He said,

> A battle is raging inside me ... it is a terrible fight between two wolves. One wolf represents fear, anger, envy, sorrow, regret, greed, arrogance, self-pity, guilt, resentment, inferiority, lies, false pride, superiority and ego. The other stands for joy, peace, love, hope, sharing, serenity, humility, kindness, benevolence, friendship, empathy, generosity, truth, compassion and faith.

The Chief looked at the children with a firm stare. "This same fight is going on inside you, and inside every other person, too." They thought about it for a minute, and then one child asked his grandfather, "Which wolf will win?"

The old Chief replied: "The one you feed."

With every situation we face, our brain will process it along two pathways for cognitive appraisal: we interpret it as either a threat or as an opportunity; something that will cause us pain or something that will reward us. This happens very quickly and, often, unconsciously. It is an immediate reaction to any situation we are in. In Chapter Nine: *Emotion Regulation*, we look at cognitive appraisal in more detail. If this resonates with you at this moment and you haven't yet read that chapter, perhaps read it next.

And so, do you ruminate on the negative feelings caused by the stress and derailment from the adverse situation you are in? Or do you feed the other wolf? And if so, how do we feed this other wolf?

### Building Resilience in Ourselves

#### Change Our Beliefs

In the 1980s, Albert Ellis created the ABC model based on his research into adversity[1]. He found that an adversity (A) does not lead directly to the consequence (C), but rather, it is the belief (B) we adopt that alters the consequence (see Figure 14.1). Therefore, by addressing these beliefs, we can change the conclusions that we form; thus, giving us the ability to choose the outcome we want to adopt following a setback and even during an adverse situation we are facing at the moment.

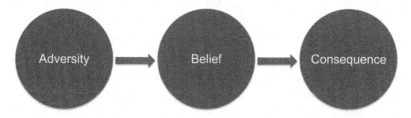

**Figure 14.1** ABC Model

For example, when we face adversity, we might, consciously or unconsciously, adopt some negative beliefs like: *"This is so hard for me." "This is a disaster."* Or *"This always happens to me."* These kinds of negative beliefs will lead us to less desirable consequences or conclusions like self-doubt or that the world is coming to an end.

There are several ways that we can change our beliefs. First of all, we can think of this as going to the balcony. Down below is the dance floor; this is where we are caught in the midst of the adversity. We need to step away from this and go to the balcony to get that bird's eye view to see the bigger and broader picture. Detach ourselves and zoom ourselves out of the adverse situation to see it from the balcony. This will broaden our perspective and deepen our understanding of the adverse situation.

Second, we need to look at ways to reappraise or reframe the situation: seeing it in as many different and positive ways as we can, and then choosing the best ones. Again, in Chapter Nine: *Emotion Regulation*, we go into much more detail about how to reappraise or reframe the situation to regulate our emotions, which will lower our cortisol levels and reduce our stress. We can use this same process as well to change our beliefs when faced with adversity. This will help us to plan and carry out a decisive course of action to resolve the stress caused by the adversity.

Moreover, if we embrace change and adversity with an attitude of challenge and opportunity, it lets us embrace and welcome this as a normal life process. We take an unbiased view toward this that helps us pursue what satisfies us for the longer term. Positive and negative experiences are simply situations we learn from. This does not mean that we jump for joy when adversity comes our way. Instead, we approach it as a meaningful challenge by seeing opportunity in every difficulty, rather than seeing it as a threat. We stay motivated despite stressful adversity, are able to learn from our experiences to do better the next time and maintain that whatever does not kill us makes us stronger. We see it as a necessary stimulus for self-discovery and growth, and it provides us an opportunity to further develop purpose and meaning.

For example, Wendy and Tim are managers in a pharmaceutical company that was losing money. Wendy regrets the decisions, some of which she had participated in, that led the company on this downward spiral. But she feels that the company can learn from these failures, and she continuously looks for alternatives that could improve the situation. Instead of panicking, she tries to see how to make the situation better, and that there is a lot to be learned. Tim, however, sees the failures as a permanent sign that he and the company are inadequate. He is flooded with the pain of what is happening, and of it becoming public. Therefore, he thinks of ways to cover up the financial mess, even if that means lying about it and being dishonest.

So, by changing our beliefs about the adversity, we can change the conclusions and consequences. It changes our mindset, which influences our thinking and feelings which, in turn, influence our actions and behavior.

### Channel Stress into Positive Stress

As we just talked about, we can regulate our emotions, which will lower our cortisol levels and reduce the amount of stress. We also want to channel our stress into positive stress.

### The Yerkes–Dodson Law

Developed by psychologists Robert M. Yerkes and John Dillingham Dodson in 1908,[2] the Yerkes–Dodson law shows the relationship between stress and performance. The law dictates that performance increases with physiological or mental arousal, but only up to a point. When levels of arousal become too high, performance decreases (see Figure 14.2).

**Figure 14.2** The Yerkes–Dobson Law: How Anxiety Affects Performance

Some of the key ways that we can channel our stress into positive stress are through: attentional deployment, getting into flow and adopting an iterative problem-solving approach. Our brain has an ability to deploy or focus our attention on different aspects of the situation. If we focus on the threatening or emotional aspects, it will bring/drive us into a downward spiral. However, if we focus on the nonemotional aspects or distance ourselves, this will start creating an upward spiral. In Chapter Four: *Mindfulness*, we go into much more detail about attentional deployment.

Getting into flow, as we deep dived into in Chapter Five: *Flow*, is the mental state of being fully immersed in a feeling of energized focus, full involvement and enjoyment in the process of the activity we are doing. In essence, it is characterized by complete absorption in what we do, performing at the edge of our capabilities, peak performance. In this state, it feels effortless, as if things are flowing together. We then go on, in Chapter Five, to outline the conditions for getting into flow. By deploying our attention to the positive or opportunity aspects of the situation, and getting ourself into flow around this, we can channel our stress into positive stress, accelerate changing the situation and growing and getting meaning from it. We turn the boiling water into coffee and we feed the other wolf.

Lastly, we also want to adopt an iterative problem-solving approach. A linear approach would look like this: what is the root cause of the problem? how can we solve it? what action do we need to take? This approach is good for simple tasks that have no emotional component. However, an iterative approach is better when there is not one clear solution and when there are emotions involved. We do not need to have the answer immediately; it may not be that clear. However, by taking a non-linear or iterative approach, we can have more insights, *aha moments*, and the path forward will unfold for us. In Chapter Seven: *Insight*, we deep dive into more about insights.

And so, these are some of the key ways that we can channel our stress into positive stress to help us feed the other wolf and change the boiling water into coffee.

---

**Reflection**

**Building Resilience in Yourself**

1. Think of an adverse situation that you are in at the moment.

2. What negative beliefs might be causing you more (undue) stress?

3. How can you change your beliefs and channel your stress into positive stress? (*Make a note here.*)

   _____

   _____

   _____

   _____

   _____

---

### Adopt a Prosocial Mindset

We should approach change and adversity in a more social way, how it affects the people around us, rather than being insular and looking out only for ourselves. Research by Adam Grant and Nancy Rothbard showed that people with prosocial concerns are more resilient than people concerned about their own security.[3]

In their research, they explored the interaction between an individual's personal values and proactive behavior in ambiguous work scenarios (i.e., during change and adversity). They found that those who exhibited high levels of "prosocial concern" (a concern for and protecting others) showed high levels of proactive adaptive behaviors. Those with high levels of security values (a concern for their own safety and security) exhibited the least proactive behavior. This is important, as a desire to protect oneself from perceived threats of change and adversity actually results in the deployment of completely ineffective behaviors during such situations.

People with strong security values perceive ambiguity as self-threatening, withhold proactivity and focus on the experience of fear and anxiety about whether it is safe. In contrast, people with strong prosocial values perceive ambiguity as an opportunity to create change for the benefit of others, and for themselves, seizing the opportunity to improve the status quo.

People with strong prosocial values are more willing to confront the challenges posed by unpleasant circumstances in order to make meaningful contributions to other people and the organizations they belong to. By being proactive, people with strong prosocial values can reduce collective uncertainty and dissatisfaction, creating better circumstances for others and for themselves. For example, people with strong prosocial values may respond to ambiguity by taking initiative to sell issues that will improve gender equity for colleagues. People with weak prosocial values, however, place less importance on improving the situation for others and themselves. As a result, they will be less likely to take advantage of ambiguity and adversity as an opportunity to proactively create change and make the situation better.

On an airplane back from Australia from a business trip in 2019, I didn't want to work, so I watched a movie. I watched *Captain Marvel*, and as I watched it, I thought superheroes are the most resilient people. They never give up, and they have a prosocial concern for others' well-being not about their own safety and security. Superheroes are a great example of resilient people.

### Building Resilience for Ourselves and Our Teams

When we work in teams, two areas that will derail us most during adverse times and increase our stress are:

1.  Unclear Expectations
2.  Dysfunctional Teams

### Clarify Expectations in Line with the Change or Adverse Situation

Under normal circumstances, we usually set our key job objectives (or KPIs) at the beginning of the year and have reinforcement on a quarterly basis. When change or adversity happens, however, we should clarify the KPIs immediately in line with the change. For example, one client of mine introduced a new performance approach, which placed more emphasis on career growth and leaders having meaningful conversations with their direct reports. This is now one of their key job objectives and is expected of them. This was clarified immediately in line with this new approach and reinforced on a monthly basis.

With daily activities, under normal circumstances, we usually reinforce these daily or weekly, depending on the level of complexity and collaboration. When change or adversity happens, we should clarify immediately how people need to change their daily activities. For example, with my client, there were now formal quarterly check-ins, plus regular ad hoc catchups and ongoing daily conversation. This needed to be reinforced in line with the new performance approach. We may not get certainty, but we can get clarity. This will also increase commitment and dedication, which is necessary for resilience.

### Maintain a High Functioning Team

In *The Five Dysfunctions of a Team*, Patrick Lencioni outlines the five dysfunctions of teams: absence of trust, fear of conflict, lack of commitment, avoidance of accountability and inattention to results.[4] He then goes on to outline the five functions of a high performing team: trust, absence of fear of conflict, commitment, accountability and attention to results. During times of change and adversity, by focusing on building a high functioning team, we appraise the people and activities in our life as important to our personal satisfaction and our interaction with them as worthwhile enough to pursue vigorously. This increases our commitment and dedication. If the opposite is true, we are more apt to deny or avoid the problem to minimize its damage to us.

For example, Eric and Tony work for a tech company, which is in the midst of a major reorganization. Eric is committed to this and wants to stay involved with the work and his coworkers, thinking through what is happening, asking others how they feel and how they're doing. He keeps working on things and participating as much as, if not more than, before the downsizing. He continues to care about the company and its members, feeling a strong sense of commitment. Tony, by contrast, sees the reorganization as just another disruption. With little commitment, he quickly concludes that the company executives are incompetent and not worth his loyalty, and that his fellow employees are fools not to see this too. He detaches himself from everything that is going on and does as little as possible during the workday, preferring to daydream of happier times. Eric is committed, more resilient and has high performance, whereas Tony is distracted and his performance has suffered.

Moreover, when we feel accountable and have attention to results, we adopt a mindset or attitude of control, which enables us to take direct, hands-on action to transform changes, adversities and the problems that they may cause. We are likely to say, "Let me find, or develop, the resources to solve this problem." If we believe that we can influence the outcome of an adverse situation, we are more apt to push ourselves to deal with it. If the opposite is true, we may question our ability to turn adversity around and stop trying.

For example, Rohaya and Cathy work for an insurance company that is being acquired by another larger firm. Rohaya feels accountable and cares about the results. She embraces the situation, thinking through the likely implications of the changes for her, for those around her, and for the company itself. Through all of this, she keeps in mind the downside of the changes, and the upside as well, and what she can do to influence it for beneficial outcomes. This mindset helps her take action to deal with it and interact in relevant, constructive ways. Cathy, by contrast, panics and has a sense of powerlessness as the changes mount. She doesn't feel accountable or care about the results. She does not believe it likely that she can do anything constructive, so she tries to decrease her pain by detaching herself from what is happening. She concludes that whatever is going to happen will happen, so it is better to think that it doesn't matter to her anyway. Rohaya is resilient; Cathy is not.

And so, when we go through times of change and adversity, if we focus on building a high functioning team – with trust, absence of fear of conflict, commitment, accountability and attention to results – it will lead to proactive behaviors and increase our resilience and the resilience in our team.

One of the best examples of a resilient high performing team is *The Avengers*. They function well together, are committed, accountable and engage in proactive behaviors to make the situation better, not only for themselves, but for everyone. They do everything they can to actively turn the boiling water into fresh, aromatic, tasty coffee.

---

**Reflection**

**Building Resilience for Yourself and Your Team**

1. Think of the changes and adverse situations that you face at the moment. This could be the changes going on at work, for example, something in your personal life or the adversity of a pandemic affecting the entire world.

2. How is this making you feel as a result of these changes and the situation?

3. How can you adopt a more prosocial mindset and see the change or adversity as an opportunity to make things better for yourself and others?

4. How can you clarify expectations (both KPIs and daily activities) in line with the change or adverse situation?

5. What can you do to help yourself and your team to be more high functioning?

---

## NOTES

1 Ellis, A. *Overcoming Resistance: Rational-Emotive Therapy with Difficult Clients.* New York, NY: Springer Publishing. 1985.
2 Yerkes, R. M. and Dodson, J. D. "The relation of strength of stimulus to rapidity of habit-formation." *Journal of Comparative Neurology and Psychology,* 18(5), 459–82. 1908.
3 Grant, A. M. and Rothbard, N. P. "When in doubt, seize the day? Security values, prosocial values, and proactivity under ambiguity." *Journal of Applied Psychology,* 98 (5), 810–19. 2013.
4 Lencioni, P. *The Five Dysfunctions of a Team: A Leadership Fable.* New York, NY: Wiley. 2002.

# Fifteen

In 1923, Austrian philosopher Martin Buber wrote the book I and Thou,[1] and it is still very relevant today. In it, he makes a distinction between two kinds of relationships: I–It, in which we turn inward, focusing only on ourselves, and treat others as things for us to get what we want; and I–Thou, in which we turn outward, seeing others as people and building authentic relationships with them.

Before we dive into how to build lasting authentic relationships with others, let's first look at what it means to be authentic, what holds us back from being authentic and why are some people "fake" or "superficial."

**What Does It Mean to Be Authentic?**

Being authentic includes:

- Being real.
- Being honest and true with yourself.
- Being vulnerable.
- Letting go of your own ego.
- Looking not only at what you like about yourself but also the "darker" part that can be improved and changed.
- Having the courage, humility and discipline to take a hard look in the mirror at who you are, recognizing the good things, but also the parts that can be improved and changed.

For example, I recently took a 360 assessment that looks at strengths and areas for improvement. Several years ago, I realized that I used to listen to people with my mouth open. So I wasn't really listening to them. I was just waiting for them to finally stop talking so that I could say something that I clearly thought was more important. But I wasn't really listening to them. I then started listening to people with my mouth closed, and this really helped me to open my ears to listen better. As my mentor

DOI: 10.4324/9781003127000-15

once told me, "Grant, there is a reason that you have two ears and only one mouth: you should be listening twice as much as you are talking." I worked on this for several years and thought I had become a better listener. So, on my self-assessment of my strengths and areas for improvement, I listed listening as one of my strengths.

Then, when I got the results from the 360 assessment, I saw a pattern. I had 11 other people, that I have worked closely with, anonymously fill it out for me as well. There was a pattern there from several people that I could improve my listening, truly listening to understand others rather than listening to reply. This was a big eye-opener for me, as I thought that this was an area I had improved and considered a strength. And so I thought about it deeply and realized that maybe in my ears and my mind I am listening to them, however, they do not feel that they are being listened to. Perhaps I was listening to them and then responding to what I heard, rather than empathically listening to them and playing back for them what I heard so they would feel heard and know that I am listening. As a result, I have now started doing more empathic listening ("You sound frustrated because of ...," "That must have been scary ...," "It seems stressful to have gone through that ..."), and I have noticed a big change because of this. When I listen empathically, others open up more and share more of what they are feeling and thinking. This, I believe, has helped me strengthen my relationships in business and personally.

For example, a friend of mine was diagnosed with breast cancer. It must have taken courage for her to tell me this and obviously is very upsetting to experience this. Rather than asking probing questions though to find out more, I listened empathically. I simply said, "That must have been scary." And then she went on to explain her feelings in detail. As a result, it helped to build trust between us and develop the relationship further. It showed that I was truly listening to her and allowing her the space to express herself as she wanted to. I listened empathically, she felt heard, and it developed a better relationship.

In Chapter Eighteen: *Empathy*, we explore more about empathy. If you haven't read it yet and this resonates with you, perhaps read it next.

So, What Holds Us Back from Being Authentic?

There are several reasons why people may not be authentic or as authentic as they could be. Here is a list of some:

- Fear of being vulnerable.
- Fear of rejection.
- Fear of judgment.
- Fear of abandonment.
- Competitiveness.
- Insecurity.
- Self-protection.
- Jealousy.
- Fear of not being good enough.
- It takes courage, humility and discipline.
- It takes effort.
- Difficulty in letting go of our ego.

It is frightening to be authentic: what if people don't like us? what if we are judged? We may feel a need to protect ourselves; we may feel inner competitiveness or jealousy, which may lead to insecurity about ourselves. As a result, we may project just a small part of ourselves to others or a polished version of ourselves.

For example, Rachel, a Senior Director in the retail industry, once told me that when she feels uncomfortable or insecure, she politely says, "I'm fine, thank you." It doesn't appear authentic; it is only surface level. Although extremely successful in business she also told me that she has self-esteem issues and, stemming from childhood, often believes that she is not good enough. When this happens, this is when she protects herself, giving only surface-level responses, and appearing inauthentic.

Also, a few years ago I did some consulting work with a major global tech company. One of the key issues they were facing was competition between people within the same team. As David, a Senior Leader in Product Development, recalls, "People were intentionally withholding information from each other and, in some cases, actively trying to sabotage other people's projects. Competition between people in the same team was rampant." This not only had a negative impact on innovation and business results but also created inauthentic and toxic relationships. We worked with Senior Leaders, like David, to create an environment that encouraged collaboration and synergy, and to change the leaders' mindsets to develop paradigms that valued collaborative interactions, teamwork and authenticity. This not only increased innovation but also helped them to develop better relationships with each other.

Have you ever felt like this? Like Rachel or David? Perhaps there was something in the environment or an incident that happened, and you felt a need to protect yourself. Has this ever happened to you? What did you do?

### Why Are Some People Fake or Superficial?

We have all seen these people – who appear fake or superficial. Perhaps, even, we have appeared this way to others. Why, though, does this happen? Why do we become fake or superficial?

- It is in our comfort zone.
- We want to be liked.
- We want to be validated.
- We feel a need for self-protection.
- It's easier.
- Our ego gets in the way.
- We don't have the courage, humility and discipline needed to take a hard look in the mirror at who we are.

Stemming from the reasons for not being authentic (insecurity, jealousy, inner competitiveness, fear, self-protection), we may project an image of ourselves which is not our true self – a persona to be liked and validated, that can protect our vulnerabilities, our insecurities and the other "darker" parts of ourselves. And so, we appear fake or superficial.

For myself, for example, I struggled to be vulnerable, to really let myself be free to open up to others. I felt a need to protect myself. If they know who I am and they reject me, it's painful. If I don't let them see that, then I can't be hurt. So, I would project an image of myself that I'd want them to see. I then had some great relationships where I was authentic and let people see the real me. It was so rewarding and felt so good, freeing. I then decided to have the courage to be authentic and real. If people like it, then we can build a great relationship; if they don't, then it's okay because other people do. Sometimes, I still feel a need to protect myself but I'm more comfortable with it, and more comfortable being authentic and real with people.

### How We Regard Others

How we behave toward others is about what we say or do toward them. Deeper inside, however, is how we regard or feel about them, how we see them in our mind. For example, if a person regards others as lazy and do not work hard, they may behave toward them in line with this paradigm, micromanaging and directing them like a child. If they change their behavior to communicate and delegate in a better way, if they still regard others as lazy and not hardworking, they will still be ineffective. It won't matter if they try managing by walking around, sitting on the edge of the chair to practice active listening, inquiring about family members in order to show interest or using any other skill they may have learned in order to be more effective. What others know and respond to is how that person is regarding them when doing those things.

John, a Senior Leader in the financial services industry, was such a person. His outward behavior and communication were such that he was listening to others and responded in a way that might flatter them or make them feel good. But there seemed to be something underlying this, something that made it seem inauthentic. Perhaps, he had his own agenda and regarded others as a way to achieve this. And it left people wondering, "What are your real intentions?"

Some people and leaders inspire devotion and commitment in others, even when they're interpersonally clumsy. The fact that they haven't attended many seminars or that they've never learned the latest techniques hardly matters. They seem to produce anyway. And they inspire those around them to do the same. Some of the best people and leaders in the world fall into this category. They don't always say or do the "right" things, but people love them and love working with them. They get results. But then there are other people who have a very different influence. Even if they do all the "right" things interpersonally – even if they apply all the latest skills and techniques to their communications and tasks – it won't matter. People ultimately resent them and their tactics. And so they end up failing as people and leaders – failing because they provoke people to resist them.

Like John, no matter what we're doing on the outside, people respond primarily to how we're feeling about them on the inside.

For example, once I was getting on an airplane after a long, tiring business trip. I found my seat and then put half of my newspaper on the seat next to me so no one would sit there and started reading the other half. I just wanted my downtime. I could see other passengers coming in and the plane was starting to fill up, but I didn't regard them as people with their own equal needs. I didn't consider the needs of those still looking for seats to be as legitimate as my own. My needs counted, and everyone else's were secondary. In a sense, I saw myself as the "kingpin," as the center of the world. My ego was in control. And I saw others as things around me.

It's like this: whatever we might be "doing" on the surface – whether it be, for example, sitting, observing others, reading the paper, whatever – we are being one of two fundamental ways when we are doing it. Either we are seeing others straightforwardly as they are – as people like us who have their own needs and desires as legitimate as our own – or we are not. One of these ways, we experience ourself as a person among people; the other way, we experience ourself as a person among objects. This is what Martin Buber described as the I–Thou relationship and the I–It relationship.

As another example, on that same airplane that I was on, there was a woman sitting by herself at the back reading her newspaper. The airplane was full, and she noticed a couple near the front who could not sit together. Immediately, she folded up her newspaper, went up to the couple and said, "There is an empty seat next to me. I will be happy to switch with one of you if you would like to sit together." She regarded them as people with their own equal and legitimate needs and took action based on this. Although her behavior was the same as mine, reading a newspaper on the airplane, she regarded people as people, not as objects in her own life.

In business, when we see people as people, these people become smarter, more skilled and harder working because they are regarded as people with their own equal and legitimate needs. And it is the same in any relationship, whether it be at work or personal. When we are regarded as people, we become better because we are recognized as the people that we really are.

One Managing Director I know, Barry, exemplifies this. He believes that purpose is important, and that aligning one's own values with their purpose and with the organization's purpose creates the kind of environment and relationships in business where people can thrive, be their best and perform at the highest level possible.

Do you know people like John or Barry? Perhaps, like John, someone whose outward behavior seems okay or even good, yet something deeper down inside – how they regard others – seems different? How did you respond to this person? Have you ever been like this to others, whether intentionally or unintentionally? How did they respond to you? Or, like Barry, someone who sees people as people, with their own needs and desires, and regards and behaves congruently toward them? How did you respond to this person? And imagine yourself, if you are like this, how will others respond to you?

### Self-Focused vs Other-Focused

Most people are happier when they succeed themselves rather than seeing others succeed. These people sometimes run over other people trying to get their own results. They might try to encourage teamwork, but they don't really mean it. These people, when they are in this frame of mind, are just focused on themselves. And they may be conscious of this or they may not even see it.

When we are self-focused, we experience others not as people with their own lives but as objects within our lives. When we are other-focused, by contrast, we experience others as people. Moreover, when we experience others in these two different ways, either as people in and of themselves or as objects in our lives, we experience ourselves differently as well. The choice to see others as either people or objects is a choice between whether we will see and experience ourselves and others truthfully and authentically.

The choice to move from being self-focused or other-focused (or vice versa) amounts to a radical shift in our way of being in the world, which is to say that it changes not only our behavior but also our thoughts, emotions, interpretations of events and views of the past, present and future.

This is what Martin Buber meant by the I–It relationship and the I–Thou relationship. When we treat others as an object, they become just a means for us to get what we want, for us to succeed. However, when we treat others as people, we fundamentally change the way we feel and think, about them, us and events.

For example, in my earlier years, I was very result-focused, driven and strived for success for myself. I may have steam-rolled over people, albeit inadvertently. Then, I became aware of this and wanted to change. I started focusing more on others, and it changed the way I saw the situation and the world. I saw it as more interconnected and where synergy thrives; and I saw people differently – as real people with their own needs and emotions. This helped me to build better relationships with them and truly understand who they are.

Where do you see yourself? Are you sometimes self-focused or always other-focused? How much of your time do you spend in each? How does this change the way you think, feel and interpret the world?

### Building More Authentic Relationships with Others

Let's now explore ways that we can build more authentic relationships with others, regarding them as people, and living an I–Thou relationship with them.

#### Connecting with People with Similar Values

We are drawn to people who are similar to us and who share similar values. These people are easy for us to connect with. This is because our brains release and build oxytocin: the neurochemical produced from the comfort of social trust either given or received. This could be feeling safe with a group of like-minded people, having social support from people similar to ourselves or physical touch from a loved one. The brain releases oxytocin cautiously in order to promote our survival and avoid harm. It can also help us to overcome some of our insecurities, inner competitiveness or self-protection, so that we can truly be more authentic to ourselves and to others.

How do you feel when you are with people similar to yourself, who share the same values? Do you feel more connected? Do you feel something in your brain, like a sense of comfort, trust or safety? What experiences or people have triggered this for you?

### Valuing Differences and Putting the Other Person First

Insecure people have a high need to clone others, to mold them into their own thinking and their own way of thinking. They may do this consciously, or perhaps they are not even aware of it. They put their needs before others and, therefore, regard and treat them as an object to help them get what they want, as an I–It relationship. In my earlier years, this is something I did, albeit inadvertently; and I worked on it, and am still working on it, to make this better.

In order to build truly authentic relationships, we need to overcome our own ego and put others first. We need to value the differences in the people around us and build on the strengths that they have. As an exercise, I recently made the following chart and identified the strengths of some of the people closest to me:

|  | Wee Ping | Grace | Yiming | Brenda |
|---|---|---|---|---|
| Strengths | Courageous | Planner | Intelligent | Creative |
|  | Relationship Builder | Good Listener | Analytical | Go-Getter |
|  | Sensible | Considerate | Insightful | Fun Loving |
|  | Natural Leader | Collaborator | Objective | Focused |

**Figure 15.1** Value Differences and Strengths (Example)

By identifying the strengths and valuing the differences with the people we work with or are close to us in our personal lives, we can help ourselves to put others first and overcome our own self ego.

**Reflection and Exercise**

*Valuing Differences and Putting Others First*

1. Think about the relationships in your life, both in business and personally. Are you regarding everyone as a person with their own legitimate needs and desires? Are there any people that you may, consciously or unconsciously, be regarding as an "object" to help you get what you want? (*Make a note here.*)

   _____

   _____

   _____

   _____

   _____

2. Use Figure 15.2 (or create your own matrix) to list up the strengths of some of the people closest to you in order to value the differences and help put them first.

**Figure 15.2** Value Differences and Strengths (Template)

Extroverts and introverts approach authenticity and relationships differently. Extroverts may be less protecting and critical of themselves, whereas introverts may be deeper, more self-protecting and inwardly critical. Extroverts can have both light surface relationships and deep relationships and can travel/float between these seamlessly. Introverts, by contrast, want to have and thrive on deep relationships only and may stay clear of light surface relationships altogether.

Understanding these differences is important to build authentic relationships with others, especially if they are different from us.

For example, I am an extrovert and my friend René is an introvert. On her birthday, I handwrote a nice note about who she is. She was touched and loved it. It was deep. A few days later, I sent a humorous photo of myself for a bit of fun and to make her laugh. She said it was strange to do that; and I felt I went three steps forward, two steps back. Whereas, as an extrovert, I can travel/float between the deep and the light-hearted, introverts, like René, thrive in keeping it deep.

Which are you – an introvert or an extrovert? Because of this, how do you approach authenticity and relationships? What's important to you?

### Understanding the Needs and Differences of the Four Social Styles

We can also put this in the context of the four social or behavioral styles:[2]

- Amiable
- Expressive
- Analytical
- Driver

This can be expressed by the figure on the next page.

Analyticals and Amiables are less assertive; Drivers and Expressives more assertive. Analyticals and Drivers are less responsive, controlling their emotions; Amiables and Expressives are more responsive, displaying their emotions. This, then, creates the four social or behavioral styles.

Analyticals are systematic, prudent and task-oriented. Amiables are supportive, dependable and people-oriented. Drivers are independent,

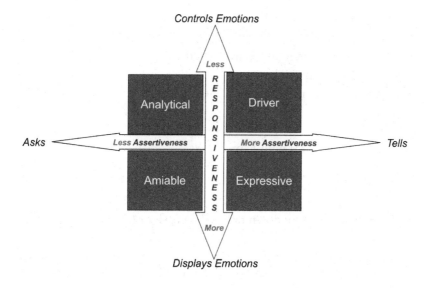

**Figure 15.3** Four Social or Behavioral Styles

candid and results focused. And Expressives are fast-paced, fun-loving and articulate. Each of these styles will also approach relationships in different ways.

Where do you fit in? What style are you? How about the people you work with, or those close to you personally – where do they fit in?

We won't deep dive into these, but rather share a few practical tips to flex ourselves to build better relationships with different people with different styles.

Building relationships with Analyticals:

- Allow them their own pace.
- Create a safe space for them to feel comfortable expressing themselves.
- Show understanding through empathic listening.

Building relationships with Amiables:

- Speak when you are calm, not stressed.
- Engage them by asking and listening to them.
- Treat their reservations with care and concern.

Building relationships with Drivers:

- Be direct and straightforward with them.
- Help them to listen better.
- Encourage them to express their feelings without pressing too hard.

Building relationships with Expressives:

- Engage and interact with them.
- Have fun.
- Help them to slow down rather than rush or be impulsive.

How can you flex yourself with the people around you? Based on their social style, what can you do to build a better relationship with them?

### The Neuroscience of Our "Social Brain"

*"Grant, what did you do this morning?" my friend asked.*
*"I stared out the window and did nothing," I replied.*

If this is not on your "to do" list, it should be.

Without getting too deep into the neuroscience, we have two systems in our brain: the X-system and the C-system. The X-system (or reflexive system) is automatic, responsive, like/dislike, reward/threat. The C-system (or reflective system) is controlled, conscious, with executive function and executive control.

You may have heard or come across the story of Phineas Gage, who, in 1848 in the United States, survived a blast while building a railroad, which shot a tamping iron through the front part of his brain. Remarkably he survived. However, his behavior had changed. Where before, he was a mild-tempered respecting person, his behavior now was to seek reward without consequences, operating only by habit; rude, course, vulgar, animalistic. He destroyed the C-system, operating on X-system only. In other words, he had no control over his automatic, reflexive system, and his behavior became unbearable as a result. He treated everybody as an object for his own personal reward.

The C-system, among other things, is important for self-reflection and understanding self/other relations. This happens in the front-medial (or front-middle) part of your brain; so there is a real need to protect it. This part of the C-system, moreover, is known as our "Default Mode," because when the brain is at a resting state, this specific system kicks in, which is focused around social understanding (thinking about yourself, others' thoughts, others' actions, etc.). During this resting state, moreover, your mind is not thinking deeply, but rather you are letting it wander.

And so, if we focus deeply only on tasks and results, we may be missing out on an important system for social processing. It is equally important for us to process, develop and understand social connections. Therefore, it is important for us to spend time, "down time" if you like, to rest in our "Default Mode," allowing our mind to wander.

And so, if you haven't already done it, go ahead and add to your "to do" list: "*Stare out the window and do nothing.*" Your life will thank you, and it will help you build better, more authentic relationships.

### Go Slow to Go Fast

In order to build truly authentic relationships with people, we need to "go slow to go fast." In other words, slow down the conversation with people, truly listen to them empathically and be fully present to them. This will then build the relationship to be deeper. So, we go slow with the conversation and communication in order to go fast with the depth of the relationship.

For example, I was having lunch with a friend of mine recently and I discovered this experientially during our conversation. We were talking about relationships and authenticity and I really wanted to deeply understand her views, ideas and feelings on this. I made myself fully present to her as she was speaking, empathically listened to her by playing back for her the feelings and ideas she said ("You sound frustrated because of ...," "It seems that this is important for you ..."). I consciously slowed down my thinking to fully understand everything she was saying and feeling. And I noticed that as I was doing this, I could understand her better as a person and develop a deeper relationship as a result.

And so, by slowing down the conversation, we can go faster to develop the relationship.

Have you ever experienced this yourself – slowing down the conversation so you can build a deeper relationship? What did you do and how did you feel?

## How to Resolve Conflict

Inevitably, conflict will arise in relationships. This could be caused by a difference of opinion, feeling that you were wronged by someone, a disagreement, a misunderstanding, being hurt by something someone did or said, differences in communication styles, feeling you were disrespected, differences in culture, not feeling listened to, differences in expectations or for other reasons. Below are some practical ways and tips to help us resolve conflict in an amicable way to go beyond the conflict and move the relationship forward:

- Fully understand the other person first, then share your feelings.
- Listen empathically; for example, "You sound upset from ..." or "You feel disrespected because ... is that right?"
- Value the strengths and differences in someone to build the relationship rather than focusing on the things that bother you.
- Let go of your own ego.
- Regard them as a person, not as something that is part of your life.
- Use nonviolent communication – expressing from your perspective and the impact on you, rather than using blaming language; for example, "I feel frustrated when I feel I'm not being listened to" or "I feel less autonomy and empowered when I receive detailed instructions rather than being asked for my thoughts and ideas," rather than "You always ..." or "You make me feel ..."
- Use inclusive, needs-affirming language; for example, "What do you think we should do?" or "We both want to make this better. Together we can find a way. Perhaps we need to go slow in order to go fast."

For example, James, an executive I know who is the Head of the Sales Division of a tech company, once told me an incident that happened to him. His direct report made a calculation error on a report and could have cost the company millions of dollars. When he saw this, he was furious. He went to his direct report's office, standing, pacing frantically, and said, "I can't believe this. We could have lost millions of dollars if I let this go through. How could this happen?" Then his direct report said, "It sounds like you are upset because of this mistake." "Yes, I'm upset. How could this happen?" he replied. His direct report then said, "I understand how you feel about this. Let's look at it and see what caused this." Turning to her computer she then said, "Here it is. There's an error in the data in our system. It looks like this has been here for a long time. Shall we contact the Purchasing and Marketing Departments to flag them and discuss it?" James then sat down and said, "Yes, I think this would be a good idea, so we can avoid this in future and so I don't feel like I'm going to explode." And then he sighed and smiled. By going slow to go fast, it not only helped prevent this financial loss, but also helped resolve the conflict and build a better relationship between them.

---

**Reflection**

*Building More Authentic Relationships*

1.  Think of one person in business and one person in your personal life that you would like to build a more authentic relationship with.

2.  How would you describe them? Are they an introvert or an extrovert? Are they an Analytical, Amiable, Driver or Expressive? How do they approach authenticity and relationships? (*Make a note here.*)

    _____

    _____

    _____

    _____

    _____

3.  Stare out the window and think: what could you do to build a more authentic relationship with each of these people? How can you "go slow to go fast?" How would you resolve conflict with them if it arouse? (*Make a note here.*)

    _____

    _____

    _____

    _____

    _____

## NOTES

1 Buber, M. *I and Thou* (second edition). New York, NY: Charles Scribner's Sons. 1962.
2 Bolton, R. and Bolton, D. G. *People Styles at Work: Making Bad Relationships Good and Good Relationships Better*. New York, NY: Amacom. 1996.

## COMPANION WORKBOOK

As you may have noticed, each chapter has exercises and reflection activities. If you would like to keep a record of your journey all in one place and have a working tool that you can go back to, there is a Companion Workbook. This is a free interactive pdf that you can save as you go along. To access it, go to the following URL or scan the QR code below.

www.selfleadershipassessment.com/workbook/

# **Sixteen**

Let's start off with a couple of exercises:

### Exercise 1

A bat and a ball cost $1.10. The bat costs $1.00 more than the ball. So how much does the ball cost?

### Exercise 2

Spot the error.

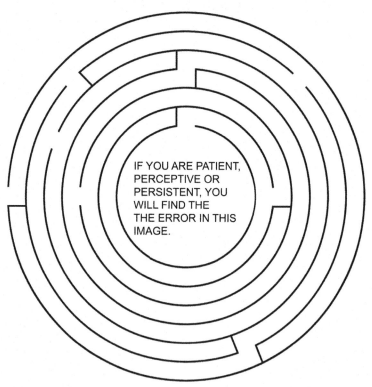

IF YOU ARE PATIENT,
PERCEPTIVE OR
PERSISTENT, YOU
WILL FIND THE
THE ERROR IN THIS
IMAGE.

**Figure 16.1** Maze

DOI: 10.4324/9781003127000-16

## Exercise 3

This exercise is from Daniel Kahneman's book *Thinking, Fast and Slow:*[1]

> As you consider the next question, please assume that Steve was selected at random from a representative sample: An individual has been described by a neighbor as follows: "Steve is very shy and withdrawn, invariably helpful but with little interest in people or in the world of reality. A meek and tidy soul, he has a need for order and structure, and a passion for detail." Is Steve more likely to be a librarian or a farmer?

A bit of fun for our minds, and some interesting insights we can glean from this too. We will return to these exercises throughout this chapter. First, though, let's explore the nature of biases and what they are.

### So, What Really Are Biases?

Biases are mental shortcuts that allow us to quickly sort, categorize and make decisions on pieces of information in order to navigate the world in an efficient way. They can be positive, negative or neutral, although most of us probably associate them more with the negative side.

They can be conscious; for example, I have a conscious bias toward extroverts and musicians because I am both of these and can relate to the kind of energy these people have. When I meet these people, I can immediately form a connection with them and it's a very good feeling.

Biases can also, and much more often, be unconscious. Unconscious biases are natural; we all have them and unknowingly use them to make judgments every day. They help us to navigate the world. However, as behavioral science tells us, they can also impact the quality of our thinking, judgment and decisions. To make better judgments and reduce bias, we need to be aware and accept that we have biases, label the biases and mitigate them using the appropriate mental and behavioral processes.

### The Neuroscience of Bias

Our brains are made up of two systems: the X-System and the C-System or, put more simply, System 1 and System 2. System 1 is the autopilot, fast-thinking, reflexive system. System 2 is the more deliberate, slow-thinking, reflective system. System 2 is much more demanding on our cognitive resources than System 1. If we were to do everything in System 2, we would burn out very quickly. We need

System 1 in order for us to navigate the world efficiently and stay sane. In fact, according to Lieberman, Kahneman and other neuroscientists, on average, only 2% of our thinking is done in System 2; 98% is in System 1.[2]

Thinking back to the exercise earlier about the cost of the bat and ball, you were likely able to arrive at a solution fairly quickly, one that felt obvious and satisfying to you (i.e., the bat costs $1.00 and the ball costs $0.10), and feel that this is correct. Feeling that we are correct is associated with contentment and certainty; it is rewarding and activates our brain's reward sensation. The enjoyment we experience from being right, moreover, is one of the main reasons that we are motivated to overlook our own biases and the errors that we may make. This is pure System 1 thinking.

On deeper reflection, kicking in our System 2 thinking, we realize that if the bat costs $1.00 and the ball costs $0.10, then the difference between them is $0.90, not $1.00. If the bat costs $1.00 more than the ball, then the bat would cost $1.05 and the ball $0.05. This is System 2 thinking.

Moreover, not only does it feel good to be right, it feels bad to be wrong. Making errors and mistakes are painful and distressing and activate regions of our brain associated with pain and negative emotion. We also often feel angry and frustrated when making errors.

As humans, we are motivated to seek out reward and avoid pain. Therefore, we want to feel right all the time. Moreover, the positive emotion and rewarding feeling of being right does not just occur when we are objectively right; it also occurs when we believe we are right, whether we are actually right or not. Believing that we are right – that we answered a question correctly, that we made the right decision, took the right action, etc. – further motivates us to seek out information and situations in which we feel that we are right and avoid information and situations that suggest we might be wrong, even if that information is right in front of us.

That being right is rewarding and being wrong is painful are important and central to understanding how our judgments and decisions are influenced by unconscious bias and why it is difficult to overcome such bias. We make judgments and decisions based on what feels right, even though what feels right may be based on information that is incomplete, not all relevant, distorted or just plain wrong.

In Exercise 2 above, how many of us were looking at the maze to find the error? Probably most of us. Perhaps we got frustrated because it is possible to solve the maze and it doesn't seem like there is any error in it at all. However, we were looking in the wrong place. Go back and read the words in center again. It says, "... find the the error ..." The word "the" is written twice. Most people overlook this, thinking that the right answer is in the maze and that they should be focused there.

This applies not only to puzzles but also in our daily life. As Daniel Kahneman wrote: "People who are cognitively busy [using System 1 thinking only] are more likely to make selfish choices, use sexist language, and make superficial judgments in social situations."[3]

For example, I remember a friend of mine recently told me about a learning session she was taking from her company on mindfulness and meditation. It was a virtual session, where only the coach had her camera on; the participants did not. My friend said that there were many good things about the session. However, she also remembers that, at the beginning of the session, the coach asked one of the participants, who has an Indian name, "Where are you from?" He said that he is from India. The coach then replied, "So, you must be very good at meditation." This is also an example of System 1 thinking and, perhaps, a little ironic given the very topic of the learning initiative.

Have you ever seen this before, where someone just uses autopilot System 1 thinking, rather than deliberate thoughtful System 2 thinking? Have you ever done it before? Or, since it is unconscious, have you ever done it and not been aware of it?

### Ladder of Inference

Created by Harvard University Professor Chris Argyris, the Ladder of Inference shows how our brain processes and selects the information we receive, how we interpret or infer from this information, which then leads us to the beliefs and actions that we take. Figure 16.2 illustrates the steps in this ladder.

Often this happens unconsciously in System 1 thinking, which helps explain how our brains form the beliefs we have that lead to the actions we take. Moreover, the beliefs we form then loop back to affect what data we select next time, creating a reinforcing loop or bias for future data selection.

For Exercise 3 above, the resemblance of Steve's personality to that of a stereotypical librarian strikes everyone immediately, and we select that information to reach our conclusion. We ignore other relevant statistical considerations. For example, there are more than 20 male farmers for each male librarian. Because there are so many more farmers than

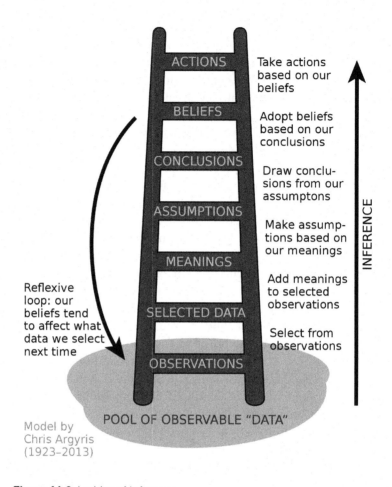

ACTIONS — Take actions based on our beliefs

BELIEFS — Adopt beliefs based on our conclusions

CONCLUSIONS — Draw conclusions from our assumptons

ASSUMPTIONS — Make assumptions based on our meanings

MEANINGS — Add meanings to selected observations

SELECTED DATA — Select from observations

Reflexive loop: our beliefs tend to affect what data we select next time

OBSERVATIONS

INFERENCE

POOL OF OBSERVABLE "DATA"

Model by Chris Argyris (1923–2013)

**Figure 16.2** Ladder of Inference

there are librarians, certainly there must be more "meek and tidy" ones found on tractors than at library information desks. Rather than reaching out for a more holistic view, we focus only on the information that is immediately available in front of our face. This is how we often draw our conclusions.

We will apply this and System 1 thinking to the various types of biases we encounter.

### Types of Biases

There are over 150 known biases in psychology. Rather than deep dive into each of them, we can group them into themes and focus on the more salient ones. We will, therefore, focus on the following three clusters of biases:

1. Similarity Bias
2. Urgency Bias
3. Experience Bias

### Similarity Bias

Categorizing people into social groups – termed *social categorization* – allows us to simplify the social world and generalize our existing knowledge about certain groups and new people. This could be based on age, ethnicity, gender, personality, education, occupation, hobbies, country of origin, etc. This helps us to navigate the world and know how to respond to and interact with different people in different situations. It can also lead to preferential treatment, inaccurate stereotypes and prejudices. In Exercise 3 above, most of us probably thought Steve was a librarian.

As a result of social categorization, we form *ingroups* and *outgroups*. *Ingroups* are people who are similar to us, part of the same group. For example, I am a male, from Canada, late-40s, consultant. This is one way of categorizing me, and others who are similar, and would be part of this *ingroup*. *Outgroups*, by contrast, refer to people who are not part of this group. When we identify, value and cooperate with *ingroup* members, we enjoy numerous benefits, including the fulfillment of many of our basic psychological needs (e.g., relatedness, security, belonging and so on), and feel a sense of connection, understanding, familiarity and trust.

Social categorization, however, can also lead us to some possible biases: the "ingroup bias" and the "outgroup bias," where we promote and protect our own group (our friends, team, colleagues, etc.), who are part of our *ingroup*. This "ingroup bias" refers to the more positive perception of people who are more similar to us compared to those who are less similar to us; the "outgroup bias" refers to the more negative perception of people who are more different than us compared to those who are less different. This perception then drives our behavior and actions – we may do favors for people in our *ingroup*, but not for the *outgroup*; allocate more resources to *ingroup* (vs *outgroup*) members; or listen and show more understanding for those in our *ingroup*.

Beyond mere group membership and identity, moreover, one key amplifier of intergroup bias is the perception of a zero-sum relationship between the different groups.[4] Therefore, we feel connected with our ingroup and potentially threatened by an outgroup. For example, with connectedness, I have lived in different countries around the world and, including my own country, there is a feeling of pride and identity associated with each of these countries. The Olympics certainly demonstrates this. More specifically, right now, I am a Canadian living in Singapore, part of the Executive Committee for the Canadian Association of Singapore and have spearheaded several events targeting Canadians in Singapore and Singaporeans interested in Canada. I am also part of a dragon boat team and actively involved in the dragon boat community. And I am a musician and feel a sense of connection and affiliation with other musicians and artists from all over the world. These are examples of connectedness that help us satisfy and fulfill our basic psychological needs.

There may be times, however, when we perceive the world as a zero-sum game, where one person's win is another person's loss. We see this in the world of competitive sports. Manchester United vs Liverpool – one team wins and the other team does not. And certainly the fans of each of these teams feel affinity with their ingroup and possibly threatened by the outgroup. We see this when we travel to new, unfamiliar places and we connect with other fellow travelers similar to us to feel safer and more secure. We also see this in work situations. For example, perhaps there are fewer jobs than candidates. Some people may see educated foreigners as a threat, show biases (whether conscious or unconscious) toward their own ingroup and devalue the competence and skills of those in the outgroup.

What groups are you a part of? Who then would the outgroups be?

Another interesting experiment was done between Manchester United and Liverpool fans.[5] Enlisting Manchester United fans as part of the experiment, in the first part of the study, each person completed a set of questionnaires about their team allegiance and feelings of identification with the team. Importantly, these questionnaires reinforced the participants' allegiance to Manchester United. The experimenters then told each participant that the second half of the study involves watching a short film on soccer, which will be screened in an adjacent building. They give them directions and send them on their way. As they make their walk, however, an actor working with the experimenters jogged along nearby, and as misfortune would have it, he slipped and fell, grabbing his ankle and shouting in pain. The experimenters changed the jogger's shirt swapping it for either a Manchester United shirt or a Liverpool shirt. When the participants in the experiment saw a fellow Manchester United fan in need, 92% stopped to help him, whereas only around 30% do anything to help when it's a Liverpool fan or when it's someone in an unbranded shirt. This clearly shows the preferential treatment we might have for an *ingroup* member vs an *outgroup* member.

Moreover, we tend to see *ingroup* members as individuals and lump *outgroup* members together as one homogenous group.[6] Therefore, we build up more of a personal connection with *ingroup* members and lowered trust with a "homogeneous" *outgroup* group.

In the world of work as well, when it comes to selecting someone for a role, this may also play out. For example, imagine you are putting together a team for a high-profile project and you need to decide which role Raj should have: Project Manager, Creative Lead, Quality Assurance or Stakeholder Engagement.

Raj is 41 years old. He describes himself as a visionary, speaks five languages and works regularly on global projects, using his multilingual abilities to work effectively with cross-functional teams. He is an early adopter of new technologies and enjoys helping others understand how things work.

When he's not working, he enjoys attending the opera and reviewing unique restaurants for his food blog. So, which role would you select for Raj?

There are different reasons we might select him for the various roles above. For example, we might select him as the Project Manager because of his global experience; or Creative Lead because of his creative interests. Earlier, we introduced the Ladder of Inference, where we select elements from the pool of information we have and make conclusions and decisions based on this. This is exactly what we did here.

We may also have some similarity with him, whether it is about age, experience or interests. This may also influence our decision. It is important to also note that the profile above is his own self-description. Perhaps if we were to speak to a former Manager of his, we might hear something different. Perhaps, for example, he may struggle to understand the scope of projects or may be difficult to work with. And so, the description above may not be complete; it may be missing some things about Raj.

**Exercise**

**Identity and Similarity Bias**

1.  Make a list of as many "I am ..." statements about yourself as you can. For example, *I am a Canadian, I am a consultant, I am humorous, I am creative, etc. (Make a note here.)*

    _____

    _____

    _____

    _____

    _____

    _____

    _____

    _____

    _____

    _____

    _____

    _____

    _____

    _____

    _____

    _____

2.  How do you feel when you meet people who identify the same as you? Which of your identifiers are most important to you? Are there any that you do not feel comfortable sharing at work or with people you do not know very well? How do you feel if you are the only person who identifies this way?

3.  Where have you seen *similarity bias* play out? What examples of connection and affinity can you think of that help you to fulfill your psychological needs? Where have you seen examples of a zero-sum game that might include scarcity or a win–lose mindset? How have *ingroup* and *outgroup biases* impacted this? *(Make a note here.)*

    _____

    _____

    _____

    _____

    _____

Urgency biases are mental shortcuts that help us make quick and efficient decisions. They are expedient; however, they may be based on incorrect judgments. We use System 1 thinking based on our intuition and impulse and make decisions based on what information is easily accessible and feels right. Recall the example of the bat and the ball earlier. The total price is $1.10; the bat costs $1 more than the ball; therefore, we think the bat costs $1 and the ball costs $0.10. This system relies on fast, easy associations and intuition. Yet, as we know, $1 for the bat and $0.10 for the ball is incorrect. Often, we need to (or should) make decisions based on more objective information, which is often not so easily accessible and takes more mental effort to access and to use when making judgments. This System 2 thinking is slower and more effortful and is the overseer of the faster, more intuitive System 1. System 2 is sometimes called the "lazy fact checker" since it can be called upon to correct System 1's mistakes. However, because it requires more cognitive effort to engage, we often do not call upon it and leave contented with our System 1 answer.

In addition, focusing intensely on a task can make us effectively blind, even to stimuli that normally would attract our attention. As mentioned in Chapter Four: *Mindfulness*, in their book *The Invisible Gorilla*, Christopher Chabris and Daniel Simons constructed a short video of two teams passing basketballs, one team wearing white shirts, the other wearing black. The viewers of the video are then instructed to count the number of passes made by the white team, ignoring the players in black. This task is difficult and completely absorbing. Halfway through the video, a woman wearing a gorilla suit appears, crosses the court, thumps her chest and moves on. The gorilla is in view for nine seconds, however, of the many thousands of people who have seen the video, about half of them do not notice the gorilla. They are focused on the counting task and, especially, ignoring one of the teams, which causes this cognitive blindness. No one who watches the video without that task would miss the gorilla. The authors also note that people find the results very surprising. The viewers who fail to see the gorilla are initially sure that it was not there, as they cannot imagine missing such a dramatic event. This illustrates two important insights about our minds: we can be blind to the obvious, and we are also blind to our blindness.

This also plays out in our own daily lives too. For example, this may play out when we have a deadline. Greg, a consultant I know, was working on a proposal for a client and he wanted to submit it by this coming Friday. The client was open to receiving proposals later, but Greg wanted to get it in this Friday to expedite the process. As a result, his System 1 thinking kicked in, like a racehorse with blinders on, relying on his own thinking and what was immediately available to him. Then, one of his partners, Clement, shared another perspective on it and some of his concerns. This made Greg take a step back and think more effortfully, to look at a bigger picture and more ideas and insights, which led him to create a more thorough and deeper proposal, one that is more holistic, more concrete and more likely to get a favorable response from the client. If it weren't for Clement, Greg would have stuck to his System 1 thinking, rushed through his proposal and submitted it by Friday. However, it would have been partially complete, unclear and most likely not accepted.

Have you ever done this – felt rushed, like Greg, to submit your proposal or make a decision and rush through it – rather than slowing down to think more thoughtfully and deliberately? How was it? What was the result?

### Experience Bias

Experience biases are a result of our brain understanding the world as if we have a direct and objective understanding of what is really out there. It is as if we have an implicit belief that our perceptions and beliefs are objectively true, and that anyone who doesn't see what we see must be incorrect or somehow missing something to enable them to see this. This assumption that our experience corresponds to reality is referred to as "naïve realism." The problem with this bias is that it doesn't take into consideration all the varying diverse experiences and factors upon which our understanding of reality is constructed: our expectations, past history, personality, emotional state, socialization, relationships, upbringing, among others.

This type of bias is an egocentric one, which assumes that our experience and perception of reality is the objective truth. This happens outside of our awareness; therefore, it is nearly impossible to detect. And because we hold such a strong belief that we are seeing reality as it is, we tend to believe that anyone else who sees things differently must either see things incorrectly or are somehow missing something to enable them to see this.

For example, I am currently working on this large global project with several other people from across the world, many of whom are creative types, spanning time zones from California to Singapore. Originally, we only had one person from California, with others from Eastern United States, Brazil, Europe and three of us in Asia. Seven people in total. So, originally, the time for our weekly call was Wednesday 10 am Eastern Standard Time (EST), which is 10 pm in Singapore and 7 am in California. Since there was only one person in California, he didn't mind waking up at this early time, although he didn't really like it that much. We decided then to move the time ahead 30 minutes: 7:30 am for him; 10:30 am EST; and 10:30 pm in Singapore. I was still okay with this. Then, as we expanded the project, we invited seven other people to join our team. Of these people, four of them were from California. So, we had a discussion about whether we should change the meeting time, shifting it ahead an additional hour. I said that for a 90-minute meeting, given a choice of 7:30–9 am or 11:30 pm–1 am, that 7:30–9 am is much better. In my mind, this was very clear and reasonable. And then someone pointed out, "Well, Grant, not everybody thinks like you do." And they were right. Just because this was how I see it doesn't mean everybody else sees it this way too. I realized, at that moment, that I assumed that everybody thought the same as I did. So, because there are now five from California and only two of us in Singapore, I agreed to move the meeting ahead another hour to make it better for those in California.

Have you ever felt this way? Have you ever assumed that others see things and the world the same as you? Are you aware of this or just thinking it now for the first time?

---

### Reflection

#### Urgency and Experience Biases

1. When have you experienced Urgency Bias? When has your System 1 thinking kicked in and you were making decisions and acting based on impulse and autopilot? This could be because of a deadline you were meeting or because your first reaction felt right and you didn't feel a need to go deeper or engage your System 2 thinking. (Make a note here.) What would have been the benefit of taking a step back, slowing down and accessing your System 2 thinking? (Make a note here.)

_____

_____

_____

_____

_____

2. Take a moment to reflect on the way that you see the world. What is it about your experience that has led you to see the world this way: your expectations, past history, personality, emotional state, socialization, relationships, upbringing or other? Are you aware of ever having felt *Experience Bias*, where you assume that the way you see the world is correct and that others must see it the same as well? Have you ever had a revelation where you realized that others don't see the world as you do? What happened? (*Make a note here.*)

-----------------------------------------------------------------

-----------------------------------------------------------------

-----------------------------------------------------------------

-----------------------------------------------------------------

-----------------------------------------------------------------

### Managing Biases

Biases are a natural part of the human condition. We cannot get rid of them. Therefore, we need to understand them and manage them. To do this, we offer a simple three-step process:

1. Accept and admit that we are biased by virtue of our biology.
2. Label the type of bias that might be influencing us or a particular decision.
3. Mitigate the bias using an appropriate process.

#### Step 1: Accept and Admit We're Biased

We're all biased. It is a natural part of being human. Be honest with yourself. Acknowledging and being consciously aware that we have biases is the first step to help us mitigate them and make more balanced judgments and decisions.

#### Steps 2 and 3: Label the Type of Bias and Mitigate It

Next, we want to understand what type of bias might be influencing us or a particular decision we need to make. Then, look at ways to help us mitigate it. We will return back to our three broad types of bias – *Similarity Bias*, *Urgency Bias* and *Experience Bias* – and specific strategies to mitigate each.

### Similarity Bias

Similarity biases involve evaluating more positively people you feel are similar to you, or who share similar goals, and unconsciously showing them favoritism or preferential treatment. These kinds of biases will be common in people's decisions. For example, hiring decisions, promotions, who to have on our team and for what role, deciding what clients to work with or deciding who to have in our social network. Maybe a recruiter hires someone for a position because they "look the part" without considering enough about skillset. Or, a consultant who chooses clients because the decision maker is from the same country as them. Or, a Senior Leader allocating high visibility projects to someone who went to the same university as them. Or, choosing friends because they wear the same clothes and like the same music.

Before we look at strategies to mitigate this bias, let's first explore what does it feel like to be left out, excluded. Think about it. How would you feel if all of your friends are invited to a dinner party except you? How would you feel if someone else gets the promotion that you want, although they are certainly less qualified? It is not a good feeling, is it?

In a very interesting study by Eisenberger, Lieberman and Williams (2003), they had participants in a functional magnetic resonance imaging (fMRI) scanner to measure the brain activity of being excluded. Participants played a game called Cyberball, in which a participant plays a virtual game of "catch" with two other supposed players. In fact, the two other players are part of the computer simulation, but the participant is told and thinks that they are real people in different rooms doing the same as them. At first, the two computer players throw the ball equally to all players. The fMRI scanner picks up feelings of pleasure, reward and happiness in the brain. Then, after a few minutes, the two computer players then only throw the ball at each other. Self-reporting after the experiment, participants said comments like, "I felt rejected" or "I felt meaningless." Moreover, the fMRI scanner indicated activity in the brain in the same way as physical pain. It literally hurt to be excluded.

So, with this in mind, let's look at how we can mitigate *Similarity Bias*. There are two strategies to help us do this. First, we need to engage in self-affirmation (thinking about people important to us or things we value) to affirm our sense of who we are and make us less likely to be negative to people different from us. With a stronger sense of security and who we are, it will put us in a position to be more open to others.

Next, we want to find ways to think of those who are different from us to be more similar to us. This could be thinking of ways that we and those different from us share goals, values or preferences that put us in the context of a larger group. If we all feel that we are working toward the same goal or have the same values or preferences, it will increase the feeling of connection to the larger purpose and reduce a scarcity mindset of a zero-sum game.

For example, Jay J. Van Bavel and Mina Cikara cite:[7]

Recent research confirms that coalition-based preferences trump race-based preferences. For example, both Democrats and Republicans favor the resumes of those affiliated with their political party much more than they favor those who share their race. These coalition-based preferences remain powerful even in the absence of the animosity present in electoral politics. Our research has shown that the simple act of placing people on a mixed-race team can diminish their automatic racial bias.

Of course, instilling a sense of common identity and cooperation is extremely difficult in entrenched intergroup conflicts, but when it happens, the benefits are obvious. Consider how the community leaders in New York City and Ferguson responded differently to protests against police brutality – in NYC political leaders expressed grief and concern over police brutality and moved quickly to make policy changes in policing, whereas the leaders and police in Ferguson responded with high-tech military vehicles and riot gear. In the first case, multiple groups came together with a common goal – to increase the safety of everyone in the community; in the latter case, the actions of the police likely reinforced the "us" and "them" distinctions.

In another recent experiment,[8] participants were sorted into groups – red versus blue team – competing for a cash prize. Half of the participants were shown a picture of a segregated social network of all the players, in which red dots clustered together, blue dots clustered together and the two clusters were separated by white space. The other half of the participants were shown an integrated social network in which the red and blue dots were mixed together in one large cluster. Participants who thought the two teams were interconnected with one another reported greater empathy for the outgroup players compared to those who had seen the segregated network. Through this image of interconnectivity, individuals can be connected to one another despite being from different groups, and it is a way to build trust and understanding among them.

As mentioned earlier, we feel connected with our *ingroup* and potentially threatened by an *outgroup* when we divide based on our race, age, gender or team affiliation for example. However, by focusing on shared goals, values or preferences, we increase the feeling of connection and reduce the feeling of threat.

For example, I am part of a dragon boat team in Singapore called the *Canadian Dragons of Singapore*. We are a multicultural team made up of men and women from 18 different countries and ranging in ages from 25 to 60 years old. Of course we like to win, like anyone else. However, we are also part of a larger community called the *International Dragon Boat Community*, consisting of 11 teams like ours, with a larger purpose to foster international relations between expats and Singaporeans through a shared vision of camaraderie and community. And still, this is part of a larger community called the *Singapore Dragon Boat Association*, which includes all of our teams, plus the community teams, university teams and corporate teams, again sharing the common vision and value of camaraderie and community.

I am also a Director and Partner for a large online music and art festival, with over 50 artists and facilitators from 25+ countries on 6 continents, with a wide range of ages, genders, personalities and sexual orientations. With a common shared vision of bringing the world together during the unprecedented COVID pandemic through the spirit of collaboration and co-creation, we are building a sense of community that values the diversity within it to achieve this shared larger purpose.

Likewise, in a corporate environment, focusing on a shared vision and larger purpose can help us build connections and make more balanced judgments and decisions.

I remember, a few years ago, watching a global tech company's video on diversity and inclusion. It had different employees introduce themselves with this pattern, and I'll say it about myself: "I am Grant. I'm Canadian. I am a man. I am Caucasian. I am a consultant, a writer, an executive coach, a music composer, a dragon boater, a runner, a drummer, a husband, a brother, a son, a friend ... I am not only one thing." A very powerful message for all of us to remember. We are not only one thing. We are dynamic and that is what makes each of us special.

And so, rather than forming an *ingroup* with only one part of ourselves, seeing those members as individuals and lumping others as one homogeneous *outgroup*, it is far better to see the individuals in all the groups that we are a part of; and to see and appreciate all the beautiful elements in other people's identity, recognizing them as individuals too, and "not only one thing."

When we look at *Urgency Bias* and *Experience Bias*, we will look at some other strategies that can also be used to help us with *Similarity Bias* as well.

**Reflection**

*Identity and Similarity Bias*

1.  Look back at your list of "I am ..." statements from before, add more to the list if you like and reflect on all the dynamic elements you have of your identity.

2.  Think about all the people that are important to you and the things you value in your life, to affirm a strong sense of security and who you are, in order to create a deeper ability to be open to others.

3.  Think about all the people you work with and interact with in your personal life. What makes them different? What "I am ..." statements would they write about themselves? What are all the beautiful dynamic elements that they bring to their identity? (*Make a note here.*)

    _____
    _____
    _____
    _____
    _____

4.  What are the shared goals, values or preferences that you have with these people? Is it a work-related goal, or perhaps a higher-level purpose, that you are working toward? Is it a sense of community that you are building? How does everyone fit in to a bigger picture vision? (*Make a note here.*)

    _____
    _____
    _____
    _____
    _____

5.  How can you value each of them as an individual rather than lump them into one group? (*Make a note here.*)

    _____
    _____
    _____
    _____
    _____

## Urgency Bias

Urgency biases might occur in activities and decisions that involve planning, analysis, evaluation or making conclusions from data, for example, identifying the right solution for a client or project managing a project.

Earlier, we introduced Greg, a consultant I know who was trying to get his proposal submitted to his client by this coming Friday, kicking his System 1 thinking in, like a racehorse with blinders on. He was falling into an availability bias, relying only on information and ideas that were readily available to him, instead of really trying to search for the best possible ideas. He was also falling into a familiarity bias, feeling within his comfort zone with his own ideas, and a little apprehensive of ideas that fell outside of this.

Then, when one of his partners, Clement, shared another perspective and some of his concerns, this made Greg take a step back and go to the balcony. Greg was caught up on the dance floor where all the action was and could only see one piece of the whole picture. Clement's insights and perspective helped Greg to see a bigger picture, some of the pieces that were missing and some of the elements that were weak. Greg, then, kicked in his System 2 thinking and started thinking how to strengthen the weaker elements, for example, what deeper insights and value could the client get from this. He also thought about what other people and resources could he include to make the team even stronger. He then reached out to these people to set up meetings to discuss this project and proposal.

Urgency biases will be especially likely when people are in a hurry or are mentally depleted. Greg was in a hurry and therefore fell into this. Also, when we are tired, we tend to function and think on auto-pilot; as also when we are lacking glucose or dehydrated. In other words, with urgency bias we take the easy path, rather than engaging in deeper and more deliberate thinking. Therefore, to help mitigate this, we need to activate our brain's braking system to stop the automatic reflexive thinking to have more System 2 reflective thinking. We need to get off the dance floor and go to the balcony.

This is what Greg did when he discussed the proposal with Clement. Wanting to spearhead the best project and create the best proposal, Greg laid out the synopsis of the proposal, the skeleton structure of it and step-by-step logic behind it. He was then very open to any and all feedback and different perspectives and thoughts from Clement, who is more senior to Greg and has a lot more experience. This then allowed Greg to see things through a different lens and motivated him to explore alternatives and different ways to create a better project and proposal.

Have you ever felt this urgency bias – where your System 1 thinking kicks in – and you think and operate on autopilot? How would it feel to take a step back, go to the balcony and see a bigger picture?

Another strategy to help mitigate urgency biases is developing a step-by-step approach that breaks a problem down into its component parts and encourages more thoughtful, deliberate reflection and insight. For example, using a step-by-step approach such as this:

1. Define the criteria for success.
2. Brainstorm all possible ways to reach it.
3. Soundcheck these ideas with others.
4. Brainstorm more ideas with others.
5. Refine and redefine the criteria for success.
6. Reform ideas into more robust solutions.

Notice that this process is not a linear process: criteria, ideas, solutions. But rather, it is an iterative process, where we go back and forth from criteria to ideas to solution, back to ideas and back to criteria, then to ideas and to solutions again. And so on. We iterate along this approach to craft the best ideas and solutions to meet the most robust and clearest criteria.

As we can also see, it is very helpful to involve other people and get outside opinions as part of this decision-making, problem-solving or project management process. This allows us to soundcheck our ideas, get different perspectives and lenses, seek out and evaluate opposing or conflicting views, and put the ideas together in stronger, more concrete ways. This also helps us to ensure that we base our ideas, decisions and solutions on validated facts and concrete results, rather than assumptions or our impulsive feelings.

How could a step-by-step process help expand and clarify your thinking? How will involving others help expand your thinking and create stronger, more robust and clearer ideas?

### Experience Bias

Experience biases can happen anytime, anywhere and in any situation where we fail to appreciate other people's perspectives. This could be when we are excited about something and miss the fact that others are not as excited as we are. We may see the benefits of a change in our project or organization but fail to see that not everyone is onboard. Or maybe we explain something to one or a group of people; to us it's clear but we fail to notice that they don't really understand.

I mentioned earlier with a large global project I am working on, we were discussing whether to change the time for our weekly meeting. To me, I clearly thought it was better for anybody to meet from 7:30 am to 9 am, rather than having someone meet from 11:30 pm to 1 am. I assumed that everyone saw the world the same as me and must clearly think the same. Then someone pointed out, "Well, Grant, not everyone thinks the same as you." And since more people could benefit from shifting the time to an hour later, all those in California plus those in Europe too, I could see it and appreciate it from their perspective and easily agreed to the change.

Greg is also in a similar situation. For the project he is proposing, he was only seeing through his own lens and how everything fits into that lens and didn't appreciate that there may be other perspectives on this and different lenses to see this through. However, after speaking with Clement, he could see this and became very excited to explore this even further – to discuss it with more people, get their thoughts and insights and together craft the best proposal possible, taking into account all the rich array of perspectives and lenses.

And this is exactly what we need to do to help us mitigate experience bias. We need to get objective, outside opinions from others – to hear their thoughts, ideas, feedback and insights – and help us to see things in different ways. We also need to take a break and distance ourselves from our original ideas; then revisit them to see them in a fresher, more objective light and to see them through other people's eyes. This is what I do when I write proposals and also this book. I will write the proposal or chapter, then take a break for a few days or a week, then revisit it again to edit and finalize it.

Getting out of our own head, distancing ourselves, seeking out other people's perspectives and viewpoints, and then seeing it through their eyes – these are the best strategies to help us mitigate experience bias.

How would you feel if you did this – got out of your own head, distanced yourself and sought other people's perspectives? How could this benefit you to mitigate your experience bias?

### Being Mindful and Talking to Other People

When we are able to engage our mental brakes, inhibit our initial automatic responses, take a more objective view and engage our System 2 thinking, then we can mitigate the influence of bias. Moreover, it has been shown that the more mindful we are, the more we can engage our mental brakes, increase our self-awareness, reduce emotional impulses and reduce our susceptibility to unconscious bias (Creswell et al., 2007).

Talking to others is also one of the most helpful ways to mitigate bias. This will help us get out of our own experience bias and appreciate other people's perspectives. It will help us to get out of our autopilot, easy route thinking of the urgency bias to have deeper, more robust and deliberate thinking. And it will also help us to appreciate, value and embrace all the wonderful diverse people in this world and break out of our similarity bias. We can learn new things about different people, what's important to them, their concerns and struggles; see the world through their eyes and how they feel.

So, taken together, being more mindful and putting on our mental brakes, and talking to others to understand multiple, diverse perspectives, will help us mitigate the different biases we may have or face.

Another way of looking at this is to think about the incredible ability the brain has to rewire itself. The neuroplasticity of the brain is such that we actually restructure it depending upon what we are exposed to, thus changing our behavior. This means that by being mindful, talking to others and working in an environment of inclusion, we become more inclusive and mitigate our biases.

---

**Reflection**

*Urgency and Experience Biases*

1.  How can you put on your "mental brakes" to stop the automatic reflexive thinking and have more System 2 reflective thinking? How can you get off the dance floor and go to the balcony? Perhaps this is about seeing things differently, perhaps it is about slowing down, perhaps it is about being more mindful of what is around you. (*Make a note here.*)

    _____

    _____

    _____

    _____

    _____

2.  What step-by-step approach could you develop that breaks down the problem or situation you are in now into its component parts and encourages more thoughtful, deliberate

reflection and insight? Perhaps it could be like the process or approach mentioned earlier, or maybe one of your own. (*Make a note here.*)

_____

_____

_____

_____

_____

3. Who can you reach out to involve and get objective, outside opinions from others – to hear their thoughts, ideas, feedback and insights – and help you to see things in different ways? How can you take a break and distance yourself from your original ideas; then revisit them to see them in a fresher, more objective light and to see them through other people's eyes? (*Make a note here.*)

_____

_____

_____

_____

_____

## NOTES

1 Kahneman, D. *Thinking, Fast and Slow*. New York, NY: Farrar, Straus and Giroux. 2011. (pp. 6–7).

2 Kahneman, D. *Thinking, Fast and Slow*. New York, NY: Farrar, Straus and Giroux. 2011.

3 Kahneman, D. *Thinking, Fast and Slow*. New York, NY: Farrar, Straus and Giroux. 2011. (p. 41).

4 Fiske, S. T. and Ruscher, J. B. "Negative interdependence and prejudice: whence the affect?" *Affect, Cognition and Stereotyping: Interactive Processes in Group Perception*. Cambridge, MA: Academic Press. 1993 (pp. 239–68). Struch, N. and Schwartz, S. H. "Intergroup aggression: its predictors and distinctness from in-group bias." *Journal of Personality and Social Psychology*, 46(3), 364–73. 1989.

5 Levine, M., Prosser, A., Evans, D. and Reicher, S. "Identity and emergency intervention: how social group membership and inclusiveness of group boundaries shape helping behavior." *Personality and Social Psychology Bulletin*. April 1, 2005.

6 Van Bavel, J. J. and Cikara, M. "The neuroscience of intergroup relations: an integrative review." *Perspectives on Psychological Science*. 9, 245–74. May 12, 2014.

7 Van Bavel, J. J. and Cikara, M. "The neuroscience of intergroup relations: an integrative review." *Perspectives on Psychological Science*. 9, 245–74. May 12, 2014.

8 Cikara, M., Bruneau, E., Van Bavel, J. J. and Saxe, R. "Their pain gives us pleasure: how intergroup dynamics shape empathic failures and counter-empathic responses." *Journal of Experimental Social Psychology*. 55:110–25. November 2014.

# Seventeen

*"If you want to build a ship, don't drum up the men to gather wood, divide the work and give orders. Instead, teach them to yearn for the vast and endless sea."*

Antoine de Saint-Exupéry

Trust is like a bank account: we can increase it with deposits or reduce it with withdrawals. For example, when we are kind and respectful to others, we make a deposit and increase the level of trust; when we are unkind or disrespectful to others, by contrast, we make a withdrawal and lower the trust. When we keep promises, we make a deposit; when we break promises, we make a withdrawal. When we apologize, we make a deposit; when we are selfish, proud or arrogant, we make a withdrawal.

Every interaction we have with others is a chance to make a deposit or make a withdrawal. If we make many deposits and build this up over time, we can have an abundance of trust. So, if there is a time where we might have made a withdrawal, others can forgive us for this one time and still keep a high level of trust. However, if we make multiple withdrawals, these will accumulate and drive the level of trust down, which is harder to come back from. It can, in fact, go into a negative balance, where we may distrust that person, and then interpret all of their behavior in a negative light, from which they may never come back.

Two areas where we see this play out every day are how we handle our own mistakes and how we handle disagreements. These are key indicators of trust – whether we will build or erode it; whether we are making a deposit or a withdrawal.

### Acknowledging Mistakes

In 2013, The Forum Corporation conducted research into building trust in business through their Global Leadership Pulse Survey.[1] Figure 17.1 shows how often leaders acknowledge their own mistakes, as reported by the leaders and the employees who work under them.

DOI: 10.4324/9781003127000-17

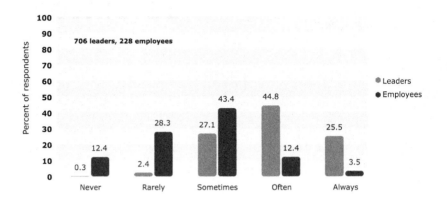

**Figure 17.1** Leaders Acknowledge Mistakes

As we can see, leaders reported acknowledging their mistakes much more often than their employees reported that their leaders did. Seventy percent of leaders reported that they often or always acknowledge their mistakes, whereas only 16% of their employees reported that their leaders acknowledge this. When asked whether leaders apologized to employees for their mistakes, the differences were even more stark: 87% of leaders responded that they often or always apologize, while only 19% of employees indicated their leaders did so. When asked why they were reluctant to apologize, the most frequent comments related to their image or reputation: they didn't want to look weak or incompetent.

Mistakes are a natural part of business, and life, and how we handle them will either build or erode trust. There are many opportunities that we have to incorporate "moments of trust" into our working day and personal lives: where we use mistakes to build trust, foster learning and develop our relationships. If we try to bury them or punish others for making them, it has a damaging effect on trust. There is a strong correlation between trust and a person's willingness to acknowledge their own mistakes, apologize for them and encourage others to acknowledge and learn from mistakes. This will also develop their relationships in the process.

For example, I used to be on a committee that organized events. I was the Second Vice President of this committee, and we had a First Vice President and President who sat above me. At the beginning of one of our online events, Sara, the First Vice President, said, "Grant, we can't get started yet because not everybody has the link. You know, when you do these events, Grant, you should make sure that everyone has the link." Now, the truth is that everybody did have the link. However, she said this and said it in front of our entire audience for the event, causing embarrassment. Later when I talked to her one-on-one about it, she got extremely upset and defensive and said, "I didn't say that; you're defaming me." She then went behind my back and complained to the President about it; the President subsequently stepped down for personal reasons. All she had to do was admit her mistake and say, something like, "I'm sorry. I didn't realize I said that." And then, bang, you're done. That's it.

As another example, I'll offer my own mistake that I had made and how I handled it. I am one of the leaders on a sports team for dragon boating. One day, I overslept and didn't make it to practice – the first and only time this ever happened. It was pouring raining outside, with lightening, and we had a Category 1 warning, which means it was too dangerous to go out on the water because of the risk of being struck by lightning. Therefore, the practice was canceled. I could have taken this as "Fine it's a Category 1 warning and it doesn't matter." However, the fact is I should have been there. So, I texted each one of the team members individually and apologized for what happened and for my mistake, and to let them know that it will not happen again ever. And it never has.

A leader I know through our consulting business, Carrie, offers yet another good example. She is a Senior Leader in her organization and oversees a team of six direct reports, who each have their own teams. One of her direct reports didn't come to a meeting once because he said that he did not have final confirmation of the meeting, although everybody else knew about it. He apologized to all the other team members about it. Moreover, Carrie took joint ownership of what happened and she apologized to all team members one-on-one as well. Her direct reports respected her even more for this, and she built more trust with them, making a very good deposit into the trust account.

We can apply this also to our personal relationships.

For example, a friend of mine, Randy, with whom I have a very good relationship, said something to me that was impolite and disrespectful and then just spoke superficially for the next several weeks. I was confused because usually we have a very good relationship, and I felt that this was making a withdrawal on that trust. Then after a few weeks, he apologized and said that he was going through some stressful times and having a hard time dealing with it. This forced him to be overprotective of himself and caused his behavior to others to be a little erratic. Because he apologized, he made a deposit into the account and rebuilt the trust.

How do the people around you handle mistakes? Have you experienced people like Sara who defend themselves and turn it on you? Have you experienced people like Carrie or Randy who take ownership of it and apologize? How do you handle mistakes? How can you handle them better to make a deposit into the account to build trust rather than erode it?

### Handling Disagreements

Handling disagreements is also a key indicator of trust – whether we will build or erode it – whether we make a deposit or a withdrawal.

For example, on the same committee I was on for organizing events, one time Sara, Sean and I were discussing about a Google form that we were going to use to pulse check all of our Executive Committee members about discussing and creating a new vision for the organization. We went back and forth with several iterations of the form and, at least Sean and I thought, reached agreement on the final iteration. We both thought that we all had agreement on it. So, I shared it with the rest of the Executive Committee. Sara then got so upset and said, "I never approved this" and it created some tension within the organization. Rather than approaching me one-on-one to discuss where this disagreement stemmed from, Sara went behind my back and got three other people to gang up and bully me at our next meeting in front all of the Executive Committee members. This is how she handled the disagreement, and it was a major withdrawal from the trust account.

By contrast, a good example of handling a disagreement was with one of my business partners, Stewart. We had a disagreement about how we should communicate externally to our customers. He thought we should do "A," and I thought we should do "B," and it escalated into a very heated argument. We didn't speak for a few days. Then, I called him up and said we should talk about this. So, we met one-on-one to clarify and understand how each of us saw the situation, listening to each other to understand rather than listening to reply. We were both flexible in our thinking and willing to explore other options. We discussed it and found a way to blend both of what we wanted. We could have just ignored this and held a grudge. But we didn't. We met as adults one-on-one to discuss it, resolve it and cocreate a new way forward. That's how we handled the disagreement and created a big deposit of trust for both of us.

And so, how do the people around you handle disagreements? Have you experienced people like Sara who gang up and bully you or talk behind your back? Have you experienced people like Stewart who take the time to have a one-on-one adult conversation to listen, understand each other and cocreate a way forward? How do you handle disagreements? How can you handle them better to make a deposit into your account to build trust rather than erode it?

### Oxytocin in Our Brain

When we trust and have trust with others, our brains release and build oxytocin: the neurochemical produced from the comfort of social trust either given or received. This could be feeling safe with a group of like-minded people, having social support from people similar to ourselves or physical touch from a loved one.

Oxytocin is produced in the human brain when we feel trust and trusted, and this molecule motivates reciprocation.[2] Researchers found that the human oxytocin response signals that another person is safe and familiar; and that this "you seem trustworthy" signal occurs even between strangers without face-to-face interactions.[3]

Paul J. Zak, the person who discovered the behavioral effect of oxytocin, said, "After years of experiments, I now consider oxytocin the neurologic substrate for the golden rule: If you treat me well, in most cases my brain will synthesize oxytocin and this will motivate me to treat you well in return."[4]

---

**Reflection**

*Making Deposits and Withdrawals*
*Acknowledging Mistakes and Handling Disagreements*

1. Think of one person you work with in business and one in your personal life where trust is important and there may have been, or is, some tension between you.

2. How do you handle mistakes with them? Do you defend yourself, or do you acknowledge them and apologize? How do you handle disagreements with them? Do you ignore them or talk behind their back, or do you meet with them one-on-one to resolve it and move it forward? (*Make a note here.*)

   _____

   _____

   _____

_____

_____

3. What could you do to make more deposits rather than withdrawals in order to build more trust with them? How will you handle mistakes and disagreements more effectively moving forward? (*Make a note here.*)

_____

_____

_____

_____

_____

### Eroding Trust

There are several obvious behaviors that erode trust, whether the person is aware of it or not. Below is a list of the kinds of behavior that clearly erodes trust.

**Table 17.1** Seven Types of Behavior that Erode Trust

| Behavior | Example |
| --- | --- |
| Being inconsistent | Talking "team" and "togetherness" but leading in a top-down, micromanaging style. |
| Lying/lacking transparency | Withholding information or telling different people different things. |
| Lacking follow through | Not following through on commitments or holding others accountable for meeting their commitments. |
| Taking undue credit/passing blame | Taking praise for others' work. Letting people take blame for your mistakes. |
| Talking behind people's back | Talking negative about another person in their absence, which makes others wonder what you might be saying about them. |
| Not "walking the talk" | Asking other people to do things that you wouldn't do yourself. |
| Poor communication/ interpersonal skills | Not listening to people. |

For example, Sara, whom I mentioned before, the First Vice President of a committee I was on, seemed to be doing everything she could to erode trust. She talked behind people's back, had secret conversations that excluded others, withheld information, took control of everything, said negative things about people for the efforts that they had done, and took tasks away from people and gave them to other people – she wrote the book on eroding trust. This not only reflected negatively on her, but made everyone in the team feel uncomfortable and uneasy, and caused several other committee members to step down as a result.

Have you ever met people like this? People who do this kind of behavior? How does it make you feel? Have you ever done any of these behaviors? How do you think it makes other people feel? Are you aware of this and the impact on them?

### How We Regard Others

In Chapter Fifteen: *Relationships and Authenticity*, we made a distinction between our outward behavior and how we regard others inwardly. If our behavior is like Sara's in the example above, perhaps it reflects something about how we regard others. In Sara's case, perhaps she sees others as a threat or as a resource for her to get what she wants, rather than regarding them as a person with their own equally legitimate needs and feelings.

How do you regard others? As a resource to get what you want? Or as person in and of themselves with their own needs and feelings?

If you haven't read Chapter Fifteen: *Relationships and Authenticity* yet and it resonates with you, perhaps read it next after this chapter.

## Being Trustworthy

Trust is invaluable in all of our relationships, both in business and in our personal lives. Ideally, we would like to increase the trust with everybody we are closely in contact with. In order to do this, however, we first need to be sure we are doing everything possible to be fully trustworthy. The very nature of the word itself means to be worthy of trust. So, how do we build and demonstrate such trustworthiness?

### The 5 Cs to be Trustworthy

There are five attributes to build and demonstrate trustworthiness: character, competency, credibility, consistency and care.

**Character** – Do I trust you? Are you a person of integrity? To be trustworthy, we need to have integrity; that is, we need to have strong moral principles and be honest with others. We need to be reliable and keep promises. If others question if we are genuine, if they feel like a pawn in our chess game – a thing to be used for our own agenda – it will be difficult for them to trust us. By being reliable, keeping promises and having strong ethical standards, it will increase our trustworthiness.

**Competency** – Are you competent? Do you have a proven track record of success? To be trustworthy, we need to demonstrate our competence – that we can do what we say we are going to do and be successful in doing it. We need to demonstrate our capacity to stay focused on our message and act successfully on this. Being honest, transparent and secure helps create awareness about our ability to meet others' needs and our ability to meet commitments. This then increases our trustworthiness.

**Credibility** – Are you credible? Can people believe that you can understand the complexity of their problems and, using your competence, design a solution that enables them to flourish and achieve their goals? To do this, we need to connect the dots between other people's problems or situations and our solutions in order for them to believe that we can benefit them. If we make assumptions and predetermine the solution before fully understanding their needs, we will not be seen as credible. We need to listen to the core issues and provide solutions that meet their specific needs. Then we will come across as credible and demonstrate that we are trustworthy.

**Consistency** – Do you do what you say you are going to do? Is there consistency in the way that you handle things? We need to create stability in the situations we face and the people we interact with. This stability helps people feel at ease and know what to expect from the group and the circumstances they encounter. This too builds and demonstrates our trustworthiness.

**Care** – Do you care about the people you interact with? Do you show them that they matter? This could take the form of giving appreciation to them and the tasks or activities they do. It could be about anticipating their needs and offering support to them, reading their cues and being there for them to help in any way we can. It is about knowing them and what works best for them, knowing the pressures they have and being able to forgive them if words get said because of these pressures. All of this demonstrates emotional intelligence, builds human connections and enhances our trustworthiness with the people we engage with.

For example, I recall an incident once where our HR consulting company accidentally undercharged a client for a piece of work we had done for them. It had gone unnoticed by our accounting department and we would not have been any the wiser had the client paid the amount invoiced. The economy was tough at this time and all companies were watching their spend. Our client, however, let us know about the discrepancy in the invoice. As a result, it increased the trust between us and demonstrated their integrity and trustworthiness. This led to more work with this client, and our consultants would go the extra mile to create even more value for them.

Another example, in 2007, is when rock band Radiohead released their album *In Rainbows* online, trusting fans to decide on the price for the album with a "pay-what-you-want" digital download. This was met by skepticism and criticism from the music industry. However, as vocalist Thom Yorke said "in terms of digital income, we've made more money out of [*In Rainbows*] than out of all the other Radiohead albums put together, forever." Showing trust with their fans, it built up a larger fan base and revenue.

This is the same with a project that I am involved with too. *Metamorfosize*, as it's called, is an online 24-hour global music and art festival, of which I am the Music Director, with over 40 artists and facilitators from 23 countries. We started off ticketing the events and attracted only a few people. We then opted to make them donation based. This allows access to the events for people in the world who come from less affluent countries and also a way for people who are more affluent to show their support. We not only increased the number of attendees, but also increased the revenue far beyond what we would have received if it was ticketed. By trusting our attendees, it is building up quite a nice community. Likewise the artists and facilitators involved log their own hours, on an honor system, and payments are made out according to this. This has created a very tight and trusting community among the artists and facilitators as well.

And yet another example, similar to the one above. Years ago, Ford, which had more than 500 employees working in its accounts payable department, decided to benchmark against Mazda. To its surprise, Ford discovered that Mazda only had five employees in payables. Ford had 500 vs Mazda's five. Mazda could do this through trust. With Ford, the account payable employees had to match the purchase order, receiving reports and supplier invoices. If there was a mismatch, there was significant rework. With Mazda, however, there was no paperwork at all. Mazda trusted its suppliers and did not bother processing invoices. When goods arrived from suppliers, Mazda built their cars. Once a car was built, it automatically transferred funds to the suppliers. Mazda had no invoicing or processing, but paid with trust, saving significant costs.

So, we can see that by building and demonstrating trustworthiness, we can build positive human connections with people, enhance trust with them and have better outcomes as a result.

Who do you know who is trustworthy? How do they demonstrate the 5 Cs of trustworthiness? What results are they getting? And for yourself – how can you be more trustworthy? Which of the 5 Cs would you like to improve for yourself?

---

**Reflection**

**Eroding Trust and Being Trustworthy**

1. Think of one person you work with in business and one in your personal life where trust is important.

2. What kind of behavior have you done with these people that might have contributed to eroding trust with them? Have you been inconsistent or lacked transparency? Have you ever missed on follow through or had poor communication? (*Make a note here.*)

   _____

   _____

   _____

   _____

   _____

3. How can you be more trustworthy in order to build more trust with them? How can you demonstrate your character, competency, credibility, consistency and care in order to be more worthy of their trust? (*Make a note here.*)

   _____

   _____

   _____

   _____

   _____

---

### Creating a Trusting Environment

So far, we have looked at trust on a character level and as individuals between people. Let's now dive into what it takes to create an environment where trust can flourish. Specifically, we will look at *psychological safety* – what it is and how to create it; and *micro-messages* – what they are and the different kinds that we may be displaying.

#### Psychological Safety

Psychological safety is the condition in which we are able to show and be our complete self without the fear of negative consequences to our self-image, status or career, where we feel included and safe to be our *expanded self* without the fear of being embarrassed or punished in any way. This is essential to create a trusting environment.

When people can be their *expanded self*, they have:

- Increased confidence
- Better sense of belonging
- More contribution
- Improved performance
- More trust

By contrast, when people operate as their *diminished self*, they have:

- Superficial behavior
- Defensiveness/attacking
- Withdrawal/shutdown
- Poorer performance
- Less trust

For example, Sara, whom I mentioned before, the First Vice President of a committee I was on, was chairing a meeting on the vision of the organization. As mentioned before, Sara, Sean and I went back and forth quite a bit to create a Google form to pulse check all of our Executive Committee members about creating a new vision for the organization. This was then to be sent out to all of them to reflect on and then openly share and discuss all of our ideas about this. When we had the meeting, however, Sara said, "This is the vision of our organization. It has always been this way and it always will be. The next item on our agenda is ..." There was no discussion on this for people to share their thoughts and feelings; rather, she announced it, silencing everybody and creating zero psychological safety.

Have you ever experienced something like this? Where somebody makes you feel your *diminished self*, withdrawn and shutdown? How did it make you feel? How did it impact the level of trust in the room? How did it impact the level of trust you felt personally?

We can contrast this with Barry, who is the Managing Director for Asia Pacific of a very large publishing company. Chairing a meeting on the vision and purpose of their organization, he said,

> I would like for all of us to consider what is the vision and purpose of our organization and how each of us fit in and would like to fit into this. Together we can craft the vision and purpose and explore how each of us see ourselves as part of this. I have drafted a few questions for each of us to consider to get us started on the conversation. It is certainly not an exhaustive list; so, please feel free to think of any other questions and any ideas that you have about this. We can take the next few days for each of us to think and reflect, and then meet on Friday to discuss this together. I very much value all of your ideas and contributions, and together let's create the best vision and purpose that we can.

Barry did just as he said, creating psychological safety for all the team members to freely contribute and feel like they all belonged. This allowed them to be their *expanded selves* and create a trusting environment.

Have you ever experienced this? Where the environment and the people there made you feel and live your *expanded self*, being able to be and express yourself freely to contribute, like you belonged there? How did it make you feel? How did it impact the level of trust in the room? How did it impact the level of trust you felt personally?

We can also tie this in with our psychological needs. In Chapter Three: *Inspiration and Motivation* and Chapter Twelve: *Change*, we introduced our *ACRES Needs*, which stands for *autonomy, competence, relatedness, equity and sureness* – the psychological needs we all have in order to thrive and perform at our peak levels. If people or the environment around us threaten our psychological needs, trust will erode; if people or the environment around us are allowing and encouraging us to satisfy all of our psychological needs, trust will be high. Creating a trusting environment makes people feel safe and not threatened and helps them to satisfy all of their psychological needs. If you haven't yet read these chapters and it resonates with you, perhaps read them after this one.

We can also apply this in our own personal lives too. For example, I was having dinner with a group of friends once and everyone was really listening to each other and respecting each other. Even though several people had different views and didn't always agree, we created an environment where everyone felt psychologically safe to be their *expanded selves*.

We can use the checklist below in Figure 17.2 to help us assess and increase the psychological safety we create in our teams at work and in our own personal relationships.

|  | Yes | No |
|---|---|---|
| Do people tell you more than they need to about themselves? |  |  |
| Are you positively surprised by what lies "beneath the surface"? |  |  |
| Do you make everyone feel valuable? |  |  |
| Do people proactively share their views and ideas with you? |  |  |
| Are you aware of assumptions you are making about people? |  |  |
| Do you actively seek out and value different points of view? |  |  |
| Do you monitor against dismissing or ignoring people? |  |  |
| Are you discrete with information that people share with you? |  |  |
| Do people feel comfortable bringing up problems and issues with you? |  |  |
| Do you connect personally with people? |  |  |

**Figure 17.2** Checklist to Create Psychological Safety

If you answer "yes" to all or most of these questions, this is what it takes to create and maintain psychological safety. If you answer "no" or "sometimes" to some of these questions, try to think for yourself how you can do more of this – both in your work and your personal life.

Micro-Messages

Micro-messages are small, subtle messages that we send and receive verbally and nonverbally. It is not intentional, but rather unconscious behavior, that could either have a negative impact or a positive impact on the person or people around us.

For example, I was having drinks with a friend of mine and he seemed always to be checking his phone or looking around. I didn't feel he was really paying attention to me. These subtle messages had a negative impact and took away from creating a trusting environment.

Have you ever experienced this before? Either at work or personally? How did it make you feel?

In another situation, I was having lunch with another friend of mine. She kept her phone in her bag (as did I), was not looking around and very much seemed to be paying attention. These subtle messages had a positive impact and helped to facilitate creating a trusting environment.

Have you ever experienced this before? Either at work or personally? How did it make you feel?

Below are a list of negative micro-messages (micro-aggressions) and positive micro-messages (micro-affirmations) and the results that they create.

**Table 17.2** Negative and Positive Micro-Messages

| Micro-aggressions | Results |
| --- | --- |
| • Checking emails/texting during F2F com | • Lower our confidence |
| • Sharing info with some but not others | • Decrease engagement |
| • Valuing one person's opinion over others | • Drive down commitment |
| • Appearing distracted | • Impact our mental and physical health |
| • Making assumptions based on looks | |
| • Seeking advice from some, not others | • Erode trust |
| • Using examples relevant only to a few | |

| Micro-affirmations | Results |
| --- | --- |
| • Focusing complete attention on someone | • Boost our confidence |
| • Asking for alternative viewpoints | • Increase engagement |
| • Using open body language | • Raise our commitment |
| • Nodding and active listening | • Contribute to a positive, inclusive culture |
| • Seeking out different perspectives | |
| • Paraphrasing understanding | • Build trust |
| • Appreciating individual strengths | |

### Reflection

#### Creating a Trusting Environment

1. Think of the people you work with in business and in your personal life, and the kind of environment you are creating for them.

2. Review the checklist for *Creating Psychological* Safety. What mindsets do you hold and what behaviors are you doing to help people to be their *expanded selves*? What areas would you like to do more of in order for them to be this even more? (*Make a note here.*)

_____

_____

_____

_____

_____

3.  What micro-messages are you doing that you may or may not
    be aware of? Who are you encouraging and affirming? Who
    might you be taking for granted and overlooking? How can
    you reduce the _micro-aggressions_ and increase the _micro-affirmations_
    to create a more trusting environment for everyone to feel
    included, respected and valued? (_Make a note here._)

_____

_____

_____

_____

### Behavior and Mindsets for Building and Maintaining Trust

There have been several surveys and studies done on the mindsets and
behaviors to build trust. Among the top include: act with integrity – be
open and transparent; listen/demonstrate care; "walk the talk;" demonstrate trust and empowerment; encourage/recognize hard work; provide
clear and consistent messages/vision; and give constructive feedback/
coaching.[5]

From these studies, the main themes that emerge to build trust are: be
consistent in messages and actions; communicate openly and frequently;
demonstrate interest in others and their ideas; be candid about mistakes;
create an environment that is emotionally "safe," and model and support
continuous growth and learning.

In 2020, myself and our consulting firm conducted our own
survey in the face of COVID-19, work from home and social distancing. Figure 17.3 below shows the top results for critical factors that
impact trust.[6]

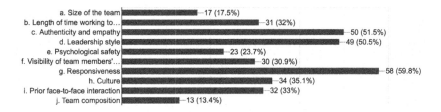

a. Size of the team —17 (17.5%)
b. Length of time working to... —31 (32%)
c. Authenticity and empathy —50 (51.5%)
d. Leadership style —49 (50.5%)
e. Psychological safety —23 (23.7%)
f. Visibility of team members'... —30 (30.9%)
g. Responsiveness —58 (59.8%)
h. Culture —34 (35.1%)
i. Prior face-to-face interaction —32 (33%)
j. Team composition —13 (13.4%)

**Figure 17.3** Critical Factors that Impact Trust

"Responsiveness" came out on top, with 60% of survey participants indicating that this is the most critical factor to build and maintain trust. This includes paying attention to people, understanding their needs and doing what you can to help them meet those needs.

Comments from survey participants include:

*Having a good team makeup who work well together and are responsive in their communication engenders trust. Unresponsive, new teams need to work together to build a bit of cohesion.*

*A strong leader and a strong work culture are important to make sure that the bus is being driven and stays on the road. From there, people have to communicate and get back to you, so responsiveness is hugely important. When you don't have that, then things fall apart.*

*Smaller teams, that have worked together face to face before, who respond promptly to asynchronous communication, develop trust more quickly when remote work is forced upon them.*

"Authenticity and empathy" came out as the second most important critical factor to build and maintain trust during this unprecedented pandemic in 2020, with 52% of respondents indicating this. This includes showing genuine positive regard for others, in our mind, intent and behavior. In Chapter Fifteen: *Relationships and Authenticity*, we dive deep into this. If this resonates with you and you haven't read it yet, perhaps read it next.

It also includes showing care and compassion for people. Again, not only on a behavioral level, but genuinely in our heart and intentions. In Chapter Eighteen: *Empathy*, we explore *empathic concern*, where we not only understand what people think and feel what they feel but also genuinely want to do something to help them. If this resonates with you, perhaps read this chapter next.

Comments from survey participants include:

*Knowing one another deeply means shared vulnerability, which is where trust tends to live in my experience. Lacking a deep relationship, I at least need to know that our intentions align, e.g. we are both here to co-create something vs you are trying to sell me something. Trust means knowing the motivations of others, the purpose of collaborating, and having the CHOICE to participate in that endeavor.*

*When people can bring their whole selves to work and work from a place of authenticity, while listening and providing their diverse point of views, it creates an environment of trust. When you have a culture that fosters psychological safety and enables all members to be themselves and has a framework of norms, goals, roles and responsibilities, the team now has guard rails to hold each other accountable and quickly work through problems, issues and conflict.*

*Authenticity is generally a key indicator that the person is trustworthy; psychological safety contributes to opportunities to build trust in more possibly difficult situations.*

*Authenticity is important in getting to know team members and building connection and trust. Empathy: because everyone wants to be heard and understood. I think overall, these 2 factors are key for any working environment but perhaps the need is even more important working remotely because you're siloed.*

Understanding our behaviors and mindsets for building and maintaining trust takes self-awareness and managing our impact on others. To do this, we need to have courage, humility and discipline. Courage to be vulnerable and open to others; and courage to want to continuously make ourselves better. Humility to be human, admitting our mistakes, admitting we are not perfect or always right, and being able to look in the mirror to continuously improve. And discipline to make the changes necessary and to maintain the consistency necessary to build, develop and prolong trust.

Communication also plays a key role in building and maintaining trust. We need to be open and honest – because secretiveness and withholding information leads to distrust. We need to make communications timely, done sensitively and with awareness of any and all the consequences or results that may follow. We need to communicate not only the what and when but also the why – to make the context clear so people can understand better what is being asked of them and how they fit in and belong. We need to set agreed ground rules and a psychologically safe space for good communications and fruitful conversations to happen. And we need to be mindful that we are speaking with and not merely to or at people, asking for their feedback and showing (by "walking the talk") that we have taken what's being said on board and doing something with it. This will help them meet their psychological needs, build trust and decrease threats. Communication is not merely transactional; it facilitates building trust and positive relationship with others.

Trust is the cornerstone of any successful relationship. Others trusting us helps to create a space where they feel they matter and belong; it creates opportunities to collaborate and cocreate, to be given the benefit of the doubt in ambiguous situations and to move quickly to action for better relationships and better outcomes. Developing our mindsets and behavior to demonstrate our character, credibility and human connection will build trust with those around us and maintain that trust for the long term and during trying times.

---

**Reflection**

**Behavior and Mindsets for Building and Maintaining Trust**

1. Think about one person you work with in business and one person in your personal life that you would like to build more trust with.

2. What will you think and feel to have a mindset and intentions so that they can see, know and feel that you want to build more trust with them? (*Make a note here.*)

   _____
   _____
   _____
   _____
   _____

3. What behaviors will you stop doing that might be taking away from this? What behaviors will you continue that are working? And what new behaviors will you start doing to build and maintain this even more? (*Make a note here.*)

   _____
   _____
   _____
   _____
   _____

## NOTES

1 The Forum Corporation. *Driving Business Results by Building Trust*. Singapore: The Forum Corporation. 2013.

2 Zak, P. J., Kurzban, R. and Matzner, W. T. "The neurobiology of trust." *Annals of the New York Academy of Sciences*, 1032, 224–7. 2004.

3 Carter, C. S. and Keverne, E. B. "The neurobiology of social affiliation and pair bonding." In D. Pfaff (Ed.), *Hormones, Brain and Behavior* (pp. 299–377). San Diego: Academic Press. 2002.

4 Zak, P. J. "Why inspiring stories make us react: the neuroscience of narrative." *Cerebrum*. Feb 2;2015:2. eCollection. 2015.

5 The Forum Corporation. *Driving Business Results by Building Trust*. Singapore: The Forum Corporation. 2013.

6 YES (Your Empowering Solutions). *Building and Maintaining Trust During COVID-19*. Singapore: YES (Your Empowering Solutions). 2020.

Empathy

# Eighteen

Empathy is the capacity to understand or feel what another person is experiencing from within their frame of reference, the capacity to place ourselves in another person's position, to put ourselves in their shoes, see it from their eyes, their perspective, their way of thinking and feeling.

For example, have you ever felt someone else's pain or frustration? Have you ever understood the situation from their viewpoint?

A few years ago, I was working with someone, myself based in Tokyo at that time, she in New York. We were working on a big project together, along with several others around the world. I was a Consultant; she was the Project Leader. I wanted to know more about the scope and big picture of the project, so I asked many questions. She felt, however, that she was being "hounded," and either didn't have the answers or felt that she didn't need to share this.

This created some tension, and I could sense this. I felt her frustration and discomfort. So, I looked at it from her perspective. I thought, "what does a day in the life of this Project Leader look like?" She is probably very busy doing several tasks for several different projects. She wants to give others enough information and feels that she is giving enough. She feels pressure to do her job. When people start questioning her too much, she gets frustrated and it erodes trust.

Have you ever experienced this? Either because of a miscommunication or some other reason, there becomes some tension?

There are many situations when we can feel empathy. When something happens to our friend or coworker, for example, we can feel their pain and understand it from their perspective. And this is a very powerful tool. It becomes even more powerful, like the example above, in times of tension between people, when there is a disagreement or conflict.

So, having felt the frustration of the Project Leader I was working with and understanding the situation through her eyes, I took action to let her know the reason for these questions (so I could know the big picture), the benefits for me and the client, as well as showing understanding for

DOI: 10.4324/9781003127000-18

the position that she is in. This helped us build trust, develop the relationship and achieve better outcomes.

As humans, we can empathize with others, feeling what they feel; however, we are also often wrong about what others are thinking, their intentions and motivations. Why would we care that we are wrong? We care because we make assumptions, which then influence our decisions and actions.

For example, Scott was going to have lunch with his friend Rebecca. Rebecca suggested Sunday. Scott said, "Sure, I will be available at 1:30 pm." Rebecca then said, "Maybe another time, I have something in the afternoon," without apologizing or explaining what it was. Scott was excited to see his friend, as it had been awhile, and he felt hurt and disappointed. The next day, he emailed her to tell her this. Then, she got very angry and said, "I had to help my friend with her kids, and maybe we should never speak to each other again."

For Scott, a simple apology at that moment would have been impactful; maybe also the reason for suddenly having to change the plan. It would have shown care, compassion and empathy, understanding Scott's thinking and his feelings. Rebecca just assumed it would be okay. For Rebecca, she got angry and reacted to Scott the next day because she felt that he didn't understand her. Scott assumed that she had made another plan and that he was not important.

And so, although we try to understand others and try to feel what they feel, we are also often wrong about what others are thinking, which leads us to make assumptions that influence our decisions and actions. We may jump to judging or blaming rather than taking a step back or going to the balcony to really empathize with and understand the other person.

---

**Reflection**

*Understanding Others*

1. When have you been wrong when thinking about the thoughts or motivations of others? What assumptions did you make? Think of one personal example and one business example. (*Make a note here.*)

   _____

   _____

   _____

```
_____

_____

2.  What behavior or actions did you, intentionally or uninten-
    tionally, do as a result? (Make a note here.)

_____

_____

_____

_____

_____
```

This chapter will help us understand more what empathy is, why we do not always empathize correctly and how we can develop our ability to empathize better.

### Distinctions Between Empathy and Other Related Concepts

First, let's look at some related concepts and how empathy is distinguished from these. *Sympathy* or *pity* is the feeling we have toward someone that might be in trouble or in need of help as they cannot fix their problems themselves, often described as "feeling sorry" for someone. Empathy is not "feeling sorry" for someone but rather, as we mentioned, understanding it from their perspective and/or feeling their emotions.

Empathy is also distinct from *emotional contagion*. Emotional contagion is when a person imitates the emotions that someone else is showing without necessarily recognizing that this is happening. For example, a child may do this, or when we are in a very large excited crowd of people. Empathy is not by accident; rather, it is a proactive mindset and behavior.

### How Empathy Works in Our Brain

Contemporary neuroscience has allowed us to understand the neural basis of our ability to understand and process emotion. Research and studies have shown the activation of "mirror" neurons in our brains, which help explain the basic process of empathy. In our brain, empathy is a spontaneous sharing of a person's feelings or thoughts by witnessing and being affected by their emotional state. In a way, we "mirror" or "mimic" the emotional response that we would expect to feel ourselves if we were in that same condition or context.

A "mirror" neuron is a neuron in our brain that fires both when we act and when we observe the same action performed by someone else. Therefore, the neuron "mirrors" the behavior, feelings or thoughts of the other person, as if we were ourselves experiencing it. The most common theory behind the origin of "mirror" neurons is that they evolved in the human brain to facilitate and understand the actions we need to take in response to others as, at least in human history, our survival would depend on it.

Neuroscience has also shown us that there is a stronger pull on our brain toward negative or threat feelings (pain, disgust, absence) compared to positive or reward feelings (joy, happiness, kindness). Again, this is linked to our evolutionary history, where our survival may depend on it.

I remember very clearly, in the theater with a large group of people in the audience, watching the movie *Dancer in the Dark*, starring Björk and directed by Lars von Trier. It is one of the most emotional movies I have ever seen. I very clearly remember at the end of the movie in the last scene, you could hear everyone in the theater crying. It was like an additional soundtrack on top of the movie itself. We were all so drawn in to the feelings that Björk had and our "mirror' neurons were firing on all cylinders as if we were all experiencing it ourselves.

### Three Kinds of Empathy

There are three kinds of empathy: *cognitive empathy, emotional empathy* and *empathic concern*.

#### Cognitive Empathy

*Cognitive empathy* is taking another person's perspective and understanding the situation as they see it. Through their words and body language, we process it logically, taking on their perspective, without "experiencing" it. This is done purely logically and the "mirror" neurons do not fire.

For example, when I go shopping, I would always pay for things by taking out all my coins and then getting rid of as many coins as I could so I would end up with less change. This seems logical to me. One of my friends, however, would pay for things with whichever coin came out first. Although I felt mine was more "logical," hers was a different kind of logic, and I could understand it from her perspective.

#### Emotional Empathy

*Emotional empathy* is feeling someone's pain or other emotion (like Bill Clinton said, "I feel your pain"), experiencing their emotion by seeing it in them and simulating/sensing it in ourself. In this case, the "mirror" neurons fire as we experience their situation as if it were our own.

For example, I was listening to two friends speaking. Julie, a Sales Person in the Financial Services industry, was telling Kim, a Sales Person in Personal Wealth Management, about an incident that had happened with one of her clients. During one particular phone call, her client got very upset and said that "we don't want to deal with your company anymore." Julie was so surprised and shocked because she has a great rapport with all of her clients, and all people for that matter, and would never disrespect anybody. After the call, Julie was very upset, crying and all she could think about was this call. When she told Kim this story, Kim listened very intensely and said, "ouch," "I feel you," and reached out to touch her. I could genuinely hear it in Kim's voice that she really felt Julie's pain, experiencing it as if it were her own.

### Cognitive vs Emotional Empathy – Which One Do We Choose?

When we are similar to the other person, we feel more *emotional empathy*. We can relate to them, who they are, what they feel, because they are similar to us. As a result, we feel their feelings as if it were really our own experience. When we are different from the other person, or perceive ourselves to be different, we do more *cognitive empathy*. We try to see it from their perspective as we see ourselves as different from them and try to put ourselves in their shoes to see it as they see it, because we ourselves may not be able to directly relate to it.

Recent neuroscience, moreover, has confirmed that different areas of the brain are activated during *emotional empathy* and *cognitive empathy*. As a result, we process it differently within our brain. It has also shown that we can control *cognitive empathy* much more than *emotional empathy* because it uses a logical part of our brain rather than an emotional center. We can also do both simultaneously to understand the other person's perspective *and* experience their emotions, thereby being even more accurate with what they really think and feel. This will help us to understand their real intentions and motivations, make fewer assumptions and really truly empathize with them.

I noticed for myself that, in business, I tend to use more *cognitive empathy* than *emotional empathy*. As a result, I have actively worked on feeling more *emotional empathy* in work and business situations to truly understand and empathize more.

**Reflection**

*Cognitive Empathy and Emotional Empathy*

1.  When have you experienced *cognitive empathy*? Think of one personal and one business example where you have taken another person's perspective and seen it through their eyes, but not experienced the emotions like they were your own. (*Make a note here.*)

    _____

    _____

    _____

    _____

    _____

2.  When have you experienced *emotional empathy*? Think of one personal and one business example where your "mirror" neurons were firing and you "experienced" their emotions as if they were your own. (*Make a note here.*)

    _____

    _____

    _____

    _____

    _____

3.  How can you benefit from experiencing both at the same time? Think of some examples where stepping into their shoes to see it from their perspective *and* firing up your "mirror" neurons to "experience" their emotions as if they were your own would help you to understand and feel them more. (*Make a note here.*)

    _____

    _____

    _____

    _____

    _____

### Empathic Concern

Empathic concern is the feeling that if I can do something that can help you, I will; the felt-sense that when I see you in trouble, I spontaneously want to help you out. It is being genuinely concerned with others and experiencing *other-oriented* emotions to help them and help themselves get better. This is when we express care, tenderness, compassion, soft-heartedness, and the like about another person, supporting them, showing trust, allowing them space. *Empathic concern* takes *emotional empathy* to a deeper level. Whereas *emotional empathy* is experiencing another person's perceived emotional state, *empathic concern* also includes having a non-fleeting concern for the other person.

And so, in my example with the Project Leader I worked with from New York, having felt her frustration *and* understanding the situation through her eyes, I took action to let her know the reason for the questions I had (so I could know the bigger picture), the benefits for me and the client, and showing understanding for the position that she was in. I felt a genuine concern and wanted to do something to make things better. As a result, we built more trust, developed the relationship and achieved better outcomes.

---

**Reflection**

**Empathic Concern**

1. When have you experienced *empathic concern*? Think of one personal and one business example where you have genuinely felt a non-fleeting concern for another person and spontaneously wanted to help them. (*Make a note here.*)

   _____

   _____

   _____

   _____

   _____

2. How can you develop yourself to experience this more with other people? Think of some examples where showing genuine spontaneous concern for others would help you to build more trust, develop better relationships and achieve better outcomes. (*Make a note here.*)

_____

_____

_____

_____

_____

### Choosing to Be Empathic

Although empathy is a natural biological process within our brains, it is not automatic. Rather, feeling empathy is a choice we make. If people don't want to be empathic, there is no way to train them or help them; they have to want to be. Like losing weight, it is about the motivation behind it. Even if other people's emotions rub off on us automatically, this process is only set in motion if we decide to put ourselves in a position for empathy to occur, and this decision is anything but automatic. Studies have shown that instead of automatically taking on other people's emotions, people make choices about whether and how much to engage in empathy. In fact, people sometimes make deliberate choices to avoid other people's emotions in attempts to stave off the discomfort or costs of empathy. A more important trait is not how *good* a person is at empathizing, but how *motivated* they are to engage with others in the first place.

We will now look at some situations in which people may, consciously or unconsciously, choose not to be empathic, before moving on to the benefits of empathy and choosing empathy.

#### Urgency and Self-Focused

In 1973 at the Princeton Theological Seminary at Princeton University, John M. Darley and C. Daniel Batson, psychology professors at Princeton, conducted a landmark psychology study. With a group of students from the Theological Seminary studying to become priests, they then divided these participants into two subgroups. For both groups, they told them that they would have to go across campus to another lecture hall and give a talk on the bible story *The Good Samaritan*, which is about helping others in need; so they had this in the forefront of their minds. They then told the participants from one of the groups that they have plenty of time to get over to the lecture hall; they told the participants from the other group, however, that they only have five minutes and must hurry to get over. To ensure that each participant would walk over to the other lecture hall one by one, they had participants report to the first building at their allocated time, giving the instructions and conditions one by one to each of them.

Enroute to the lecture hall to make their talk, each priest passed by a man who was injured and needed help, this person himself being an actor and part of the experiment. Of the priests that were told they had plenty of time to get over to the lecture hall, 61% stopped to help the injured person; of the priests who were in a hurry, however, only 10% stopped to help. Although helping others was at the forefront of their mind because of the nature of the talk they had to give, the immediacy of their own situation (i.e., being late vs not being late) affected their ability to be empathic and help the person who needed it.

So, what does this mean? It means that when we are caught up in our own immediate issues and thoughts, we do not feel empathy for others. Our focus may be too focused on ourselves, and we don't notice others. We deploy our attention solely to our own immediate situation (e.g., I'm in a hurry; I need to do this for myself) and we turn off the part of our brain that "includes others."

We can tie this in with business too. Kim, the Sales Person we mentioned before for Personal Wealth Management, has a boss whom she thinks does not understand her situation or has empathy. Her boss is under a lot of pressure from the Senior Leaders to hit the extremely aggressive sales targets that they have, as well as dealing with an emergency that just came up, adding to his pressure. Perhaps, then, he does not have empathy because he is focused on what is immediately in front of his face.

Is this behavior justified because we know the cause? No. Can we learn from this and become better? Yes. It is indeed possible for us to focus on ourselves *and* others simultaneously, even under pressure; we just need to be more proactive in what we do.

### The Social Brain vs the Analytical Brain

The "*social brain*" and the "*analytical brain*" are different. Or more precisely, they are different parts of our brain and function very differently and independently. In fact, according to recent neuroscience discovery, they are mutually exclusive (i.e., we will engage one or the other, not both, depending on the situation).[1] In some situations, it may be better to use an analytical mindset (e.g., solving a purely technical problem); in others, a social mindset (e.g., engaging with others). When people are at rest with nothing to do, which we call the resting state, we naturally cycle between the two networks.

There are some people, however, who tend to think very analytically; so much so that the human element is often lost. This then has an impact on people, relationships, motivation, performance and other people-related issues. As a result, these analytical thinkers may engage the *analytical brain* for all situations, which is why they may not be as empathic as they could be, because we need to engage the *social brain* to be empathic. They treat everything as a "task," in which an *analytical brain* is appropriate; however, for different situations, it is not appropriate to treat everything as a "task." Rather, we need to know in which situations an *analytical brain* would be most appropriate, and in which situations a *social* or *empathic brain* would be most appropriate.

There is a need, therefore, especially for analytical thinkers, to develop a more social and empathic mindset in order to have better people relationships in business and engage with others more effectively.

### The Emotional Burden of Feeling Empathic

Excessive empathy can lead to empathic fatigue. It requires enormous energy and can be extremely draining to try and have literally the same experience as another person, particularly another who is in distress and pain. We risk being flooded with pain, fear and uncertainty if we remain too often in a truly empathic state. Moreover, if as a result, we feel personal distress (i.e., feelings such as distress, alarm and worry), because it can focus attention on addressing self needs, can interfere with truly compassionate behavior that is generally associated with *empathic concern*.

I recall a friend of mine who called herself an "empath" because of deeply feeling what others feel. She said that she was also diagnosed with borderline personality disorder. In psychiatry, borderline traits have been associated with deficits in *cognitive empathy* and a more acute sense of *emotional empathy*.[2] As a result, someone with borderline personality disorder can be completely flooded with other people's emotions.

This can happen, perhaps not to such a degree, in all of us. If we take on too much of the other person's emotions internally within ourselves, we can also become flooded and feel personal distress.

In some cases, there could also be something in the situation that affects us emotionally, for example, if there is a disagreement between two people because of a misunderstanding. As a result, we feel our own emotions, which will hinder our ability to be empathic toward them because we may feel the need to protect ourself.

In all of these cases, we need to regulate our own emotions. In Chapter Nine: *Emotion Regulation*, we deep dive into all the different strategies for regulating our own emotions. If this piece resonates with you and you have not yet read Chapter Nine: *Emotion Regulation*, I would recommend to read that one after this.

### The Bully

There are also cases where someone intentionally hurts you. This could be a bully or power harassment, or any other kind of toxic or destructive behavior where someone intentionally tries to hurt you.

For example, four years ago, I was the Team Manager of an amateur sports team and was being defamed by the former Team Manager. Out of jealousy or ego or whatever reason, the former Team Manager started spreading lies about me in an attempt to defame me. Certainly, in such a case, for me to feel empathy toward him would be ridiculous.

So, if we are being bullied or harassed by someone and they are intentionally trying to hurt us, it is justified not to choose to feel empathy for them.

### Narcissism

It is worth pointing out as well about narcissism. Narcissism is characterized by a grandiose sense of self-importance, a need for admiration, and the belief that one is entitled and deserving of special treatment. A narcissist cares only about themselves and does not care about the impact they have on others. In psychiatry, narcissistic traits have been associated with a deficit in *emotional empathy*.[3] Some people, although not diagnosed with narcissistic personality disorder, may exhibit narcissistic traits. If you have, or have seen, this in yourself or others, it is a good idea to focus proactively on developing yours or their empathic mindsets and skills.

## Why We Should Choose to Be Empathic

We're going to deep dive now into the benefits of empathy and why we should choose to be empathic. As we mentioned before, although empathy is a natural biological process within our brains, it is not automatic. Rather, feeling empathy is a choice we make. To be empathic, we have to want to be empathic. Like losing weight, it is about the motivation behind it. We choose the foods we eat and the exercise we do in order to lose weight. It is the same with empathy and engaging with others.

Psychologist Carl Rogers said, "The gentle and sensitive companionship of an empathic stance ... provides illumination and healing. In such situations, deep understanding is, I believe, the most precious gift one can give to another."

First of all, for social beings, like humans, negotiating interpersonal decisions is as important to survival as being able to navigate the physical landscape. Our brains need to understand others in order to facilitate and understand the actions we need to take in response to them. We live in a social context and to survive in this we need to understand others.

Now, survival is not our only goal; we want to build relationships with people, which will simultaneously enhance ourselves and them. Psychological and neuroscientific research has shown that having social connections is important for both our physical and psychological well-being. Empathy is an essential ingredient for building such connections with others and building relationships. It enables us to establish rapport with another person, make them feel that they are being heard and feel respected and valued. When someone feels seen and heard by you, they begin to trust you and it establishes positive relationships.

Empathizing with others can also help us learn to regulate our own emotions, which will allow us to manage our own feelings without becoming overwhelmed. It also promotes helping behaviors. So, not only are we more likely to engage in helpful behaviors toward others, but others are also more likely to help us when they experience empathy. It is reciprocal, and we both grow as a result.

In business, moreover, empathy can build a more effective organization and company culture. In his book *Wired to Care*, strategy consultant Dev Patnaik argues that a major flaw in contemporary business practice is a lack of empathy inside large organizations. He states that by lacking empathy, people inside companies struggle to make intuitive decisions and often get fooled into believing they understand their business if they have quantitative research to rely upon. Patnaik claims that the real opportunity for companies doing business in the 21st century is to create a widely held sense of empathy for customers, pointing to Nike, Harley-Davidson and IBM as examples of "Open Empathy Organizations." Such institutions, he claims, see new opportunities more quickly than competitors, adapt to change more easily and create workplaces that offer employees a greater sense of mission in their jobs.[4] In addition, studies by the Management Research Group found that empathy was one of the three strongest predictors of senior executive effectiveness.[5]

And so, there are multiple reasons and benefits why we would choose to be empathic.

### How to Be More Empathic

At the most basic level, there are two main factors that contribute to the ability to experience empathy: genetics and socialization. Parents pass down genes that contribute to overall personality, including the propensity toward empathy and compassion. Also, people are socialized by their parents, peers, communities and society. How people treat others as well as how they feel about others is often a reflection of the beliefs and values that were instilled in them at a very young age.

As is the case with any ability, some people are simply better at being empathic than others, just as some people are better at kicking goals in soccer or persuasive arguments in team meetings. Moreover, in our modern society, more and more, we live in bubbles. Most of us are surrounded by people who look like us, think like us, earn like us, spend money like us, have educations like us and see the world like us. Because of people's homogeneous social circles, the result is an *empathy deficit*.

Empathy, however, is like a muscle. It can be weak. And we can also grow it and make it strong. That is, empathy can be developed, and there are steps we can take and habits we can form to acknowledge our own mindsets, behavior, biases and worldviews, and move beyond this to try to understand people better, build better relationships and better outcomes. And, as a bonus, we will make new friends along the way and enrich and develop ourselves personally.

First of all, let's introduce a checklist to assess some of our habits now.

Early Indicators for a Lack of Empathy
Here are some of the early indicators for a lack of empathy:

1. Not listening when spoken to.
2. Creating opinions early and defending them strongly.
3. Often having prolonged arguments with others.
4. Thinking that other people are overly sensitive.
5. Not open to other points of view.
6. Blaming others for mistakes.
7. Holding grudges and struggling to forgive others.
8. Lack of ability to work in a team.

If you have, or have seen, any of these in yourself or others, it is a good sign that something needs to be done.

Let's now deep dive into some habits for effective empathy.

### Habit 1: Cultivate Curiosity About New People and Strangers

Empathic people have an insatiable curiosity about new people and strangers. They will start a conversation with a stranger or invite new people they meet to lunch or coffee. They find other people more interesting than themselves and are curious to know who they are without interrogating them. Try it out for yourself. Go beyond small talk and be curious about who they are, especially people who have a different background or are different from you. Follow them on social media as well to find out more about their different views, religions and way of thinking.

### Habit 2: Try Out Someone Else's Life

Empathic people expand their empathy by gaining direct experience of other people's lives, "walking a mile in their shoes." Attend someone else's church, mosque, synagogue or other house of worship for a few weeks, or volunteer with a new organization. Spend time in a new neighborhood that you have never been to, striking up a conversation with someone from that community to really understand what a day in life looks like from their perspective. If someone's behavior is bother-some, think about why. If it's someone you don't know very well, for instance, start by acknowledging that they might feel stressed, and go further: what it is like to live their daily life – what is bothering them, what might they be thinking, what does life look like to them. For people leaders, what does "a day in the life of" your direct report look like.

### Habit 3: Challenge Your Biases and Discover Commonalities

We are all biased. Acknowledging this is the first step. The second step is taking action to overcome it. Empathic people challenge their own biases by searching for what they share with people rather than what divides them. Be honest with yourself. Biases are a natural part of the human condition; we use them to take mental shortcuts to navigate the people and world around us. Actively working to challenge this is what matters. Check your privileges. Your privileges are things that give you special status and that you didn't earn and don't necessarily realize you benefit from. For example, when someone raised with enough money has never thought about whether they can afford to eat; not everybody is the same. Talk to other people. One of the most important ways to confront bias and privilege in our life is to hear from others about their everyday lives and consider how they're different from ours. For example, maybe one of your colleagues leaves early to care for a family member or drives a different commute because they're afraid of interacting with police.

Perhaps they never feel heard in meetings or struggle to find the time and place to pump breast milk during the day.

### Habit 4: Listen Hard – and Open Up

There are two traits required for being an empathic conversationalist: to master the art of listening and to make ourselves vulnerable. Empathic people listen hard to others and do all they can to understand the other person's emotional state and needs. They also remove their masks and reveal their own feelings to the other person. Empathy is a two-way street. First of all, learn to be quiet. Rather than focusing on your own feelings, focus on the other person's and make the conversation about them. To listen fully to someone, use your body language to show that you're open to listening: uncross your arms, lean slightly forward, make eye contact; pay close attention to the other person's facial expressions and body language, which can convey more emotions than their words; ask open-ended questions, do not interrupt or criticize, and play back for them what you heard to show them that you are truly listening.

Also, be vulnerable yourself. This will help you be more comfortable with tough emotions during conversations with others. It will also help the other person to open up more to you. For some people, this comes easier than others. Analytical thinkers, for example, may need to make a little more effort to access their emotions. "Labelling" is a great skill to develop; that is, the ability to put words to our emotions, differentiating and defining them. In Chapter Nine: *Emotion Regulation*, we look in detail at this. Also, be open to changing your mind. Bring to the table ideas, feelings and thoughts, and be flexible and open to other people's ideas, feelings and thoughts, and willing to change your mind.

### Habit 5: Stand Up for Others

Empathy should drive us to act compassionately toward others. Empathic people stand up for others and are allies with them for the greater good of the team, group, organization, society and the world. Speak up when someone interrupts or makes a discriminating comment. For example, you could say, "I think she was still sharing her idea; let's make sure she has a chance to finish before we move on," or if someone makes a discriminating comment, you could say: "What you just said is offensive." Also, create space for other voices. Step aside and allow others to speak. It is a very powerful thing to do – to proactively create space for all the voices in the room to be heard.

### Habit 6: Read Books

Reading is one of the best ways to open our mind to the experiences of others. Empathic people read literary fiction, allowing them to enter characters' lives and minds, which, in turn, increases their capacity to understand other people's thoughts and feelings. Choose novels with narrators who have lives and backgrounds unlike yours, or who live in a different place or time, and choose diverse authors. Also, expand your research. Read and watch first-person accounts of the experiences of others in magazines, newspapers, social media, podcasts and documentaries to expand your knowledge about people who are different from you.

### Habit 7: Raise Empathic Kids

Children can learn empathy and empathic parents socialize and raise their children to treat others with respect, value who they are and where they come from, and act with compassion. Teach them empathy. Children show empathy from the time they are babies, when they mimic facial expressions and learn to smile back at people. Help your children name or label their emotions. When they're crying in frustration or anger, or don't want bedtime to come or school to start, give them words for their feelings. Express your feelings in front of them, too, using the full range of emotional vocabulary. When you're discussing problems they're having, like with a sibling or friend at school, ask them to consider the other person's perspective. Model empathy and compassion in your own actions. Also read to them. Ask them what they think characters in books are feeling, based on their facial expressions or what's happening to them in the story. Choose books with a diverse cast of characters – different races, strong female characters, diverse worldviews – so they can see characters they identify with and those that they don't.

All of these habits can help us develop our capacity and ability for empathy; and the more we do this, the more we can develop this over time. They can also *prime* our brains to be more empathic. Priming, in psychology or neuroscience, is the phenomenon whereby exposure to one stimulus influences a response to a subsequent stimulus. In other words, we could use these habits to influence our mind prior to, say, a meeting with diverse colleagues, lunch with a person we may not know so well and so on. For example, in studies when women were told they were being tested on empathy, they were more empathic than when they were told they are being tested for decision-making; with men, when told that women like men who are more sensitive, men were more empathic than when they were told they are being tested for decision-making.

So, we can use these habits, not only over the long term to develop our empathy, but also immediately before activities we may do or situations we are in, in order to *prime* our brain to be more empathic.

---

**Reflection**

*Choosing to Be Empathic and Developing Your Capacity for Empathy*

1. When have you not chosen to be empathic? What was the reason for this? (*Make a note here.*)

   _____

   _____

   _____

   _____

   _____

2. What are the benefits for you of being more empathic? How can this enhance your life and grow you as a person? (*Make a note here.*)

   _____

   _____

   _____

   _____

   _____

3. What new habits will you develop to be more empathic? How will you apply this? Think of one personal and one business example where you will apply these new habits to enhance your life and grow you as a person. (*Make a note here.*)

   _____

   _____

   _____

   _____

   _____

## NOTES

1 Jack, A. I., Dawson, A. J., Begany, K. L., Leckie, R. L., Barry, K. P., Ciccia, A. H. and Snyder, A. Z. "fMRI reveals reciprocal inhibition between social and physical cognitive domains." *NeuroImage.* 66, 385–401. Feb 1, 2012.

2 Cox C. L., Uddin, L. Q., Di Martino, A., Castellanos, F. X., Milham, M. P. and Kelly, C. "The balance between feeling and knowing: affective and cognitive empathy are reflected in the brain's intrinsic functional dynamics." *Social Cognitive and Affective Neuroscience, 7*(6), 727–37. August 2012.

3 Cox C. L., Uddin, L. Q., Di Martino, A., Castellanos, F. X., Milham, M. P. and Kelly, C. "The balance between feeling and knowing: affective and cognitive empathy are reflected in the brain's intrinsic functional dynamics." *Social Cognitive and Affective Neuroscience, 7*(6), 727–37. August 2012.

4 Patnaik, D. *Wired to Care: How Companies Prosper When They Create Widespread Empathy.* Upper Saddle River, NJ: FT Press. 2009.

5 Dowden, C. "Forget ethics training: Focus on empathy." *The National Post.* June 21, 2013.

# Nineteen

Presence is a product of our internal thoughts, external behaviors and interactions with others. It's something that we carry with us at all times, whether we're walking into a meeting room or sitting at a bus stop. It is the display and perception of our body language, speech, delivery, appearance, attire, command of the room, gravitas, passion, enthusiasm, focus, comfort, authenticity, confidence and so on.

In a study analyzing videos of 185 venture capital presentations, Lakshmi Balachandra concluded that the strongest predictors of who got the money was not the person's credentials or the content of the pitch, but rather their confidence, comfort level and passionate enthusiasm. In other words, those who succeeded were fully present, and their presence was felt, and coming through mostly in nonverbal ways – gravitas, appearance, vocal qualities, gestures, facial expressions and so on.[1]

Ultimately, our presence is interpreted by the people we are interacting with through their eyes – it's a big part of how they perceive us. Having presence is like "self-branding;" it is the perception that others have of us. If we don't brand ourselves, others will brand us. So, to ensure our behavior is perceived as we want it to be, we can develop our self-awareness of our presence and take practical actions to enhance it.

### Presence Framework (Direct, Subtle, Controlled, Uncontrolled)

Our presence can be direct or subtle presence; and it can be controlled or uncontrolled. The framework in Figure 19.1 illustrates this.

With direct controlled presence, we can be the most interesting person in the room – being assertive, measured and engaging. With subtle controlled presence, we can be the most interested person in the room – being observant, connected and attentive. Both of these add value in different situations. Sometimes, however, our presence can become uncontrolled and detract from the situation we are in, causing an unintentional negative impression. Direct uncontrolled presence is

DOI: 10.4324/9781003127000-19

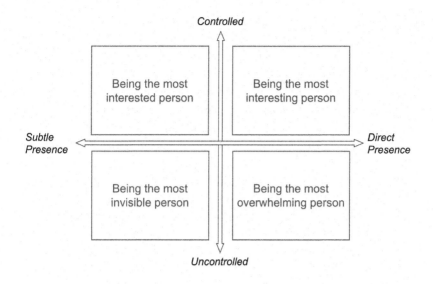

**Figure 19.1** Presence Framework

overwhelming for others and we appear loud, dominant and egocentric. Subtle uncontrolled presence makes us look invisible to others and we appear unsure, diminished and disengaged.

Some people are naturally skilled at controlling and flexing between levels of presence, however, for most of us we need to consciously work at it to bring it into our control and use it to our best advantage.

For example, as a kid growing up in the 1980s, I loved watching Tony Robbins on TV and I wanted to be like Tony Robbins – getting on a large stage with an excited crowd. And I still love him today. I always thought this meant presence – to be at the center of the room to show who I am and get noticed. But I learned that some people, however, thought this made me appear arrogant. I was, unintentionally creating this perception – this branding – and unaware of it. This is an example of uncontrolled direct presence.

While decisiveness and toughness signal conviction and courage, without empathy or compassion these come off as arrogance and insensitivity. The difference between controlled presence and uncontrolled presence, therefore, is understanding others – having emotional intelligence.

Over the course of several years, as I became more aware of this perception and as I developed empathy and emotional intelligence, I then took more control of my presence, being more measured and aware of what I was saying, how I was saying it and the impact it had on others. And I saw the difference. People saw me as "interesting," not overwhelming; they respected me because I was aware of them.

Then, however, I noticed something else that happened in my life. About 12 years ago, I noticed that one consulting company that I had worked for pigeon-holed me as "the presentation guy for mid-level managers and salespeople, but certainly we cannot put him in front of Senior Leaders." I was gregarious, outgoing and assertive, and I was good at speaking in front of an audience. Therefore, this was all they saw and pigeon-holed me such.

It was also around this time that I met Aki Sumitomo, or Sumitomo-san as I called him, and first became aware of the difference between subtle and direct presence. Through Sumitomo-san, I realized that I had only known direct presence. I had learned to become more aware of my behavior, style of communication, and fostered empathy and emotional intelligence to develop controlled direct presence rather than uncontrolled direct presence, but I had never imagined subtle presence at all until this moment.

Now back to the first meeting with Sumitomo-san, which I still remember so clearly. I was doing some leadership development work for the American Management Association in Japan (AMA Japan), where I had lived at that point for about 15 years. It was the then President of AMA Japan who introduced me to Sumitomo-san. Sumitomo-san was a retired Managing Director, having held that top position with three different companies, who then became the top Executive Coach in Japan. Fukuda-san, the President of AMA Japan, told me that Sumitomo-san was looking for a coaching partner to develop and execute what we eventually called 2-on-1 Executive Coaching.

So, the day that I met Sumitomo-san, Fukuda-san opened the door to the meeting room to let me in, and there I see, immediately sitting opposite the door at the center of the table is Sumitomo-san (and for any of you who know about Japanese business culture, this is the most respectful place for anyone to sit, as no one would need to walk behind them to get to their seat). He was dressed immaculately, with a pressed tailored suit and cufflinks; his hair trimmed and styled back; and he sat there in stillness with an aura around him that just commanded respect. You knew, as soon you saw him, that this man in his late 70s was someone important. His presence was felt immediately when I entered the room. This is controlled subtle presence – being attentive, connected, mindful.

As Amy Cuddy said, "One need not be loud or gregarious to be passionate and effective. In fact, a bit of quiet seems to go a long way toward being present."[2]

Likewise, someone can have uncontrolled subtle presence. My friend Rachel is like this, although she is working on it. She said that sometimes she feels invisible, that she doesn't feel like she is seen. And it's impossible to be present when no one sees us. It becomes a self-perpetuating process, because the more that people don't acknowledge us, the more we feel we don't exist, that there is no space for us. She also told me that she often protects herself because she feels powerless and worn down. And if we're protecting ourselves against harm – emotional harm or humiliation – we can't be present either, because we're too protected. This is something she is working on – to be more assertive and engaging with others.

Later in this chapter, we will look at other ways to have more control over our presence and learn to flex ourselves between direct and subtle presence, as the situation may call for.

Tech-entrepreneur Elon Musk is an example of someone who has mastered the art of charismatic interested presence but is a pretty quiet guy by nature. He counterbalances his introverted inclinations with intense focus and presence. He doesn't need to be the extroverted life of the party to seem magnetic; instead of chatting everybody up and offering a little of himself to a lot of people, he concentrates on giving his full, intense attention to a few; in so doing, he makes them feel incredibly special. For him, presence isn't necessarily about quantity, but quality. Elon Musk is a great example of controlled subtle presence, where there are natural tendencies to be introverted and withdrawn.

## Reflection

### Your Presence

1.  Have you ever felt, like myself, uncontrolled direct presence, where you might be overdoing it and, maybe unintentionally, appearing aggressive, overbearing or overwhelming to others? Or, have you ever felt, like Rachel, uncontrolled subtle presence where you feel invisible and may be overprotecting yourself, feeling diminished?

2. The difference between controlled and uncontrolled presence is understanding others, having empathy and emotional intelligence. What can you do to help yourself be more aware and mindful of others? (*Make a note here.*)

_____

_____

_____

_____

_____

3. Who do you know who might embody controlled direct presence? Who comes to mind when you think of this? This could be someone you know personally or a famous person. What is it about them that gives you this impression? (*Make a note here.*)

_____

_____

_____

_____

_____

4. Who do you know who might embody controlled subtle presence? Who comes to mind when you think of this? This could be someone you know personally or a famous person. What is it about them that gives you this impression? (*Make a note here.*)

_____

_____

_____

_____

_____

### The Components of Presence

Let's look at the components of presence – the elements that create our personal branding and from which others perceive us. Specifically, we will look at:

• Mindset
• Gravitas

- Posture/Body Language
- Appearance/Clothes/Physical Fitness
- Communication

### Mindset

The way we think affects the way we behave, and therefore changing the way we think can help us to bring our presence under control, and to flex it in different situations.

One way to do this is to focus on our core values and affirm our authentic self.

In a study led by David Creswell, David Sherman and their collaborators, participants were asked to deliver an impromptu speech before a panel of judges.[3] This is stressful enough, however, the judges were also told to seem very stern and unapproachable (think Simon Cowell), and after delivering their speeches participants then had to count out loud backwards from 2,083, in intervals of 13 for five minutes, while the judges repeatedly shouted at them, "Go faster!"

Just picturing this gets your heart rate up; imagine being in there. And this is precisely the point. This particular task – known as the Trier Social Stress Test (TSST)[4] – is designed to maximize stress so that psychologists can study how people respond to it. It is a social-anxiety nightmare.

Let's tie this in with focusing on our core values and affirming our authentic self. Before the speeches, the researchers randomly assigned participants to do one of two tasks: either write about a personal core value that is important to them or write about a value that is not particularly important to them – that doesn't affect their self-identity.

After the speeches and the counting backwards test, the researchers then measured the subjects' emotional state, by testing their saliva for cortisol, a hormone we release when we're under stress, especially stress involving social judgment.[5] The TSST experience in general, across many, many studies, has been shown to cause a spike in cortisol. But in this particular study, the participants who had written about core values that are important to them had significantly lower levels of cortisol than the group who wrote about one that's not important. In fact, the group that focused on their personal core values and authentic self experienced no increase in cortisol at all. And so, recalling their most valued strengths and personal core values protected them from anxiety.

When we are in a non-stressful situation and one where we want to inspire or motivate others, having high testosterone and adrenaline (and controlling it) is important so we can have controlled direct presence. In stressful situations, however, this can act against us. Instead we need to have low cortisol so we can then have controlled subtle presence in these situations. We need to be able to do both, depending on the situation we are in.

### Gravitas

Gravitas means having high seriousness, dignity and solemnity of manner. It is about being in control and how we act.

Already, I told the story of when I first met Sumitomo-san. He had such poise, such awareness and such control of himself and the situation. You could feel it in his manners and the way he carried himself. You could feel his presence and gravitas.

According to research done by Sylvia Hewlett and the Center for Talent Innovation, executive presence rests on three pillars: How you act (gravitas); How you speak (communication) and How you look (appearance).[6]

Moreover, these pillars are not equally important – not by a long shot. Gravitas is the core characteristic. Some 67% of the 268 senior executives surveyed said that gravitas is what really matters. Signaling that "you know your stuff cold," that you can go "six questions deep" in your domains of knowledge, is more salient than either communication (which got 28% of the senior executive vote) or appearance (which got a mere 5%).

Projecting an aura of calm and competence that instills faith, demonstrating courage and emotional intelligence that secures followership – these are the qualities that connote gravitas, that weightiness or heft that marks us worthy of following into the fire. Gravitas is the very essence of executive presence. Without it, we simply won't be perceived as a leader, no matter what our title or level of authority, no matter how well we dress or speak. Gravitas is what signals to the world that we are made of the right stuff and can be entrusted with serious responsibility.

How do people know that we have gravitas? We communicate the authority of a leader – displaying confidence, having "grace under fire," being decisive and having integrity – through our speaking skills and ability to command a room. These two communication traits top the list of the senior executives in the survey, whether presenting to a small team or addressing a plenary session of a large conference.

Gravitas is a big part in projecting controlled subtle presence. Presence is not about having high energy all the time, but about having the *correct* energy. Here is an example of maintaining controlled subtle presence.

In an interview with then BP CEO Bob Dudley, in an attempt to credit him with BP's recovery, he replied with characteristic humility,

There were a lot of people who performed unbelievably well, but nothing, is more important in troubled times than a leader who projects calm and confidence. I want people around me who can be clear-thinking and calm in a crisis. I don't believe I've ever been able to judge or trust a person unless I can see what they're like under fire.[7]

### Posture/Body Language

Our posture and body language affect how others see us and it may also change how we see ourselves.

In the study by Lakshmi Balachandra that we cited before, those who succeeded were fully present, and their presence was felt, and came through mostly in nonverbal ways – vocal qualities, gestures, facial expressions and so on. Posture and body language show a lot of a person's gravitas and presence.

When we are feeling powerless, in virtually every way that we can, we make ourselves smaller. Rather than take up more space, we take up less – through our postures, our gestures, our walking and even our voices. We shorten, slouch, collapse and restrict our body language. And when other people watch us doing these things, they can't help but see us as powerless and frightened.

All of us deserve to adopt open, comfortable postures and to take up our fair share of space regardless of gender, age, personality or any other aspect of our identity.

In some situations, the opposite may happen – some people take up more space than they should. For example, have you ever seen some men on the subway, spread their legs wide to take up the space of two seats, so-called manspreading? In this situation, they are getting bigger just to make others smaller, which makes it more difficult to establish rapport. We want to look confident and relaxed, not as though we're trying to dominate. The goal is intimacy, not intimidation. Commanding a room as though you were an alpha-male gorilla leaves little space, physically or emotionally, for anyone else. We want to tone down the dominating body posture so we can have power *to* not power *over*.

Harvard University professor, Amy Cuddy, who has the second most popular TED Talk, has done a lot of research into what she calls "power poses" (e.g., Wonder Woman pose with hands on hips, or "V" for victory pose with arms outstretched in a "V"). According to her research, these "power poses" increase our testosterone and adrenaline, and lower our cortisol.[8] This then gives us the mindset to be mindful and aware of what is inside us and around us, and to have more control over our behavior. This is something to do before a meeting or interview, by ourself, as we prepare beforehand. This can help us a lot to project the right kind of presence that we want and to show our gravitas.

### Appearance/Clothes/Physical Fitness

Our appearance, clothes and physical fitness all play a role in creating and showing our presence. Although not as important as mindset or gravitas, if we do not look the part, we may never even get a chance to show them. We need to look the part – our appearance, clothes and physical fitness – and through this, show them our mindset and gravitas.

"When I look in control I feel in control – and that's how others perceive me,"[9] said D'Army Bailey, Memphis-based lawyer and former judge, with a remarkable career litigating and adjudicating landmark cases and founding the National Civil Rights Museum in Memphis.

I remember also in 2015, when I first moved to Singapore. I was working for a consulting company and very much liked the people I worked with. Then, one day, one of my colleagues (who is still a very close friend now) told me that the company didn't think I looked "consultant" enough for them. At that time in my life, I had my hair slicked back and I was wearing pin-striped "power suits." They said that I looked like front line sales in finance, not a "Consultant." At first, I was a little surprised and taken aback, but then took it on as a fun makeover. So, one of my other colleagues then, another consultant, who happens also to be an expert in fashion and style, introduced me to his tailor and barber. So, I got my hair cut and styled differently and bought some new tailored suits with his help and recommendation. And then I looked more like a Consultant. It was still me. But the outward appearance projected the kind of executive presence the clients expected. Although I was a little surprised at first, I took it on as a chance to redefine my branding to have greater impact on clients, partners and others that I meet.

Mindset, gravitas and communication skills are more important than appearance, but appearance is the filter through which these are evaluated. This is why high-performing junior employees sometimes get passed over for key roles and promotions: they simply don't look the part. In other words, if we don't get the appearance thing right, then we are struck off the list. No one bothers to assess our communication skills or our thought leadership if our appearance projects we are clueless or unapproachable or aggressive or anything else of the sort.

According to the CTI Executive Presence survey, "Being polished and groomed" is by far most important; coming a little later in second is "Physically attractive, fit, slim."[10] So, the intrinsic stuff (body type, height) is not what matters most; rather, it's what you do with what you've got. You have to look as though you've tried, that you pulled yourself together, that you look the part.

There are famous people who carved an image for themselves based on their appearance. Steve Jobs, with his classic black turtlenecks and blue jeans. Or Oprah Winfrey, with her well-groomed and styled hair, polished conservative dress and radiant smile.

Previously, I had mentioned, Sumitomo-san, at the age of 75, with his tailored Italian suit, patent leather shoes, red tie, looking stately and commanding respect by his very appearance. Or of another person I know, the Managing Director for Asia of a major publishing company, who always dresses with his pressed collars, ironed ties, adorned with classic cufflinks. He is always like this – always dressing the part of his presence.

I remember also, when I lived in Japan, a former client – the Head of HR at a major global media company – said that when interviewing, he always looks at the person's shoes because everyone wears a nice suit or business skirt; shoes show attention to detail. He said, "Dress for the job you want, not the job you have."

In terms of physical fitness, it doesn't mean we have to look like a star athlete, but we do have to look healthy and fit. Being healthy and fit not only gives us more energy, focus and flow but also increases people's confidence that we will take care of what we are asked to do, because we are taking care of and grooming ourselves.

And so, our appearance, clothes and physical fitness are the medium for our message and, as such, it should neither distract nor detract from what we want to say. Rather, it should augment who we are and what we stand for. Perhaps, this could also mean having something distinctive about us – a strong tie, colorful socks, a brooch, a particular handbag – something that will make us stand out. Like Steve Jobs' turtlenecks and round glasses, Margaret Thatcher's Launer handbags or Richard Branson's red goatee.

Even in our online presence, we still need to look the part, including the background behind us. For me, I have a professional bookshelf with all the top leadership books on it, and something to set me apart: a set of bongos (because I also play drums) on the right side at the back. I also play drums, and this is a part of who I am.

As a final note, perception, and therefore presence, comes mostly from visual, nonverbal elements – from the visual appearance of it. In 2013, Dr Chia-Jung Tsay, Assistant Professor and Concert Pianist,

University College London, studied the idea that we see music competence with our eyes not ears.[11] More than 1,000 participants in the study were given samples of either audio, silent video or video with sound and asked to rate the top three finalists from ten international classical music competitions. The actual competition winners were only correctly identified by those who were randomly assigned the silent videos. When the volunteers viewed video with sound, the accuracy dropped back to chance levels that were found with sound alone. This shows how important the physical and visual element of our presence is, and how powerful it is on other people's perception.

### Communication

Messaging matters. Enormously. The wrong message and the wrong messenger can damage image, destroy careers and lower branding.

I remember in early 2021 talking to the CHRO of a very large global multinational company, someone whom I had met before but we didn't know each other very well. In our video conference, when she asked about what we do, I started by saying, "We have several new programs on Inclusive Leadership and the Neuroscience of High Performing Teams," thinking that these topics are fresh and would resonate with someone who is very focused on DE&I (diversity, equity and inclusion) and developing leaders to be inclusive. Although I and our company focus on behavioral change and shifting mindsets and paradigms, I failed to bring this out. What she heard was "programs" and this meant to her, "training," and said, "Oh, we don't want training." Although I never said the word and in fact do not "do training," this is what she heard. I projected the wrong image; the wrong branding. Through my communication, I projected an image of "training topics" rather than "changing behavior and shifting mindsets through discussion and self-awareness to form lasting new habits." The latter is what we actually do (and what she wanted); the former is what my communication said. As a result, I did not communicate the branding or presence I wanted. From this experience, I have learned, and now very carefully position and communicate the branding more elegantly.

According to the CTI Executive Presence survey, Senior Leaders cite the following as the top communication traits: Superior speaking skills, Ability to command a room, Assertiveness and the Ability to read a client/a boss/a room.[12]

Regarding speaking skills and tone of voice, our brains are wired to tune into lower frequencies, pay attention longer to these voices and are drawn toward them. Consider, for example, comparing James Earl Jones's voice (at 85 Hz) with Roseanne Barr (at 377 Hz). There is something commanding and soothing about James Earl Jones's voice that just shows presence. Also, Duke University's Fuqua School of Business and the University of California, San Diego's Rady School of Management did a study showing that optimally pleasing voices win the biggest leadership roles and earn the biggest salaries. The researchers analyzed recordings of 792 US chief executives at public companies as they made investor presentations or earnings calls. They also gathered data on their salaries, length of tenure and company size. After controlling for experience, education and other influential factors, the scientists found that a drop of 22 Hz in voice frequency correlated with a $187,000 increase in compensation and a larger company size ($440 million larger, in fact). The implication? The lower your voice, the greater your leadership presence, which correlates to an increased likelihood of running a large company and making a substantial salary.[13]

There is also a need to understand others or our audience; there is a need for emotional intelligence. If we do not know the needs of our audience, it will undermine perceptions of our authority. There are three reasons for this. First, it projects an image that we are someone who is closed-off and can't or won't take in new information. Second, it implies that we don't care about our audience, destroying any chance of connection with them. Finally, it implies that we are not agile enough to adapt to rapidly changing circumstances. So, understanding others or our audience is important.

---

### Reflection

**Your Presence**

1. Reflect on each of the following components of presence with respect to your own presence: (*Make a note here.*)
   a. **Mindset** – What are one or two values important to you? What stressful situations have you been in recently or are currently in? How do you manage or control your stress to keep your cortisol level low?

   _____

   _____

   _____

b. *Gravitas* – How do you behave under fire? How do you keep your grace?

_____

_____

_____

c. **Posture/Body Language** – What posture and body language do you adopt? How do you project your presence through this?

_____

_____

_____

d. *Appearance/Clothes/Physical Fitness* – What kind of image do you want to project through your appearance, clothes and physical fitness? What branding do you want to portray?

_____

_____

_____

e. **Communication** – What message are you trying to convey? What do you understand about your audience? How are you using your speaking skills, assertiveness and ability to command a room to project your presence and gravitas?

_____

_____

_____

### How to Increase Our Presence

We can divide this into psychological presence (developing from the inside-out) to project our best selves; and branding presence (developing from the outside-in) to create the brand we want for ourself and to be perceived by others the way we want.

Psychological Presence (Developing from the Inside-Out)

Appreciative Inquiry

We can reduce our anxiety by reaffirming the parts of our authentic best selves we value most, by self-affirming our core values and recalling the things that are great about ourselves. This will make us feel calm and positive and put our minds in a "toward state" that opens us up to more positivity. When we feel calm and positive with ourselves, we become less defensive, more open to feedback and differing ideas, and become better problem solvers, too.[14] This helps us project our best selves to others.

### Be Seen: Feeling Seen Makes Us Feel Present

"People feel the least present when they don't feel seen," my friend Rachel told me. We cannot be present when no one sees us. And it becomes a self-perpetuating process, because the more that people don't acknowledge us, the more we feel that we are invisible and that there is no space for us. Conversely, we are the most present when we are the most seen; and then people are always confirming our sense of self. So, be seen, and find ways to make yourself seen to others.

### Don't Over-Protect: Over-Protection Lowers Our Presence

Rachel said that she often protects herself because she feels powerless and worn down. If we are protecting ourselves against harm – emotional harm or humiliation – we cannot be present either, because we're too protected. We need to learn to be more assertive and more engaging with others. More on this below.

### Don't Over-Attend; But Rather Be Aware and Mindful

When we are truly present, even in challenging moments, our verbal and nonverbal communication flows. We do not focus and analyze what we think others think of us, what we said a minute earlier, what we think they will think of us after we leave, and try to adjust what we're saying and doing to create the impression we think they want to see. Rather, when we stop trying to manage all the little details, the synchrony comes together and flows. Being mindful and aware of our bodies, rather than over-attending, helps us to be more natural and truly present.

### Branding Presence (Developing from the Outside-In)

### Build the Brand You Want

Ultimately, our presence is interpreted by the people we are interacting with through their eyes – it's a big part of how they perceive us. Having presence is like "self-branding;" it is the perception that others have of us. If we don't brand ourselves, others will brand us. So, therefore, we want to build the brand for ourselves that we want. We want to think: What do we want people to say about us when we are not in the room? What do we want to be known for? What value do we want others to see in us? Having clear answers to these questions will help us to build the brand we want.

### Build Your Gravitas

Gravitas means having high seriousness, dignity and solemnity of manner. It is about being in control and how you act. Here is a list of some tips to help build your gravitas:

- Surround yourself with people you respect and admire.
- Be generous with credit.
- Focus on what you know.
- Show humility.
- Smile.
- Help empower others.
- Drive change rather than be changed.
- Turn failure or defeat into positive learning and victory.

### Improve Your Communication

Communication ability is important – not what we say, but how we say it. Here is a list of some tips to help improve your communication:

- Control your voice.
- Reduce fillers such as "um," "like" and "you know."
- Speak in a low voice that is still natural for you.
- Over prepare.
- Broaden your small talk.
- Don't rely on props like slides or handouts.
- Do not allow challenges to your authority to go unanswered.
- Understand others/the audience and deploy emotional intelligence – to effectively read a room, tune yourself out in order to tune in to the needs and wants of others, and then course-correct on the spot to establish connection with them.

### Increase Your Controlled Direct Presence

If you want to increase your controlled direct presence, to be the most interesting person in the room, here is a list of some tips to help you with this:

- Be assertive: speak confidently, make a point and then stop.
- Use emotive and descriptive language, like "burst," "upbeat" and "incredible."
- Practice power poses and be mindful and aware of your body posture.

- Make natural controlled eye contact with people while speaking.
- Express your message through your voice, face and body.
- Tell stories to bring your ideas to life.

If you want to increase your controlled subtle presence, to be the most interested person in the room, here is a list of some tips to help you with this:

- Ask open questions and let the discussion progress at its own pace.
- Be comfortable with silence and pauses, without feeling the need to speak.
- Listen attentively to what is being said, by whom, and the meaning behind the words.
- Make eye contact when people are speaking to you.
- Wait until people finish speaking, pause, then respond.
- Be concise when answering questions.

---

**Reflection**

**Increase Your Presence**

1. Increase your psychological presence (developing from the inside-out) to project your best self. Reflect on the questions below: (*Make a note here.*)

   a. What are your core values? What are the things that you are great at doing?

   _____

   _____

   b. How can you be seen rather than feel invisible?

   _____

   _____

   c. How can you refrain from overprotecting yourself? In Chapter Fifteen: *Relationships and Authenticity*, we talk about this as well. Perhaps review that chapter also if this resonates with you.

   _____

   _____

d. What can you do to be aware and mindful of your body, rather than over-attending and trying to manage every small detail?

_____

_____

2. Increase your branding presence (developing from the outside-in) to create the brand you want for yourself and be perceived by others the way you want. Reflect on the questions below: (*Make a note here.*)

   a. What do you want people to say about you when you are not in the room? What do you want to be known for? What value do you want others to see in you?

   _____

   _____

   b. How can you build your gravitas? Which tip mentioned earlier will help you the most?

   _____

   _____

   c. How can you improve your communication? Which tip mentioned earlier will help you the most?

   _____

   _____

   d. Do you want to increase your controlled direct presence or increase your controlled subtle presence? Which tip mentioned earlier will help you the most?

   _____

   _____

3. In what situations, personally and in business, would you like to project your presence more? (*Make a note here.*)

   _____

   _____

   _____

   _____

4. How will you measure your increase in presence? How will you know you have more? (*Make a note here.*)

_____

_____

_____

_____

## NOTES

1  Balachandra, L. *Keep Calm and Pitch On: Balancing and Moderating Affect in the Entrepreneur's Pitch.* Manuscript submitted for publication. Quoted in Amy Cuddy, *Presence* (p. 19). Boston, MA: Little, Brown. 2015.

2  Cuddy, A. *Presence: Bringing Your Boldest Self to Your Biggest Challenges* (p. 30). Boston, MA: Little, Brown and Company. 2015.

3  Creswell, J. D., Welch,, W. T., Taylor, S. E., Sherman, D. K., Gruenewald, T. L. and Mann, T. "Affirmation of personal values buffers neuroendocrine and psychological stress responses." *Psychological Science*, 16, 846–51. 2005.

4  Kirschbaum, C., Pirke, K. M. and Hellhammer, D. H. "The trier social stress test—a tool for investigating psychobiological stress responses in a laboratory setting." *Neuropsychobiology*, 28, 76–81. 1993.

5  For a review of how acute stressors affect the cortisol response and what that means for psychological well-being, see Dickerson, S. S. and Kemeny, M. E. "Acute stressors and cortisol responses: a theoretical integration and synthesis of laboratory research." *Psychological Bulletin*, 130, 355–91. 2004.

6  Hewlett, S. A., Leader-Chivée, L., Sherbin, L. and Gordon, J. with Dieudonné, F. *Executive Presence: Key Findings.* New York, NY: Center for Talent Innovation. 2013.

7  Hewlett, S. A. *Executive Presence* (p. 13). New York, NY: Harper Business. 2014.

8  Cuddy, A. *Your Body Language May Shape Who You Are.* Edinburgh: TEDGlobal. 2012.

9  Hewlett, S. A. *Executive Presence* (p. 80). New York, NY: Harper Business. 2014.

10  Hewlett, S. A., Leader-Chivée, L., Sherbin, L. and Gordon, J. with Dieudonné, F. *Executive Presence: Key Findings.* New York, NY: Center for Talent Innovation. 2013.

11  Tsay, C-J. "Sight over sound in the judgment of music performance." *PNAS.* 110(36), 14580–5. September 3, 2013.

12  Hewlett, S. A., Leader-Chivée, L., Sherbin, L. and Gordon, J. with Dieudonné, F. *Executive Presence: Key Findings.* New York, NY: Center for Talent Innovation. 2013.

13  Mayew, W. J. and Venkatachalam, M. "Voice pitch and the labor market success of male chief executive officers." *Sidney Winter Lecture Series.* April 12, 2013.

14  Creswell, J. D., Dutcher, J. M., Klein, W. M., Harris, P. R. and Levine, J. M. "Self-affirmation improves problem-solving under stress." *PLoS ONE.* 8(5):e62593. May 1, 2013.

# **Twenty**

In *Thus Spoke Zarathustra*, Friedrich Nietzsche wrote about the *Ubermensch* or, translated into English, the "Beyond-Human," "Overhuman," or "Superhuman;" the ability of humans to go beyond average and reach a heightened transformational state of being. We adopted this thinking in this book, with real practical tools and exercises to engage you, the reader, and take your learning journey deeper and help transform your self-leadership style.

It was designed as a bite-size approach to develop awareness (of self, others and one's environment) to help us – whatever level of leader we are in an organization or if we are just getting started or if we are in a career transition – to reach a higher level of self-leadership through real behavioral change.

Each of the 18 content chapters explored a different theme related to self-leadership, and each one is a bite-size stand-alone unit. We think of it like going to the gym. When we go to the gym, we bench press to work our back muscles, do arm curls to work our biceps, leg press to work our quads and so on. It is the same with our brain and our behavior. Each of the chapters in this book was designed to work a different part of our brain and behavior, and together will then help us lead ourselves better to transform our self-leadership style.

You can read any of the chapters from time to time as a refresher. And you can apply all of the exercises and reflections to different challenges or situations and do the exercises/reflections again. Feel free also to take the assessment again (and from time to time) to see how your priorities may have changed. Then, focus on these chapters again if you like. You can access the assessment here anytime: www.selfleadershipassessment. com/book (or scan the QR code in the introduction).

Overall, this journey is about having more executive control of our brain and our conscious experience. This is the key to leading ourselves and leading a fulfilling life.

Rather than presenting a list of dos and don'ts, this book intended to be a voyage through the realms of our mind, charted with navigation

DOI: 10.4324/9781003127000-20

tools of psychology and neuroscience. Like all adventures worth having, it was not and should not be an easy one. It required, and still will require, some mental effort, a commitment to reflect and think hard about your own experience. Without this, you would not have gained all that you have gained so far.

This challenge was/is both easier and more difficult than it sounds: easier because the ability to do so is entirely within your hands; difficult because it requires a discipline and tenacity that are relatively rare in this present era. Congratulate yourself for the discipline and tenacity that you showed. Well done, indeed!

Control over our consciousness and behavior is not simply a cognitive skill. At least as much as rational thinking, it requires the commitment of emotions and will. It is not enough to know how to do it; you must do it. It is not only about "know how," it is, even more so, about "show how." And this is never easy. It is a challenging journey, but definitely one that is worthwhile and full of rewards.

Being the best self-leader in the world is like being the best driver in the world. Just because you have a driver's license doesn't mean you're going to be the best driver in the world. To become the best driver in the world, you need to put into practice the skills of a great driver: good eyesight, technical skill, foresight, judgment and so on. It's the same with being the best self-leader in the world. If you want to be the best self-leader in the world, you need to put into practice the skills of a great self-leader: goals, flow, insight, change, agility, resilience, trust, empathy and so on. By putting it into practice – the "show how" – you will become the best self-leader.

Also, backed by neuroscientific research and adult learning theories, two ways to embed our learning is by putting yourself in the *role of a teacher* and sharing your learning with other people (your husband, wife, friend, colleague) and creating *implementation intentions*: "If … then …" statements that will guide your mindsets and behavior through the various situations and changes you encounter.

So, choose some people to share your learning with. This could be your husband, wife, boyfriend, girlfriend, friend, brother, sister, colleague or anyone else you can think of. And then share what you've learned from this journey of self-leadership with them. One of these people could become an accountability partner for you, or part of your social accountability network. In the last section of Chapter Two: *Goals*, we talk about *social accountability*. Perhaps, review this now and think how you can apply this for yourself overall.

Also, create some *implementation intentions*. Likewise in the last section of Chapter Two: *Goals*, we talk about *implementation intentions* – "If ... then ..." statements to help us plan for various future scenarios and how we can be proactive for our intended mindset and behavior if/when we face those scenarios. Again perhaps review this as well, applying it to your continued journey.

And so, share your learning and plan your intentions, and help continuously lead yourself better – now and for the future.

Finally, I want to wish you all the best on your continued adventure!

Enjoy the deep journey of applying your transformed self-leadership style!

Grant

## COMPANION WORKBOOK AND INFOGRAPHIC

As you may have noticed, each chapter has exercises and reflection activities. If you would like to keep a record of your journey all in one place and have a working tool that you can go back to, there is a Companion Workbook. This is a free interactive pdf that you can save as you go along. To access it, go to the following URL or scan the QR code below.

www.selfleadershipassessment.com/workbook/

### INFOGRAPHIC

There is also a summary infographic that outlines the whole self-leadership journey. This is an A4 single-page document that visually captures this adventure that can easily be printed and kept by your table. To access it, go to the following URL or scan the QR code below.

http://selfleadershipassessment.com/infographic/

# About the Author

Grant Bosnick is the Managing Director of YES (Your Empowering Solutions), author, consultant, keynote speaker and executive coach. For over 20 years, he has partnered with clients, using psychology and neuroscience, to cocreate people strategies to help organizations build a trusting, collaborative culture, now and for the future, and develop leaders to transform their behavior to lead others, manage change, innovate and perform at a higher level.

He has worked with 100+ Fortune 500 and FTSE 100 companies in the tech, financial services, retail, advertising, pharmaceutical, FMCG, service and chemical industries.

Originally from Toronto, Canada, now based in Singapore, he has lived in Asia Pacific for over 20 years, given face-to-face keynotes and leadership sessions all across Asia Pacific and the Middle East, and virtually with 38 countries on six continents.

Grant thrives on developing leaders around the world and helping organizations transfer best practices.

Abbasi, A. M., Motamedzade H., Aliabadi, M., Golmohammadi, R. and Tapak, L. "The impact of indoor air temperature on the executive functions of human brain and the physiological responses of body." *Health Promotion Perspectives*, 9(1), 55–64. January 23, 2019.

Ashby, F. G., Isen, A. M. and Turken, A. U. "A neuropsychological theory of positive affect and its influence on cognition." *Psychological Review*, 106(3), 529–50. 1999.

Batson, C. D. "Prosocial motivation: Is it ever truly altruistic?" In L. Berkowitz (Ed.), *Advances in Experimental Social Psychology* (Vol. 20, pp. 65–122). New York, NY: Academic Press. 1987.

Batson, C. D. *The Altruism Question: Toward a Social-Psychological Answer.* Hillsdale, NJ: Erlbaum Associates. 1991.

Batson, C. D. "These things called empathy: eight related but distinct phenomena." In J. Decety and W. Ickes (Eds.), *The Social Neuroscience of Empathy* (pp. 3–15). Cambridge, MA: MIT Press. 2009.

Batson, C. D., Polycarpou, M. P., Harmon-Jones, E., Imhoff, H. J., Mitchener, E. C., Bednar, L. L., Klein, T. R. and Highberger, L. "Empathy and attitudes: can feeling for a member of a stigmatized group improve feelings toward the group?" *Journal of Personality and Social Psychology*, 72, 105–18. 1997.

Bazerman, M. H. and Neale, M. A. "Improving negotiation effectiveness under final offer arbitration: the role of selection and training." *Journal of Applied Psychology*, 67, 543–8. 1982.

Beaumeister, R., Bratslavsky, E., Finkenauer, F. and Vohs, K. D. "Bad is stronger than good." *Review of General Psychology*, 5(4), 323–70. 2001.

Berka, C., Levendowski, D. J., Cvetinovic, M. M., Petrovic, M., Davis, G., Lumicao, M. N., Zivkovic, T., Popovic, M. V. and Olmstead, R. E. "Real-time analysis of EEG indexes of alertness, cognition, and memory acquired with a wireless EEG headset." *International Journal of Human–Computer Interaction*, 17(2), 151–170. June 9, 2010.

Bloom, P. "Empathy and its discontents." *Trends in Cognitive Sciences*, 21(1), 24–31. January 2017.

Bolton, R. and Bolton, D. G. *People Styles at Work: Making Bad Relationships Good and Good Relationships Better.* New York, NY: Amacom. 1996.

Breheny Wallace, J. "Being empathetic is good, but it can hurt your health." *The Washington Post.* September 25, 2017.

Broda-Bahm, K. "Switch between analysis and empathy (because you won't get both at the same time)." *Persuasive Litigator.* December 13, 2012.

Buber, M. *I and Thou* (second edition). New York, NY: Charles Scribner's Sons. 1962.

Carnegie, D. *How to Win Friends and Influence People.* New Delhi: Digital Fire. 1936.

Carter, C. S. and Keverne, E. B. "The neurobiology of social affiliation and pair bonding." In D. Pfaff (Ed.), *Hormones, Brain and Behavior* (pp. 299–377). San Diego: Academic Press. 2002.

Carver, C. S. and Scheier, M. *Attention and Self-Regulation: A Control-Theory Approach to Human Behavior (Springer Series in Social Psychology)*. New York, NY: Springer. 2012.

Case Western Reserve University. "Empathy represses analytic thought, and vice versa: Brain physiology limits simultaneous use of both networks." *ScienceDaily*. October 30, 2012.

Cedeño-Laurent, J. G., Williams, A., Oulhote, Y., Zanobetti, A., Allen, J. G. and Spengler, J. D. "Reduced cognitive function during a heat wave among residents of non-air-conditioned buildings: an observational study of young adults in the summer of 2016." *PLOS Medicine*, 15(7), e1002605. July 10, 2018.

Chabris, C. and Simons, D. *The Invisible Gorilla*. Broadway. 2011.

Cheema, A. and Patrick, V. M. "Influence of warm versus cool temperatures on consumer choice: a resource depletion account." *Journal of Marketing Research*, 49(6), 984–95. December 1, 2012.

Chi, R. P. and Snyder, A. W. "Facilitate insight by non-invasive brain stimulation." *Plos One*, 6(2), e16655. February 2, 2011.

Chismar, D. "Empathy and sympathy: the important difference." *The Journal of Value Inquiry*, 22, 257–66. 1988.

Cialdini, R. B. *Influence: The Psychology of Persuasion*. HarperCollins. New York. 2009.

Cikara, M., Bruneau, E., Van Bavel, J. J. and Saxe, R. "Their pain gives us pleasure: how intergroup dynamics shape empathic failures and counter-empathic responses." *Journal of Experimental Social Psychology*, 55, 110–25. November 2014.

Clear, J. *Atomic Habits: An Easy & Proven Way to Build Good Habits & Break Bad Ones*. New York, NY: Avery. 2018.

Covey, S. R. *The 7 Habits of Highly Effective People: Powerful Lessons in Personal Change*. New York, NY: Free Press. 1989.

Covey, S. R. *First Things First*. New York, NY: Free Press. New York. 1994.

Cox, C. L., Uddin, L. Q., Di Martino, A., Castellanos, F. X., Milham, M. P. and Kelly, C. "The balance between feeling and knowing: affective and cognitive empathy are reflected in the brain's intrinsic functional dynamics." *Social Cognitive and Affective Neuroscience*, 7(6), 727–37. August 2012.

Cranston, S. and Keller, S. "Increasing the 'meaning quotient' of work." *McKinsey Quarterly*. January 1, 2013.

Creswell, J. D., Dutcher, J. M., Klein, W. M., Harris, P. R. and Levine, J. M. "Self-affirmation improves problem-solving under stress." *PLoS One*, 8(5), e62593. May 1, 2013.

Creswell, J. D., Way, B. M., Eisenberger, N. I. and Lieberman, M. D. "Neural correlates of dispositional mindfulness during affect labeling." *Psychosomatic Medicine*, 69(6), 560–5. Jul–Aug 2007.

Creswell, J. D., Welch, W. T., Taylor, S. E., Sherman, D. K., Gruenewald, T. L. and Mann, T. "Affirmation of personal values buffers neuroendocrine and psychological stress responses." *Psychological Science*, 16, 846–51. 2005.

Csikszentmihalyi, M. *Flow*. New York, NY: HarperCollins. 1990.

Cuddy, A. *Your Body Language May Shape Who You Are*. Edinburgh: TEDGlobal. 2012.

Cuddy, A. *Presence: Bringing Your Boldest Self to Your Biggest Challenges*. Boston, MA: Little, Brown and Company. 2015.

Darley, J. M. and Batson, C. D. "From Jerusalem to Jericho: a study of situational and dispositional variables in helping behavior." *Journal of Personality and Social Psychology*, 27, 100–8. 1973.

Davidson, R. J., Kabat-Zinn, J., Schumacher, J., Rosenkranz, M., Muller, D., Santorelli, S. F., Urbanowski, F., Harrington, A., Bonus, K. and Sheridan, J. F. "Alterations in brain and immune function produced by mindfulness meditation." *Psychosomatic Medicine*, 65, 564–70. 2003.

Davis, M. H. "Measuring individual differences in empathy: evidence for a multidimensional approach." *Journal of Personality and Social Psychology*, 44(1), 113–26. 1983.

Decety, J. "Naturaliser l'empathie [Empathy naturalized]." *L'Encéphale*, 28, 9–20. 2002.

Decety, J. and Jackson, P. L. "The functional architecture of human empathy." *Behavioral and Cognitive Neuroscience Reviews*, 3(2), 71–100. 2004.

Deci, E. L. and Ryan, R. M. *Handbook of Self-Determination Research*. Rochester, NY: The University of Rochester Press. 2002.

Demerouti, E., Bakker, A., Nachreiner, F. and Schaufeli, W. B. "The job demands-resources model of burnout". *Journal of Applied Psychology*, 86(3), 499–512. June 2001.

Depue, R. A. and Collins, P. F. "Neurobiology of the structure of personality: Dopamine, facilitation of incentive motivation, and extraversion." *Behavioral and Brain Sciences*, 22(3), 491–517. June 1999.

Dickerson, S. S. and Kemeny, M. E. "Acute stressors and cortisol responses: a theoretical integration and synthesis of laboratory research." *Psychological Bulletin*, 130, 355–91. 2004.

Dietrich, A. "Neurocognitive mechanisms underlying the experience of flow." *Consciousness and Cognition*, 13(4), 746–61. December 2004.

Dowden, C. "Forget ethics training: Focus on empathy." *The National Post*. June 21, 2013.

Drexler, M. "Looking under the hood and seeing an incubator." *The New York Times*. December 15, 2008.

Eisenberger, N. I., Lieberman, M. D. and Williams, K. D. "Does rejection hurt? An FMRI study of social exclusion." *Science*, 302(5643), 290–2. Oct 10, 2003.

Ellis, A. *Overcoming Resistance: Rational-Emotive Therapy with Difficult Clients*. Springer Publishing. New York. 1985.

Falk, D. R. and Johnson, D. W. "The effects of perspective-taking and egocentrism on problem solving in heterogeneous and homogeneous groups." *The Journal of Social Psychology*, 102, 63–72. 1977.

Fan, Y., Duncan, N. W., de Greck, M. and Northoff, G. "Is there a core neural network in empathy? An fMRI based quantitative meta-analysis." *Neuroscience and Biobehavioral Reviews*, 35(3), 903–11. January 2011.

Ferrari, J. R. *Still Procrastinating? The No Regrets Guide to Getting It Done*. Hoboken, NJ: Wiley. 2010.

Fiske, S. T. and Ruscher, J. B. "Chapter 11 - Negative interdependence and prejudice: whence the affect?" *Affect, Cognition and Stereotyping: Interactive Processes in Group Perception* (pp. 239–68). Cambridge, MA: Academic Press. 1993.

Fitzsimons, G. M. and Shah, J. Y. "How goal instrumentality shapes relationship evaluations." *Journal of Personality and Social Psychology*. 95(2):319–37. 2008.

Foster, R. and Kreitzman, L. *The Rhythms of Life*. London: Profile Books. 2004.

Galinsky, A. D., Maddux, W. W., Gilin, D. and White, J.B. "Why it pays to get inside the head of your opponent." *Psychological Science*, 19, 378–84. 2008.

Gallese, V. "The "Shared Manifold" hypothesis: from mirror neurons to empathy." *Journal of Consciousness Studies*, 8, 33–50. 2001.

Gallese, V. and Goldman, A. "Mirror neurons and the simulation theory of mind-reading." *Trends in Cognitive Sciences*, 2(12), 493–501. December 1998.

Gerrig, R. J. *Experiencing Narrative Worlds: On the Psychological Activities of Reading*. New Haven, CT: Yale University Press. 1993.

Gimbel, S., Kaplan, J., Immordino-Yang, M., Tipper, Gordon, C. A., Dehghani, M., Sagae, S., Damasio, H. and Damasio, A. "Neural response to narratives framed with sacred values." *Annual Meeting of the Society for Neuroscience, San Diego*. 2013.

Goleman, D. *Why Aren't We More Compassionate?* Monterey, CA: TED Talk. 2007.

Gollwitzer, P. M. "Implementation intentions: Strong effects of simple plans." *American Psychologist.* 54(7):493–503. 1999.

Grant, A. M. and Rothbard, N. P. "When in doubt, seize the day? Security values, prosocial values, and proactivity under ambiguity." *Journal of Applied Psychology*, 98(5), 810–19. 2013.

Hewlett, S. A. *Executive Presence.* New York, NY: Harper Business. 2014.

Hewlett, S. A., Leader-Chivée, L., Sherbin, L. and Gordon, J. with Dieudonné, F. *Executive Presence: Key Findings.* New York, NY: Center for Talent Innovation. 2013.

Hodges, S. D. and Klein, K. J. "Regulating the costs of empathy: the price of being human." *Journal of Socio-Economics*, 30(2001), 437–52. 2001.

Iacoboni, M. "Grasping the intentions of others with one's own mirror neuron system." *PLOS Biology*, 3(3), e79. February 22, 2005.

Jack, A. I., Dawson, A. J., Begany, K. L., Leckie, R. L., Barry, K. P., Ciccia, A. H. and Snyder, A. Z. "fMRI reveals reciprocal inhibition between social and physical cognitive domains." *NeuroImage*, 66, 385–401. Feb 1, 2012.

Johnston, G. "What's the downside of empathy?" *Welldoing.* April 14, 2017.

Kahneman, D. *Thinking, Fast and Slow.* New York, NY: Farrar, Straus and Giroux. 2011.

Keysers, C. *The Empathic Brain.* Amsterdam: Social Brain Press. 2011.

Keysers, C. and Gazzola, V. "Expanding the mirror: vicarious activity for actions, emotions, and sensations." *Current Opinion in Neurobiology*, 19(6), 666–71. December 2009.

Kirschbaum, C., Pirke, K. M. and Hellhammer, D. H. "The Trier Social Stress Test—a tool for investigating psychobiological stress responses in a laboratory setting." *Neuropsychobiology*, 28, 76–81. 1993.

Krznaric, R. "Six habits of highly empathic people." *Greater Good Magazine.* November 27, 2012.

Lally, P., van Jaarsveld, C. H. M., Potts, H. W. W. and Wardle, J. "How are habits formed: Modelling habit formation in the real world." *European Journal of Social Psychology.* 40(6):998–1009, October 2010.

Lencioni, P. *The Five Dysfunctions of a Team: A Leadership Fable.* New York, NY: Wiley. 2002.

Levine, M., Prosser, A., Evans, D. and Reicher, S. "Identity and emergency intervention: how social group membership and inclusiveness of group boundaries shape helping behavior." *Personality and Social Psychology Bulletin.* April 1, 2005.

Lewin, K. "Field theory and experiment in social psychology." *American Journal of Sociology*, 44(6), 868–96. May 1939.

Lieberman, M. D. *Social: Why Our Brains Are Wired to Connect.* Crown. New York. 2013.

Loehr, J. and Schwartz, T. *The Power of Full Engagement.* New York, NY: Free Press. 2003.

Maddi, S. and Khosaba, D. *Resilience at Work: How to Succeed No Matter What Life Throws at You.* New York, NY: Amacom. 2005.

Mahoney, M. J. *Human Change Processes: The Scientific Foundations of Psychotherapy.* New York, NY: Basic Books. 1991.

Mayew, W. J. and Venkatachalam, M. "Voice pitch and the labor market success of male chief executive officers." *Sidney Winter Lecture Series.* April 12, 2013.

Melnychuk, M. C., Dockree, P. M., O'Connell, R. G., Murphy, P. R., Balsters, J. H. and Robertson, I. H. "Coupling of respiration and attention via the locus coeruleus: effects of meditation and pranayama." *Psychophysiology*, e13091. 2018.

Millar, C. C. "How to be more empathetic." *The New York Times.* January, 31, 2019.

Nietzsche, F. *Thus Spoke Zarathustra: A Book for All and None.* London: Penguin Books.. 1961.

Ochsner, K. N. and Gross, J. J. "Cognitive emotion regulation: insights from social cognitive and affective neuroscience." *Current Directions in Psychological Science*, 17(1), 153–8. 2008.

Pancer, S. M., McMullen, L. M., Kabatoff, R. A., Johnson, K. G. and Pond, C. A. "Conflict and avoidance in the helping situation." *Journal of Personality and Social Psychology*, 37(8), 1406–11. 1979.

Patnaik, D. *Wired to Care: How Companies Prosper When They Create Widespread Empathy*. Upper Saddle River, NJ: FT Press. 2009.

Payne, B. K., Hall, D., Cameron, C. D. and Bishara, A. J. "A process model of affect misattribution." *Personality and Social Psychology Bulletin*. 2010.

Perry, J. *The Art of Procrastination*. New York, NY: Workman Publishing Company. 2012.

Phelps, E. A., Ling, S. and Carrasco, M. "Emotion facilitates perception and potentiates the perceptual benefits of attention." *Psychological Science*, 17(4), 292–9. 2006.

Plassmann, H., O'Doherty, J., Shiv, B. and Rangel A. "Marketing actions can modulate neural representations of experienced pleasantness." *Proceedings of the National Academy of Sciences U S A*, 105(3), 1050–4. Jan 22, 2008.

Prehn, A. "Create reframing mindsets through framestorm." *NeuroLeadership Journal*, Issue 4. 2012.

Preston, S. D. and de Waal, F. B. M. "Empathy: its ultimate and proximate bases." *Behavioral and Brain Sciences*, 25(1), 1–72. 2002.

Pychyl, T. A. *Solving the Procrastination Puzzle: A Concise Guide to Strategies*. Los Angeles, CA: TarcherPerigee. 2013.

Raji, C. A., Erickson, K. O., Lopez, O. L., Kuller, L. H., Gach, H. M., Thompson, P. M., Riverol, M. and Becker, J. T. "Regular fish consumption and age-related brain gray matter loss." *American Journal of Preventive Medicine*, 47(4), 444–51. Oct 2014.

Rock, D. *Quiet Leadership: Six Steps to Transforming Performance at Work*. New York, NY: HarperCollins. 2006.

Rock, D. *Your Brain at Work: Strategies for Overcoming Distraction, Regaining Focus, and Working Smarter All Day Long*. New York, NY: HarperCollins. 2009.

Rogers, T. and Bazerman, M. H. *Future Lock-in: Future Implementation Increases Selection of 'Should' Choices*. Amsterdam: Elsevier. 2007.

Sacchet, M. D., LaPlante, R. A., Wan, Q. Pritchett, D. L., Lee, A. K. C., Hämäläinen, M., Moore, C. I., Kerr, C. E. and Jones, S. R. "Attention drives synchronization of alpha and beta rhythms between right inferior frontal and primary sensory neocortex." *Journal of Neuroscience*, 35(5), 2074–82. February 4, 2015.

Seligman, M. *Learned Optimism*. New York, NY: Vintage Press. 1990.

Seligman, M. and Perrson, C. *Character Strengths and Virtues: A Handbook and Classification*. New York, NY: Oxford University Press. 2004.

Siegel, D. J. *The Mindful Brain: Reflection and Attunement in the Cultivation of Well-Being*. New York, NY: Norton & Company. 2007.

Spunt, R. P., Falk, E. B. and Lieberman, M. D. "Dissociable neural systems support retrieval of how and why action knowledge." *Psychological Science*, 21(11), 1593–8. 2010.

Steimer, T. "The biology of fear- and anxiety-related behaviors." *Dialogues in Clinical Neuroscience*, 4(3), 231–49. September 2002.

Struch, N. and Schwartz, S. H. "Intergroup aggression: its predictors and distinctness from in-group bias." *Journal of Personality and Social Psychology*, 56(3), 364–73. 1989.

Subramaniam, K., Kounios, J., Parrish, T. B. and Jung-Beeman, M. "A brain mechanism for facilitation of insight by positive affect." *Journal of Cognitive Neuroscience*, 21(3), 415–32. March 2009.

Talib, N. M. *Antifragile*. New York, NY: Random House. 2012.

The Arbinger Institute. *The Outward Mindset: Seeing Beyond Ourselves, How to Change Lives & Transform Organizations*. San Francisco, CA: Berrett-Koehler Publishers. 2016.